I0006360

Building Scalable Apps with Redis and Node.js

Develop customized, scalable web apps through the integration of powerful Node.js frameworks

Joshua Johanan

PUBLISHING

BIRMINGHAM - MUMBAI

Building Scalable Apps with Redis and Node.js

Copyright © 2014 Packt Publishing

All rights reserved. No part of this book may be reproduced, stored in a retrieval system, or transmitted in any form or by any means, without the prior written permission of the publisher, except in the case of brief quotations embedded in critical articles or reviews.

Every effort has been made in the preparation of this book to ensure the accuracy of the information presented. However, the information contained in this book is sold without warranty, either express or implied. Neither the author, nor Packt Publishing, and its dealers and distributors will be held liable for any damages caused or alleged to be caused directly or indirectly by this book.

Packt Publishing has endeavored to provide trademark information about all of the companies and products mentioned in this book by the appropriate use of capitals. However, Packt Publishing cannot guarantee the accuracy of this information.

First published: September 2014

Production reference: 1190914

Published by Packt Publishing Ltd.
Livery Place
35 Livery Street
Birmingham B3 2PB, UK.

ISBN 978-1-78398-448-0

www.packtpub.com

Cover image by Siddhart Ravishankar (sidd.ravishankar@gmail.com)

Credits

Author

Joshua Johanan

Reviewers

Harrison Dahme

Sven Kreiss, PhD

Andrew Long

Jari Timonen

Commissioning Editor

Kunal Parikh

Acquisition Editor

Richard Harvey

Content Development Editor

Arun Nadar

Technical Editors

Kunal Anil Gaikwad

Shruti Rawool

Copy Editors

Mradula Hegde

Dipti Kapadia

Sayanee Mukherjee

Deepa Nambiar

Alfida Paiva

Project Coordinator

Neha Bhatnagar

Proofreaders

Simran Bhogal

Lauren Harkins

Linda Morris

Indexers

Rekha Nair

Priya Sane

Graphics

Sheetal Aute

Production Coordinator

Nitesh Thakur

Cover Work

Nitesh Thakur

About the Author

Joshua Johanan is a web developer who currently lives in South Bend, Indiana. He has been a web developer for 5 years. He has built sites using many different languages, including PHP, Python, JavaScript, and C#, although if asked, he would prefer using Python and JavaScript. These languages have led him to use different MVC frameworks such as Zend Framework, Django, and .NET's MVC.

As you can tell from this book, he has used JavaScript on both the backend with Node.js and the frontend using many different libraries. These include Backbone, React, jQuery, and plain old JavaScript.

He currently works for a health care organization, writing websites in C#. This does not allow him to utilize the latest flashy browser technologies, but it does enforce good development skills such as maintainability and scalability.

This is his first book, but he posts regularly on his blog at `http://ejosh.co/de`.

I would like to thank my wife, Liz, for her support through the writing of this book. I would also like to thank Dexter and Gizmo, who hung out with me at my feet as I wrote most of this book.

About the Reviewers

Harrison Dahme is a full-stack software engineer in San Francisco, born and raised in Toronto. He's driven by an addiction to learning and a love for adventure. He has a specialist degree in Artificial Intelligence from the University of Toronto, and he has years of experience working with the frontend, backend, app development, and system design. When he's not making things or breaking things, you can find him surfing, rock climbing, skiing, or mountain biking. Find him on social media as @IsTheBaron, or connect with him on LinkedIn as hdahme.

Sven Kreiss, PhD, is a data scientist in New York City with a background in particle physics. He holds a Master's degree from the University of Edinburgh, Scotland, and a PhD from New York University (NYU). His thesis included software development for applied statistics tools. Together with other physicists of the ATLAS collaboration, he used these tools to discover the Higgs Boson in 2012 at CERN, Switzerland. He is also the author of Databench, an open source tool for interactive data analysis and visualization.

To learn more about him, visit his website at www.svenkreiss.com and follow him on Twitter at @svenkreiss.

Andrew Long is an entrepreneur working in San Francisco, California. He has extensive battle-worn experience in building and scaling out both the frontend and backend services of popular consumer applications. Currently, he is working as a senior software engineer at Hall, Inc. Previously, he was building Mailbox at Orchestra, prior to being acquired by Dropbox. He also worked on mobile technologies at Palm, Inc. for the WebOS platform. After Palm's acquisition by HP, he helped build the first official native Facebook application on a tablet form factor.

Follow him at @aslong on Twitter, or visit www.andrewslong.com.

I'd like to thank Katherine for her never-ending support and encouragement in producing this book.

Jari Timonen is an experienced software enthusiast with over 10 years of experience in the software industry. His experience includes successful team leadership combined with understanding complex business domains and delivering them into practice. He has been building enterprise architectures, designing software, and programming. Although he started his career in the finance industry, he currently works as a service architect in a telecommunications company. He practices pair programming and is keen on studying new technologies. When he is not building software, he spends time with his family, fishing, exercising, or flying his radio-controlled model helicopter.

He currently holds the following certifications:

- Sun Certified Programmer for Java 2 Platform, Standard Edition 5
- Sun Certified Developer for Java 2 Platform
- Oracle Certified Master, Java EE 5 Enterprise Architect

www.PacktPub.com

Support files, eBooks, discount offers, and more

You might want to visit www.PacktPub.com for support files and downloads related to your book.

Did you know that Packt offers eBook versions of every book published, with PDF and ePub files available? You can upgrade to the eBook version at www.PacktPub.com and as a print book customer, you are entitled to a discount on the eBook copy. Get in touch with us at service@packtpub.com for more details.

At www.PacktPub.com, you can also read a collection of free technical articles, sign up for a range of free newsletters and receive exclusive discounts and offers on Packt books and eBooks.

http://PacktLib.PacktPub.com

Do you need instant solutions to your IT questions? PacktLib is Packt's online digital book library. Here, you can access, read and search across Packt's entire library of books.

Why subscribe?

- Fully searchable across every book published by Packt
- Copy and paste, print and bookmark content
- On demand and accessible via web browser

Free access for Packt account holders

If you have an account with Packt at www.PacktPub.com, you can use this to access PacktLib today and view nine entirely free books. Simply use your login credentials for immediate access.

Table of Contents

Preface	**1**
Chapter 1: Backend Development with Express	**9**
Node.js and Node Package Manager	**9**
Using Express in Node	**12**
Using middleware in Express	**14**
Creating our own middleware	15
Adding templates to the mix	**18**
Layouts	20
Using sessions in Express	**23**
Using cookies in Express	23
Adding sessions	25
Redis as a session store	28
Processing forms	**31**
Cross-Site Request Forgery (CSRF)	34
Very simple authentication	**36**
Setting up a config file for our app	**42**
Route mapping	43
Updating our app to use the config	43
Methods to extend an application	**45**
Summary	**46**
Chapter 2: Extending Our Development with Socket.IO	**47**
Node package versions	**47**
Building a simple Socket.IO app	**48**
Installing the package	48
Building the client	49
Using Python to serve our site	50
Ping-Pong	51

Creating some interaction   51
Adding the browser side   52
Acknowledgments   54
Broadcasting a message   **56**
Using the disconnect event   **58**
Creating namespaces   **59**
Building our namespace client   61
Adding rooms   **66**
Using namespaces or rooms   **69**
Namespaces   69
Finding namespaces   70
When to use rooms   70
Finding rooms   71
Using namespaces and rooms together   **71**
Using Socket.IO and Express together   **72**
Adding Socket.IO to the config   72
Who are you?   74
Authorization in Socket.IO   75
Adding application-specific events   **79**
Using Redis as the store for Socket.IO   **79**
Socket.IO inner workings   **80**
WebSockets   80
Ideas to take away from this chapter   **81**
Summary   **82**
Chapter 3: Authenticating Users   **83**
Node package versions   **83**
Let's build our authentication   **84**
Registering a Facebook application   **85**
Using Passport to authenticate to Facebook   **88**
Using Google for authentication   **94**
Adding Google authentication to our application   **98**
Adding more OAuth providers   **101**
Adding secure local authentication   **102**
Adding registration   108
Adding a database   110
Password-storing theory   **111**
OAuth process   **112**
Summary   **113**

Chapter 4: RabbitMQ for Message Queuing   115

Node package versions   **115**
Getting RabbitMQ   **116**
  Installing on Mac OS X   116
    The RabbitMQ management plugin   118
  Installing on Linux   118
  Installing on Windows   119
Our first message queue   **120**
  Using the management interface   123
  Sending messages   124
  Queuing messages   125
  Adding another worker   126
Sending messages back   **127**
  Creating StartServer   129
  Building the worker   130
  Charging cards in real time   131
Adding message queues to PacktChat   **133**
  Topic exchange   133
  Building the worker   138
Message queuing in RabbitMQ   **139**
Summary   **141**

Chapter 5: Adopting Redis for Application Data   143

Node package versions   **143**
Installing Redis   **144**
  Installing on Mac OS X   145
  Installing on Linux   146
  Installing on Windows   148
Using Redis data structures   **149**
  Building a simple Redis application   150
Redis schema   **158**
  Using a hash   159
  Keys in Redis   159
Redis persistence   **160**
  Removing Redis keys   160
Using Redis as a message queue   **163**
Adding Redis to PacktChat   **167**
  Defining the Redis structures   167
  Creating our Redis functions   168
Redis is for application state   **172**
Summary   **173**

Chapter 6: Using Bower to Manage Our Frontend Dependencies   **175**
Node package versions   **175**
Installing and using Bower   **176**
Introducing React   **176**
Introducing Backbone   **184**
  Using Backbone models   185
  Using Backbone collections   186
Summary   **188**

Chapter 7: Using Backbone and React for DOM Events   **189**
Bower package versions   **189**
Finishing Socket.IO   **190**
Creating React components   **195**
  React summary   203
Backbone models   **203**
  Syncing the models with Socket.IO   203
  Creating the model   205
  Creating collections   206
The Backbone router   **208**
Putting it all together   **208**
Updating CSS and the layout   **212**
Adding a new worker   **213**
Trying out our application   **216**
Summary   **216**

Chapter 8: JavaScript Best Practices for Application Development   **217**
Node package versions   **218**
Setting up tests   **218**
  Using Istanbul for code coverage   222
Setting up different environments   **224**
  Twelve Factor App   224
  Fixing the config file   224
  Creating our environment files   225
  Adding more environments   227
Introducing Grunt   **227**
  Building a basic Grunt file   227
  Automating our tests   228
  Preprocessing our files   229
  Using Grunt to clean out a folder   231

JSHinting our source files · 231
Concatenating our code 232
Minifying our code 233
Grunt summary 234
Static files and CDNs **235**
Creating an S3 bucket 236
Python and installing virtual environments 238
Scripting our new tools **240**
Summary **242**
Chapter 9: Deployment and Scalability **243**
Creating servers on EC2 **243**
AWS EC2 summary 245
What is Ansible? **246**
Installing Ansible 246
Using Ansible roles 248
Installing RabbitMQ 251
Installing our application 253
Installing the workers 261
Load balancing multiple application servers 261
Automating roles 265
A summary of Ansible 266
Creating new environments 267
Scalability **268**
Different types of scalability 269
Horizontal 269
Vertical 270
Summary **270**
Chapter 10: Debugging and Troubleshooting **271**
Node packages **271**
Using Chrome Developer Tools **272**
Elements 272
Network 272
Sources 273
Timeline 273
Profiles 273
Resources 274
Audits 274
Console 274
Inspecting requests **274**

Debugging	**277**
Frontend debugging	278
Backend debugging	280
Debugging summary	281
CPU profiling our application	**281**
Taking heap snapshots	**283**
Frontend memory leaks	286
Memory leak summary	289
Summary	**289**
Index	**291**

Preface

Node.js is a fantastic way to begin your journey in building scalable applications. As it was built using non-blocking I/O, it can serve more concurrent requests than a blocking server, such as Apache, which can be achieved through asynchronous events. When a function call blocks, Node.js will reply via a callback. The great foundation of Node.js has led to many libraries that allow you to build a scalable application.

Redis is another vital building block of scalable applications. While Redis is not Node.js-specific, it offers great support. It fills up the need of shared memory between web servers that scalable applications require. Redis also has bindings in some other frameworks, which will be covered in this book. This prevents us from falling into the trap of needing five different data stores for five different frameworks, which only adds to the complexity of our environment and system administration overhead.

Building Scalable Apps with Redis and Node.js combines both of these essential building blocks into one comprehensive and straightforward project guide. It shows you how to build an application from scratch, straight from having an idea all the way to deploying it. The first seven chapters show you a specific problem or issue you might come across during development. The following chapter will cover some best practices when developing. The final two chapters will cover the deployment of your site to Amazon Web Services. These particular chapters will also show you how you can troubleshoot and debug your application. Although the book covers one project, the chapters are organized in such a way that you can jump straight into them, to be shown how to create a certain feature or learn a specific topic. It is recommended, though, that you work from the beginning of the book. You will find that because we will be building an entire site, the code from one chapter will have relevance to another. However, most code samples will be usable in other contexts.

On a personal note, I will say that using JavaScript for backend development is refreshing. I readily admit that when I first heard about Node.js and the idea of using JavaScript in the backend, my initial reaction was "Why would I want to do that?" I have run the gamut of server-side languages (PHP to Ruby and Python, and C# .NET). I have worked with many different web servers (Apache, IIS, built-in servers, Unicorn, Gunicorn, and so on). Throw in the fact that all modern web applications require some JavaScript and you start to build mental barriers, which is especially true if the syntax is different (consider comparing Ruby to JavaScript, for example). Node.js allows you to remain in the JavaScript mode, utilizing the same design patterns and even the same tools. You will also be glad to hear there is not much to set up. You build your Node.js app and then you simply run it. All these reasons are exactly why Node.js is one of the best web application/serving frameworks and why I, personally, love to use it.

What this book covers

Chapter 1, Backend Development with Express, shows us how to serve our pages using Express. Express is a full-featured web application framework that provides us with many features while writing very little code. It also has a rich middleware system that others have extended. This middleware allows us to work with form data as well as use templates and sessions. We will build the foundation of the application, on which all the other chapters will be based.

Chapter 2, Extending Our Development with Socket.IO, shows us how to build real-time applications using WebSockets. WebSockets are the next step in the evolution of dynamic web pages that allow users to interact instantaneously. This chapter also covers the use of tying Socket.IO to the sessions that Express creates.

Chapter 3, Authenticating Users, shows us how to build a login page that actually works! We will be using the Passport framework to build our authentication functions. Passport has performed a lot of heavy lifting in building connectors to different providers. Many of these implemented OAuth or OAuth 2.0. If you have ever had to develop against these different OAuth providers, you can appreciate the work that went into each library. You will also be shown how to store local passwords securely.

Chapter 4, RabbitMQ for Message Queuing, covers the topic of message queues. These are a requirement of any scalable application, allowing you to break your application up, that serves both its complexity and scope. In this chapter, we will cover some great use cases for this. In addition, you will be able to build your own message queues and tie them to functions.

Chapter 5, Adopting Redis for Application Data, shows us how to use the store information and retrieve it from Redis. This is important, as the Redis data storage engine is unlike any relational database. Thinking of it as such can actually create issues! We will cover the commands you will use the most throughout your application, as well as take a look at how Redis implements message queuing in your application.

Chapter 6, Using Bower to Manage Our Frontend Dependencies, begins to take a look at how you can begin the frontend development of your application. We will not have an application without a frontend. We will talk about the frameworks that will be used and why they are chosen.

Chapter 7, Using Backbone and React for DOM Events, covers the backbone, if you can excuse the pun, of the frontend of our application. The two most important tasks when using JavaScript in a browser are DOM manipulation and responding to events. You will learn how to listen for real-time events and then interact with the page. Backbone and React will help us build the maintainable code to do this.

Chapter 8, JavaScript Best Practices for Application Development, shows us how to build better JavaScript. JavaScript, as a scripting language, will run despite making many mistakes, which is both a good and a bad thing. However, you will still need to know if you have forgotten a semicolon or caused a runtime error. We will achieve this by building a repeatable build system. You will also be shown modules and how to module proof the code.

Chapter 9, Deployment and Scalability, shows us how to remove our site off localhost. It is critical to get a deployment script right, as it is very easy to miss a step when deploying. We will cover how to deploy to one, two, or more servers, including having different environments from which we can deploy. The advantage of these multiple servers for your application is that it is horizontally scalable, making it easy to add more servers.

Chapter 10, Debugging and Troubleshooting, shows us how to look at the context of a function call because strewing console.log() functions everywhere is a horrible method to debug. We will also learn how to track memory leaks in both the frontend and backend. If you have had experience in debugging JavaScript in Chrome, you will feel right at home here.

What you need for this book

A computer and an editor! Node.js is cross-platform; so Windows, Mac OS X, or Linux will all work. You can use any text editor, although I will be using Sublime Text 2 for some of the coding. I will also use an IDE for other parts, which is JetBrains PyCharm, with its Node.js module installed. You can use PyCharm, WebStorm, or IntelliJ IDEA from JetBrains, as they are all cross-platform.

You will also need the latest (at the time of this writing) version of Node.js, which is v0.10.26. The API could change (it has changed previously), so later versions could cause issues. The version of each Node package will be shown to you when you first go to install and use it.

The level of expertise you will need is just a little familiarity with Node and experience with building applications. We will touch upon many different frameworks throughout the book. You do not need to know about any of them in depth, and that is why you are reading this book! You should also know how to run things from the console (whether it is Mac OS X, Linux, or Windows) and how to get and install software packages.

Here is a summary of the version of different technologies you will be using in some of the chapters:

- Each chapter will list out all of the npm packages that will be needed for development.

- *Chapter 4, RabbitMQ for Message Queuing*, will require RabbitMQ Version 3.2.3.

- *Chapter 5, Adopting Redis for Application Data*, will be using Redis Version 2.8.6.

- *Chapter 9, Deployment and Scalability*, will require Python 2.7+ or Python 3+ to be installed. It will be used for building the deploy script. You don't need to be fluent in Python, as the syntax is very straightforward and I will cover what you will need to know. We will also need an SSH client. Mac OS X already has both installed. Linux will have an SSH client and will most likely have Python installed already, and you can install both in Windows.

- *Chapter 10, Debugging and Troubleshooting*, will be using Google Chrome. If you have worked in web development, you probably already have this installed. If you do not have Chrome, it is free and can be easily downloaded from Google.

I will personally be using Mac OS X using iTerm as my terminal application and Homebrew for installing software packages. If I run any commands, it will be in this context.

Who this book is for

This book is geared toward an intermediate JavaScript developer. It is assumed you have built applications using Node.js and that you may have used some of the frameworks before. We will work through each framework separately and also explain how to tie them all together. This book also touches upon the backend and frontend of JavaScript development. You will find this book helpful if you are well-versed in one, but lacking in the other.

This book is also perfect for someone who has read about scalability but is not sure what exactly this means for their projects. We will cover how to build applications that are horizontally scalable.

Conventions

In this book, you will find a number of styles of text that distinguish between different kinds of information. Here are some examples of these styles, and an explanation of their meaning.

Code words in text, database table names, folder names, filenames, file extensions, pathnames, dummy URLs, user input, and Twitter handles are shown as follows: "Our app.js file kicks off everything that deals with Express."

A block of code is set as follows:

```
var sayMyName = function(name){
//please don't alert anything
//this is not 1992
alert(name);
}
```

When we wish to draw your attention to a particular part of a code block, the relevant lines or items are set in bold:

```
//get the err and data
function(err, data) {
//you have access to data here
var id = data.objects[0].id;
}
```

Any command-line input or output is written as follows:

```
# npm install express --save
```

New terms and **important words** are shown in bold. Words that you see on the screen, in menus or dialog boxes, for example, appear in the text like this: "Click on the **Login** button to log in."

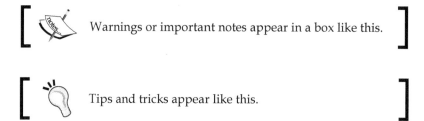

Warnings or important notes appear in a box like this.

Tips and tricks appear like this.

Reader feedback

Feedback from our readers is always welcome. Let us know what you think about this book—what you liked or may have disliked. Reader feedback is important for us to develop titles you really get the most out of.

To send us general feedback, simply send an e-mail to feedback@packtpub.com, and mention the book title through the subject of your message.

If there is a topic you have expertise in and you are interested in either writing or contributing to a book, see our author guide at www.packtpub.com/authors.

Customer support

Now that you are the proud owner of a Packt book, we have a number of things to help you to get the most from your purchase.

Downloading the example code

You can download the example code files for all Packt books you have purchased from your account at http://www.packtpub.com. If you purchased this book elsewhere, you can visit http://www.packtpub.com/support and register to have the files e-mailed directly to you.

Downloading the color images of this book

We also provide you at a PDF file that has color images of the screenshots/diagrams used in this book. The color images will help you better understand the changes in the output. You can download this file from: `https://www.packtpub.com/sites/default/files/downloads/4480OS_ColoredImages.pdf`.

Errata

Although we have taken every care to ensure the accuracy of our content, mistakes do happen. If you find a mistake in one of our books—maybe a mistake in the text or the code—we would be grateful if you would report this to us. By doing so, you can save other readers from frustration and help us improve subsequent versions of this book. If you find any errata, please report them by visiting `http://www.packtpub.com/support`, selecting your book, clicking on the **errata submission form** link, and entering the details of your errata. Once your errata are verified, your submission will be accepted and the errata will be uploaded to our website, or added to any list of existing errata, under the Errata section of that title.

Piracy

Piracy of copyrighted material on the Internet is an ongoing problem across all media. At Packt, we take the protection of our copyright and licenses very seriously. If you come across any illegal copies of our works, in any form, on the Internet, please provide us with the location address or website name immediately so we can pursue a remedy.

Please contact us at `copyright@packtpub.com` with a link to the suspected pirated material.

We appreciate your help in protecting our authors, and our ability to bring you valuable content.

Questions

You can contact us at `questions@packtpub.com` if you are having a problem with any aspect of the book, and we will do our best to address it.

1

Backend Development with Express

This chapter will show how to set up Express for our application. Express is the application framework for Node.js. If Node.js is the foundation, Express will be the framework of our house. Express provides us with routing, sessions, form processing, and so on. Entire books have been written on it, so we will just touch on what we require. If you have never used Express before in a Node project, don't worry, you will get a good feel of it by the end of this chapter. If you were lucky enough to use Express before, then hopefully I can show you something you don't already know.

The topics that we will cover in this chapter are as follows:

- Serving and responding to HTTP requests
- Routing
- Middleware
- Templating
- Creating sessions
- Parsing form data
- Integrating everything together

Node.js and Node Package Manager

Node.js is a platform that uses Google Chrome's JavaScript engine. This means that we can create server applications using JavaScript. We do not need an in-depth knowledge of everything on Node.js, we only need it to be installed. Node.js binaries are packaged for all the major platforms at `http://nodejs.org/download/`.

We will use npm (also known as Node Package Manager) to install all the libraries that we are going to use. Most languages/platforms/frameworks move to a managed packaging system. This will be familiar if you have ever used Python's pip with virtualenv, Debian's apt-get, or Microsoft's NuGet, to name a few. Managed packaging allows developers to explicitly define what dependencies your application requires. We will install almost all the Node packages locally. This allows us to install and test new dependencies separately without creating conflicts on the system. By default, npm installs the packages to a folder named `node_modules` in the root of our project. When a package is used in a file, Node will check this directory for the package. The code that accompanies each chapter will not have the `node_modules` directory included, but it will have the file that defines what is needed. When we install something globally, we will use the `-g` flag for npm. This installs the packages to a central `node_modules` directory so that every Node project can use the package. If you have built a Node.js project before, this should not be new. I will write out the commands for anyone that has not used npm.

Node packages are very notorious for having fast release cycles, which means that by the time you have read this, some of the packages you will use might be of a different version. There are a few ways to combat this. We can use `npm shrinkwrap`, which will explicitly define each package and all its dependencies. Another way, is to include all the dependencies into source control, so we are completely sure what package and version is installed. I will list out the versions I have used, so that you can install the same versions. As an example, Express has already gone through a major version upgrade (from Version 3.x to 4.x), which was not completely backwards compatible.

The following are the versions that we will use:

- body-parser: 1.4.3
- connect: 3.0.2
- cookie-parser: 1.3.2
- csurf: 1.3.0
- ejs: 0.8.5
- express: 4.6.1
- express-partials: 0.2.0
- express-session: 1.6.5
- redis: 0.10.1
- connect-redis: 1.4.7
- connect-flash: 0.1.1

To ensure that these are the versions installed, you can create a file in the root of the project named `package.json`. The file should look similar to the following code:

```
{
  "name": "NodeChat",
  "version": "0.0.0",
  "main": "app.js",
  "scripts": {
    "stop": "echo not implemented",
    "start": "node ./app.js"
  },
  "dependencies": {
    "ejs": "0.8.5",
    "express": "4.6.1",
    "express-partials": "0.2.0",
    "redis": "0.10.1",
    "connect-redis": "1.4.7",
    "connect-flash": "0.1.1"
  }
}
```

Downloading the example code

You can download the example code files for all Packt books you have purchased from your account at http://www.packtpub.com. If you purchased this book elsewhere, you can visit http://www.packtpub.com/support and register to have the files e-mailed directly to you.

The `package.json` file defines attributes about our project using JSON. The key property that we are concerned with here is dependencies. We define each one in the dependency object along with the version. Note that each dependency is pinned to a specific version. We can add a line to install Express 4 or above as follows:

```
"express": ">=4.0.0"
```

The issue with this is that we will not know what version we can get. Always prefer explicit dependencies to implicit ones.

We can then install the required packages by running the following command:

```
npm install
```

Using Express in Node

With everything installed, we can create our project directory. It does not matter where you create it (I created a `projects` directory under my user folder), but all the files we created will be referenced from the root of this folder. To do this, create an `app.js` file. Note that the aim here is to build our very own, simple Express application. To get started, open `app.js` and add the following code to it:

```
var express = require('express');
var app = express();

app.get('*',function(req, res){
  res.send('Express Response');
});

app.listen(3000);
console.log("App server running on port 3000");
```

To start the Express server, we will run the following commands:

node app.js

npm start

The first tells Node to run using this file. The other uses the value from our `package.json` file under `scripts.start`. We can then open our browser to `http://localhost:3000`. Any path we put into our browser will return the Express response, which you can see in the following screenshot:

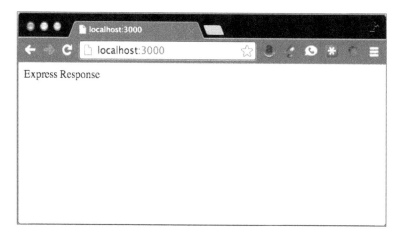

In order to receive this response, the `app.get` function uses a regular expression to match any GET request, no matter the path. The `req` and `res` objects are the request and response objects. The `res.send` Express function adds all the basic headers for us, before sending the response back.

The Express application can respond to all the common HTTP verbs such as GET, POST, PUT, and DELETE. As you have guessed by now, we will use these verbs in order to use the method call passing in the path, as well as the callback.

Although this works well, it is in fact not very useful. We will need to define routes, which are specific HTTP verbs matching with the URL. We need to add all of our routes and connect them to functions. Our application is very simple from a routing standpoint. We will have an index page, a login page that has a form, and a chat page. Although we can just as easily add all of these functions to `app.js`, `app.js`, it will then become very difficult to maintain quickly. Instead, we will create a routes folder and then add an `index.js` file. Our folder structure should then look similar to the one in the following screenshot:

Inside the `index.js` file in `routes`, we will create all our routes with the following code:

```
module.exports.index = index;
module.exports.login = login;
module.exports.loginProcess = loginProcess;
module.exports.chat = chat;
function index(req, res){
  res.send('Index');
};
function login(req, res){
  res.send('Login');
};
function loginProcess(req, res){
  res.redirect('/');
};
function chat(req, res){
  res.send('Chat');
};
```

Following this, `app.js` should only use our routes. Our `app.js` file should look similar to the following code:

```
var express = require('express');
var app = express();
var routes = require('./routes');

app.get('/', routes.index);
app.get('/login', routes.login);
app.post('/login', routes.loginProcess);
app.get('/chat', routes.chat);

app.listen(3000);
console.log("App server running on port 3000");
```

Our routes are now nice and clean, which also lends itself to aliases. If we want people to be able to see the login form from /login and /account/login, we just have to add the following line:

```
app.get('/account/login', routes.login);
```

We can also group related functions together in the same file. Our example is simple, but it will be easy to have as many files mapping to specific routes. Each file would just have the functions that relate to its primary duty, which means you could then wire them to any route you wanted.

You may already be asking, "What happens when a route is not defined?". This is, in fact, a great question, and it was something I was just about to discuss. By default, Express will respond with Cannot GET /notfoundURL. Usually, it is a bad idea to keep this as our 404 response. What we actually want is to tell the user that they have made a wrong turn somewhere. This naturally leads us to our next major idea — using middleware in Express.

Using middleware in Express

One of the greatest things about Express is that it is easily extended, which is achieved by using middleware. Every request makes its way through the middleware layer. In fact, our routes are just the final middleware function. We return a response, which means that at this point, the request is done and no more middleware functions are executed.

Creating our own middleware

To create our own middleware, all we have to do is create a function that accepts the parameters `req`, `res`, and `next`. Inside of this function, we should have access to request and response, and the ability to tell Express to move on to the next piece of middleware.

To add a middleware layer to Express, we use `app.use()`, which allows us to take a middleware function. So, let's create our own 404 middleware function! Create a directory named middleware and a file called `errorhandlers.js`, before putting the following code in the file:

```
exports.notFound = function notFound(req, res, next){
   res.send(404, 'You seem lost. You must have taken a wrong turn back
there.');
};
```

Now, update `app.js` and put this code right after the initial block of variable declarations, but before we define `routes`. This should be line 4. This is shown as follows:

```
var errorHandlers = require('./middleware/errorhandlers');
app.use(errorHandlers.notFound);
```

We didn't call the next function here because no other middleware matches this route at this point. We can safely send the response by letting the user know that they are lost. Let's fire this up and check it out. We will type a nonexistent route, `http://localhost:3000/notfound`, into our browser. So far, everything looks good. Now, let's try a known route, `http://localhost:3000/`. Uh-oh! Everything is responding as not found. What did we do wrong?

If you can keep a secret, I'll let you know that I knew this wasn't going to work. Middleware runs in the order they are added in Express. We only added one middleware, which means it runs on every request. This middleware also returns a response and does not run the `next()` function.

Since I trust that you can keep secrets, I will tell you another one. You can actually call `next()` after sending a response. You will, in all probability, create an error because another middleware/route will try to send a response that you cannot. To sum this up, if you send a response from middleware, do not call `next()`. The default action of our routes is to just return a response and not run `next`.

How do we fix this issue? Pretty easily, in fact. We will add in another piece of middleware before our notFound handler. It will be the app.router middleware, since this is the function that maps all the routes. If a request matches a defined route, then it will execute the function we have defined for that route and return a response. If it doesn't match anything, the next middleware will be called. You should then open up app.js and move app.use(errorHandlers.notFound) under the routes we have created:

```
app.get('/', routes.index);
app.get('/login', routes.login);
app.post('/login', routes.loginProcess);
app.get('/chat', routes.chat);
app.use(errorHandlers.notFound);
```

This will check the request to see if it matches a route. If not, run the next middleware, which is the notFound function. Our app is now running how we expect it to. Try loading all the routes, and then run the routes that we know will create a 404 error to test our new middleware.

Let's add a few more pieces of middleware. First off, let's add a logging middleware. Create log.js under the middleware folder and put the following code in:

```
exports.logger = function logger(req, res, next){
  console.log(req.url);
  next();
};
```

Then, modify app.js, and add this as the first middleware:

```
var errorHandlers = require('./middleware/errorhandlers');
var log = require('./middleware/log');
app.use(log.logger);

app.get('/', routes.index);
app.get('/login', routes.login);
app.post('/login', routes.loginProcess);
app.get('/chat', routes.chat);
app.use(errorHandlers.notFound);
```

Each request will log the URL to the console. We did not modify the request in any way, so it continues down the middleware path to the route or the notFound handler. We can change this to write to a file or a database, but we are keeping things simple for now (is this foreshadowing? It probably is!). Also, we do not need to modify the request or response in any way.

Although we built our own logging middleware for demonstration purposes, Express comes with its own logging middleware, which is `express.logger()`.

Next, we will add the ability to serve static assets. Most sites use CSS and JavaScript, and we don't want to send these files through the view rendering engine (a concept we will get to later in this chapter). Express comes with middleware that can serve static files. So, create a folder in our project called `static`, and then create a file called `static.txt`, putting whatever you want in the file. Now, add the static middleware right above the router, as follows:

```
app.use(log.logger);
app.use(express.static(__dirname + '/static'));
```

Anything you put in this folder will be served. Browse to `http://localhost:3000/static.txt`, and you should see whatever you added to the file.

Finally, let's add an error handler. This middleware has a different function signature. It takes the four parameter functions of `err`, `req`, `res`, and `next`. This conforms to the node practice of passing the error as the first parameter. We will add the error handler inside `middleware/errorhandlers.js`. To conclude, add the following code to the file:

```
exports.error = function error(err, req, res, next){
  console.log(err);
  res.send(500, 'Something broke. What did you do?');
};
```

Here is our final middleware stack in `app.js`:

```
app.use(log.logger);
app.use(express.static(__dirname + '/static'));
app.get('/', routes.index);
app.get('/login', routes.login);
app.post('/login', routes.loginProcess);
app.get('/chat', routes.chat);

app.use(errorHandlers.error);
app.use(errorHandlers.notFound);
```

At this point, we cannot test the error handler. Every request we create does not throw an error, so let's create a route that actually does. Add this to the end of our route definitions:

```
app.get('/error', function(req, res, next){
  next(new Error('A contrived error'));
});
```

Remember that a route is just another piece of middleware. We create an error here to pass to the error handler. The only middleware that will match the function signature with an error is our new error handler. If we go to /error, we will see that our logging middleware writes to the console, followed by the error middleware writing our error to the console. It then concludes with **Something broke. What did you do?**. Our little website is now not blowing up on errors and logging everything.

Right now, we are serving HTTP responses based on routes and wired-up logging, 404 not found error page, and error handling middleware. This is all in roughly 20 lines of code in app.js. Not too bad!

Adding templates to the mix

We now have a working site that has routes and middleware, but we are missing one import thing—HTML. Our requests come back with a Content-Type of text/html. Although res.send() adds this header for us, it is just text. It is missing a document type, head, and body, which is where another feature of Express comes in: templates.

We will use **Embedded JavaScript** (**EJS**) as our view template engine. I must notify you here that many tutorials, and even the Express command-line utility, default the view engine to Jade. I have used a few other template systems, which are not limited to PHP (which by itself is a kind of template system), Python's Django template, and Microsoft's Razor engine in MVC, to name a few. Luckily, EJS feels closer to all of these. I also feel that I don't need a parser to build my HTML. I want to write HTML and then add my variables where I need them. These are just a few reasons why we will continue using EJS.

 If you like to use Jade, a major part of the application configuration will be the same. You will just have to build your own templates.

On a side note, I will reiterate that we don't want to install Express globally. You will see answers on Stack Overflow asking if the questioner has installed it locally or globally. Everything we need to do can be done locally. There is nothing that Express installed globally can do differently, where even the command-line utility works in this way:

```
./node_modules/.bin/express --help.
```

We need to enable Express's view engine using the Express command `app.set()`. Before our middleware stack (`app.use()`), we should add the following:

```
app.set('view engine', 'ejs');
app.use(log.logger);
app.use(express.static(__dirname + '/static'));
```

To see a list of possible settings, visit `http://expressjs.com/api.html#app-settings`. The two settings we are concerned with now are view engine and views. The `views` setting is used to set the view directory. By default, it is set to the `views` directory under the current directory. We will use the default value, so now we should create a directory named `views`. Our current folder structure should then look as shown in the following screenshot:

```
.
├── app.js
├── middleware
│   ├── errorhandlers.js
│   └── log.js
├── node_modules
├── routes
│   └── index.js
├── static
│   └── static.txt
└── views
```

Under `views`, create a file named `index.ejs` and add the following HTML code to it:

```
<!DOCTYPE html>
<html>
<head>
  <title>Index</title>
</head>
<body>
Index
</body>
</html>
```

Following this, open up `index.js` from `routes`, and modify the index function as follows:

```
exports.index = function index(req, res){
  res.render('index');
};
```

Restart node and load the root. Alright, you now have a valid HTML5 document. Express knows to look in the `views` directory (views setting) for `index.ejs` (view engine setting). This is working great, but it is not very dynamic. We want to be able to change the response. We will need to modify the `index.ejs` file and change the head element, which you can do in the following way:

```
<head>
  <title><%= title %></title>
</head>
```

The main features we will use from EJS are `<%= %>`, which will output the value of the variable into the HTML document and `<% %>`, which allows us to execute JavaScript. Any `if` or `for` loop will also be used, in addition to any plain JavaScript.

Now, we have to pass a title variable to the view, so you can add the following code to the index function:

```
res.render('index', {title: 'Index'});
```

Browse to `http://localhost:3000/`, and you should see that the title of the tab is now **Index**. You can view the source of this page and see that it is rendered in HTML. This is great but not very maintainable. Essentially, this is no different than running a completely static website. So, we next need to add a layout.

Layouts

Express 3 lets each template-rendering library implement its own layout, which means it does not force any set way on the layout. This is different from Express 2 as it's defaulted to using a file named `layout` in the `views` directory. You will have to be careful that you do not get information about Express 2 when searching on the Internet. Our package of EJS does not have layout support, but we have already installed a package that does, which is `express-partials`.

We have to do a little setup to let Express know that we are using partials. The first step is to get a reference to our new library, which you can do by:

```
//all the other variables declarations at the top of app.js
var partials = require('express-partials');
```

Next, we add it as middleware. The only caveat here is that it has to be before our routes. This makes sense because we will have to render our complete page before the server sends a response.

```
app.use(partials());
//all other middleware functions
```

Finally, we can add a view option for the default layout.

```
//after variable declarations
app.set('view options', {defaultLayout: 'layout'});
//but before the middleware
```

Setting the default layout is not required, but I will recommend it. Otherwise, we will have to define the layout for every view. We can override the default layout (or set it in the first place) using the render function:

```
res.render('index', {layout: 'layout', title: 'Index'});
```

Now that we have our layout setup, we can create it and update all our routes to use the layout. Create a file called `layout.ejs` in the views folder. Add the following code to it:

```
<!DOCTYPE html>
<html>
<head>
  <title><%= title %></title>
</head>
<body>
<%- body %>
</body>
</html>
```

Now, we can create two more files called `login.ejs` and `chat.ejs`. Finally, we have to update each `res.render` function to have the name of the file to render and a title.

```
exports.login = function chat(req, res){
  res.render('login', {title: 'Login'});
};
exports.chat = function chat(req, res){
  res.render('chat', {title: 'Chat'});
};
```

Now, all the routes will return valid HTML.

Let's go ahead and make our layout pretty. We will add the HTML code that our app will use, and the CSS framework we will be using is Bootstrap. It's great to get projects off the ground as we can start to be concerned with the code as opposed to the design. We will use a theme named **Cosmo** from http://bootswatch. com/ so that our site does not look like a default Bootstrap site. We can get the CSS framework from http://bootswatch.com/cosmo/. Once you have downloaded the CSS file, create a new directory named `css` under the static directory. The path from root should be `static/css/cosmo.min.css`.

You can recognize Bootstrap sites as they have the same font, buttons, color, and CSS elements. If you are going to build something, you will want to differentiate it from other sites. You want users to associate with your site with just a look.

After carrying out all of these tasks, here is what our layout should look like:

```html
<!DOCTYPE html>
<html>
<head>
    <title><%= title %></title>
    <link rel="stylesheet" href="css/cosmo.min.css">
</head>
<body>
<div class="container">
  <div class="row">
      <div class="col-sm-4"><h1>PacktChat</h1></div>
  </div>
  <div class="row">
  <%- body %>
  </div>
</div>
</body>
</html>
```

Refer to the following screenshot to see the index page in the new layout:

PacktChat

Index

I recommend using Bootstrap when you start your projects. You can easily get a good-looking site without spending any time in design. Another great option is to use Zurb's Foundation. Using either of these frameworks is a good idea if you do not have much design experience. You can always go back and change the look.

Using sessions in Express

Express uses the same methods, cookies, as most other web frameworks to track sessions. A cookie will have the session ID so that Express can look it up on each request.

Using cookies in Express

The latest version of Express has taken out much of the middleware that was previously included in Express. This is important when migrating from Express 3 to 4. We will use the `cookie-parser` package, which should already be installed. We will now add cookie parsing to our app. It is a middleware, so we will put it with all the other middleware. Remember that the middleware is processed in order, so that we can add each before the middleware that will actually use it, which is our routes. We will do this by adding a variable declaration and another function in the middleware stack.

```
//with all the other requires at the top of the file
var cookieParser = require('cookie-parser');
//in the middleware stack
app.use(express.static(__dirname + '/static'));
app.use(cookieParser());
```

We will repeat this pattern many times over this chapter and the next. Anytime there is `require`, it will be at the top of the file. The code that comes along with the book will also declare all the variables together. There will be one `var`, and each line will have `require` with a comma instead of a semicolon. Whether there is one `var` declaration or many, the code will still run. Further down in the file, we will use our new variable. I will try to include landmarks in the code to help, but we will add a lot of code in many places at times. Refer to the code that is supplied with the book.

The cookie parser gives us access to `req.cookies`. This will be an object that we can read the values out of. At this point, if we run our application, nothing will be different. We have not set cookies, nor are we trying to access them. Let's change that.

First, let's set up our views to show us the cookies in the request. In `index.ejs` under `views`, let's add the section. The file should look similar to the following code:

```
Index
<div>Cookie passed: <%= cookie %></div>
```

We now have to pass the cookie to our view. You should edit `routes/index.js` and add this to our `view` function. Note that we do not need to specify a layout because we have a default layout set with `app.set('view options', {defaultLayout: 'layout'})`.

```
exports.index = function index(req, res){
  res.render('index', {title: 'Index', cookie: JSON.stringify(req.
cookies)});
};
```

Let's check it out in the browser. We should see that we have a blank cookie object in our request. It is time to create our own cookie. Open the JavaScript console in the browser (I am using Google Chrome) and type this in:

```
document.cookie="test=Test Cookie"
```

Refresh the page and see that it has our cookie in it. We can see that the request cookie object is just a simple JavaScript object, as seen in the following screenshot:

PacktChat

Index
Cookie passed: {"test":"Test Cookie"}

Next, we will set a cookie from the server. Express has a simple way to do this: in our `index.js` file under `routes`, let's add a cookie in the `index` function:

```
exports.index = function index(req, res){
  res.cookie('IndexCookie', 'This was set from Index');

res.render('index', {title: 'Index', cookie: JSON.stringify(req.
cookies)});
};
```

Restart the node and load the page twice. The first restart will set the cookie, and the second restart will read it into our response. From the following screenshot, you should now see both cookies on our page:

PacktChat

Index
Cookie passed: {"test":"Test Cookie","IndexCookie":"This was set from Index"}

You can also easily get rid of cookies by using `clearCookie` off the response object:

```
res.clearCookie('IndexCookie');
```

If you want to do it from the browser side, you can usually get a list of current cookies. In Chrome, this is in the developer tools. Click on the menu button in the upper right and navigate to **Tools | Developer Tools**. Then click on **Resources | Cookies**. You can then right-click on a specific cookie in the list and delete the cookie or select **Clear All** to delete all the cookies, as shown in the following screenshot:

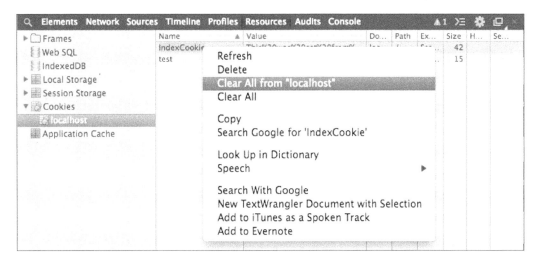

By now, you should be feeling good about adding and removing cookies to requests and responses, so now let's see how to tie these cookies to a session.

 Hopefully, I have demonstrated how easily any attacker can forge cookies. Do not store sensitive information in your cookie. For example, storing a Boolean variable whether or not the user is logged in is a bad idea. We will shortly cover how to do all of this securely.

Adding sessions

Sessions allow us to store data about requests that are tied together with a cookie. HTTP is stateless, but cookies that map back to a session allow us to know that this is the same browser making multiple requests. You should be able to guess by now that Express comes with a great session middleware.

The first thing to know is that we need to store our sessions somewhere. For now, we will use a memory store.

You should add this to our variable declarations at the top of `app.js`:

```
var session = require('express-session');
```

Next, add the middleware. You should remember to add it under our `cookieParser` middleware, as follows:

```
app.use(cookieParser());
app.use(session());
```

The `express session` uses cookies, so the cookie object needs to be present before it can use the session.

Now, we can use our session. We will update our index page to show what is stored in our session. Edit `index.ejs` under `views` to display a session:

```
Index
<div>Cookie passed: <%= cookie %></div>
<div>Session: <%= session %></div>
```

The session middleware adds a new object to our request, which is `req.session`. Let's pass this to the view from `index.js` under `middleware`:

```
function index(req, res){
  res.cookie('IndexCookie', 'This was set from Index');
  res.render('index', {title: 'Index', cookie: JSON.stringify(req.
cookies), session: JSON.stringify(req.session)});
};
```

Once you load this up, you will find that we get an error. If we check our console, as you can see from the following screenshot, we need to add a secret option for sessions:

```
/
[Error: `secret` option required for sessions]
```

We can now do this by revisiting our session middleware and adding a secret option:

```
app.use(session({secret: 'secret'}));
```

The `secret` option uses the string we pass in to create a hash of our session ID, so we can tell if someone has tried to tamper with our cookie (also known as a request forgery). We just covered ways by which users can easily delete and create any cookie that they want. If our cookie had a session ID in it, which for example could be 1234, a user could delete that cookie and create a new one with a session ID of 1235. As far as the server knows, the next request comes from the user who has session 1235. A hashed session ID makes this much more difficult. If the user does not know the secret (don't actually use secret or 123456, use something such as `http://randomkeygen.com/` or `http://www.guidgenerator.com/` to get a unique secure secret), then their ability to create a valid token is reduced. This is a very contrived example, but it should illustrate why we need this.

Reload the node and refresh twice. We can now see our session and the cookie that was created in the following screenshot:

PacktChat

Index
Cookie passed: {"test":"Test
Cookie","connect.sid":"s:l9vJYsdMJ5DquOUqTDp0HhjD.ZWbMdo/J6oD6qqExln94TP5PgilnU4wC+Olm76yCjaM","IndexCookie":"This was set
from Index"}
Session: {"cookie":{"originalMaxAge":null,"expires":null,"httpOnly":true,"path":"/"}}

We can test our security by deleting our `connect.sid` cookie and creating a new one. On the next request, we will get a new `connect.sid` cookie set.

Let's build a simple page counter in the session. On each request, we will increment a counter. We can do this easily by adding a middleware function. We only need to remember to add it under the session middleware so that we have access to `req.session`; we will write this function inline as we are not going to keep it in our final middleware stack. Add this to the stack right under session:

```
app.use(function(req, res, next){
  if(req.session.pageCount)
    req.session.pageCount++;
  else
    req.session.pageCount = 1;
  next();
});
```

Test it by going around and loading a bunch of pages. The `pageCount` session variable should track each different request you make. The request could be a 404 or even an error. Our middleware runs and adds to the total before any error handling. One thing to remember is that only our index view will output `pageCount`. After testing this, we can remove the middleware.

One limitation to how we have set this up is that only the node instance that created the session also has access to it. If you run multiple node instances, you will need to have a different session store from memory.

Redis as a session store

Redis is an in-memory key-value store. We will use Redis to hold the session ID as a key and the session data as a value. It is important to note that we will not get into what Redis is and how to install it here as *Chapter 5, Adopting Redis for Application Data,* will cover the topic. Also, we will not cover the security issues with Redis now as we just want to get it working for our sessions. However, we will cover how to add it as an Express session store.

We will use the two packages `redis` and `connect-redis`. To use a Redis store, we assume that we are running Redis locally and that Redis' version is above 2.0.0 (the latest version, as of writing this book, is 2.8.6, so this isn't a huge hurdle). First, let's change our reference to the memory store so that our variable session will point to a `connect-redis` instance. Change these variable declarations in `app.js`:

```
var session = require('express-session');
var RedisStore = require('connect-redis')(session);
```

Connect-redis extends the session. We can now set up our middleware. Change our session middleware to this:

```
app.use(session({
  secret: 'secret',
  saveUninitialized: true,
  resave: true,
  store: new RedisStore(
    {url: 'redis://localhost'})
  })
);
```

We use the same secret, but we will now create a new `RedisStore` object with an options object using the Redis server's URL. This URL can take a username, password, and port, if all of these were not the default values. At this point, we can restart our server and load up our index page. It should be working in exactly the same way as it was with an in-memory store. We also have a couple of other options. If these are not added, a warning is thrown.

Let's actually take a peek into what is happening here. We know at this point that our session is tracked with a cookie, but unfortunately, this is a signed value. We can get access to this by changing our `cookieParser` middleware to use the same secret as the session middleware. The following line of code is what our new `cookieParser` line should look like:

```
app.use(cookieParser('secret'));
```

Remember that the secret passed must match the one used for the session. This is because the session middleware creates the cookie and the `cookieParser` middleware reads it out. We will now have `req.signedCookies`. Any signed cookie will be here, so it is time to test this out. We will need to update `index.ejs` in the `View` folder and `index.js` in the `routes` folder provided in the code bundle.

The `index.ejs` file in the `views` folder looks like:

```
Index
<div>Cookie passed: <%= cookie %></div>
<div>Signed Cookie passed: <%= signedCookie %></div>
<div>Session: <%= session %></div>
```

The `index.js` file in the `routes` folder looks like:

```
exports.index = function index(req, res){
  res.cookie('IndexCookie', 'This was set from Index');
  res.render('index', {title: 'Index',
    cookie: JSON.stringify(req.cookies),
    session: JSON.stringify(req.session),
    signedCookie: JSON.stringify(req.signedCookies)});
};
```

From the following screenshot, you can see that our unsigned cookies will be first and our `connect.sid` cookie will be second:

PacktChat

Index
Cookie passed: {"test":"Test Cookie","IndexCookie":"This was set from Index"}
Signed Cookie passed: {"connect.sid":"0DMsXhobExvbCL3FFeYqRGWE"}
Session: {"cookie":{"originalMaxAge":null,"expires":null,"httpOnly":true,"path":"/"}}

The browser will still get the signed cookie, as you can see in the following screenshot:

Name	Value
test	Test Cookie
connect.sid	s%3A0DMsXhobExvbCL3FFeYqRGWE.vhahB%2BEEv7gy2FgTXB2u1X8fbGoZw8roEUnxGxrWP7c
IndexCookie	This%20was%20set%20from%20Index

Without getting too much into Redis, we will look up our session in Redis. We can quickly install Redis on Mac OS X by running the following command:

```
brew install redis
```

We can then launch `redis-cli` (which we should now have if we have Redis installed. If you face issues, jump to *Chapter 5, Adopting Redis for Application Data*). We can now run a command against Redis. connect-redis will prepend `sess:` to all the session keys in Redis. To see our session, we will run `GET sess:YOUR-SESSION-ID`, as shown in the following command line:

```
$ redis-cli

127.0.0.1:6379> GET sess:0DMsXhobExvbCL3FFeYqRGWE

"{\"cookie\":{\"originalMaxAge\":null,\"expires\":null,\"httpOnly\":true,
\"path\":\"/\"}}"
```

We can see that this returns our session object as an escaped string. You can compare this to the object that was returned from our response and see that it is the same. We have successfully moved our sessions to a data store that can be accessed from multiple servers. One of the most basic ideas of creating a scalable application is not to keep any shared state on the local instance. Previously, with the memory store for sessions, each server had its own state. Now, we can have multiple servers share the state. Here, we are using Redis, but you can use any data store to do this (which is not limited to memcache, MongoDB, Postgres, and many others). We are not going to do this here in this chapter, but we have started to prepare our app to be scalable. Another thing to note is that the Redis server is running on localhost. For a production-ready scalable application, Redis will be moved to a separate server or even several servers.

Let's clean up our views a little. You definitely do not want to send all of a user's session data to them. In `index.ejs` in the `views` folder, remove everything except for Index. In `index.js` in the `routes` folder, drop all the other attributes except for title, and remove the line that sets the cookie. This is shown as follows:

```
exports.index = function index(req, res){
  res.render('index', {title: 'Index'});
};
```

Processing forms

All web frameworks that are useful allow you to process forms. We have a route that we have not tested yet, which is `app.post('/login', routes.loginProcess);`. We have only been using and testing GET routes, so let's build a form and then do something with it.

We will create the form on the `/login` GET request. Before we modify our template, we will need some local styles that extend Bootstrap. Firstly, create a file that is called `style.css` in `static/css`, and add the following styles to it:

```
.facebook {background: #3b5998; color: #ffffff;}
.google {background: #dd4b39; color: #ffffff;}
.top-margin {margin-top: 20px;}
```

These are the styles that we will use to extend base Bootstrap. The styles are mainly for making sure that we color our social buttons correctly.

Please don't forget to add this to our layout:

```
<link rel="stylesheet" href="css/style.css">
```

We can now create our login form, which you can do by opening up `login.ejs` in `login.ejs` and adding the following code:

```
<div class="row">
    <div class="col-sm-8 col-sm-offset-2">
        <div class="row">
            <div class="col-sm-12">
              <form method="post">
                <div class="form-group">
                    <label for="username">Username</label>
                    <input type="text" class="form-control"
id="username" placeholder="username" name="username">
                </div>
                <div class="form-group">
                    <label for="password">Password</label>
                    <input type="password" class="form-control"
id="password" placeholder="password" name="password">
                </div>
                <button class="btn btn-primary btn-block">Login</
button>
            </div>
        </form>
```

```
            </div>
            <div class="row top-margin">
                <div class="col-sm-6">
                    <button class="btn btn-block facebook"><i class="fa
fa-facebook"></i> Facebook</button>
                </div>
                <div class="col-sm-6">
                    <button class="btn btn-block google"><i class="fa
fa-google-plus"></i> Google</button>
                </div>
            </div>
        </div>
    </div>
```

We will not spend a lot of time on all the classes for the elements because the Bootstrap documents are a quick-and-easy read if you are looking for a quick reference of each class. We should now have a nice-looking form, as shown in the following screenshot, although it cannot currently do much:

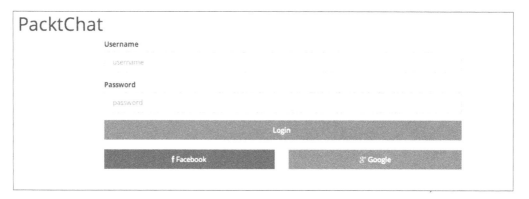

This should demonstrate why using Bootstrap can get your app running quickly. I am only using around a dozen different classes, and already, the form does not look like the basic browser style.

The form will make a POST request to /login, with the route responding with a redirect back to root. Express is not doing anything with our POST info, so let's change it.

We will first need to add a new piece of middleware (you should be seeing a trend now). Without parsing the body, our POST request will not see the data that we are sending. Add this variable declaration and middleware to the stack:

```
//variable declarations
var bodyParser = require('body-parser');
//middleware stack right after session
app.use(bodyParser.json());
app.use(bodyParser.urlencoded({extended: false}));
```

The middleware will process POST data that has a content type of `application/json` and `application/x-www-form-urlencoded`. We do not have the middleware for multipart as it can lead to a **denial-of-service (DOS)** attack. The multipart middleware creates a new `tmp` file for each new request, which can eventually kill your server. Since we are not processing files, we do not need to include it. The reason we do not use it is because it is merely a reference to all three of the parsers, as you can see in the following code line:

```
app.use(bodyParser());
```

Let's make sure that this is working how we expect it to. Open up the `index.js` file from `routes` and modify the `loginProcess` function to the following:

```
function loginProcess(req, res){
  console.log(req.body);
  res.send(req.body.username + ' ' + req.body.password);
};
```

Now, each post should show us what was entered into the form, instead of redirecting and writing it to the console. We can use the form we created, or we can use curl. Curl should be available if you are using Mac OS X or Linux, although it can be installed on Windows. Run the command below and check your node console:

```
$ curl -X POST -H "Content-Type: application/json" -d '{"username":"josh"
,"password":"password"}' http://localhost:3000/login
```

It should log { username: 'josh', password: 'password' } in the console. Let's test a URL encoded form now, so run the following curl command:

```
$ curl -X POST -H "Content-Type: application/x-www-form-urlencoded" -d
'username=josh&password=password' http://localhost:3000/login
```

It should log { username: 'josh', password: 'password' } in exactly the same way as the `json` request.

We have just built a form that will post back to itself and then parse out the form values.

Cross-Site Request Forgery (CSRF)

We are missing one huge security piece—the **Cross-Site Request Forgery (CSRF)** protection. Anyone can create a form and then tell it to process against our site. As far as Express is concerned, it is just another request, which is where CSRF comes in. It is essentially a token that is put into the form and a store on the server in the session. When the form is submitted, the server checks the token. If they do not match, the server knows the form is not from us and rejects it. It is time to implement it!

First, we add a..., you've got it, a middleware! Add the following code after your session and body parsing middleware:

```
//variable declarations
Var csrf = require('csurf');
//middleware stack
app.use(bodyParser.json());
app.use(bodyParser.urlencoded());
app.use(csrf());
```

By doing this, it will add the CSRF token to our session.

With CSRF loaded, let's try to submit our form using the POST method.
As you can see in the following screenshot, we get the error **Something broke. What did you do?**

```
{ [Error: Forbidden] status: 403 }
```

The CSRF middleware threw a 403 status code forbidden error. Our CSRF protection is working exactly as planned as we did not add the token to the form. This is exactly what will happen if someone with nefarious purposes tried to submit a form against our site with the token.

To fix this, let's add another piece of middleware (note that our app is 90 percent middleware and only 10 percent views). We will create a utility function file by creating a utilities.js file under the middleware directory. Inside this file, add the following:

```
module.exports.csrf = function csrf(req, res, next){
  res.locals.token = req.csrfToken();
  next();
};
```

Res.locals is a special object that is available to all templates that have access to this response. It will make all of its attributes available for the template to use. This is great for middleware as the only other way that we covered to get variables to the template was by passing them in through render(). Create a new variable at the top of app.js:

```
Var util = require('./middleware/utilities');
```

Add it as middleware directly under our CSRF middleware:

```
app.use(csrf());
app.use(util.csrf);
```

It seems a little redundant to add two straight CSRF middlewares, but they serve different functions. The first is the built-in middleware that will add the token to the session. The other is our utility that will take it from the session and make it available to the template. Maintainable middleware should have one simple single focus.

We can now edit our form to send this token, so right under the form declaration, add the following input tag:

```
<input type="hidden" name="_csrf" value="<%= token %>">
```

If you get errors while following along, I can almost guarantee that it is a middleware out-of-order issue. If you try to set the CSRF token in the session before the session is added to the request, you will get an error. When errors arise, step through your middleware and make sure that they are being executed in the correct order.

Our forms should now process and our middle stack should look similar to the following code:

```
app.use(partials());
app.use(log.logger);
app.use(express.static(__dirname + '/static'));
app.use(cookieParser('secret'));
app.use(session({
  secret: 'secret',
  saveUninitialized: true,
  resave: true,
  store: new RedisStore(
    {url: 'redis://localhost'})
  })
```

```
);app.use(bodyParser.json());
app.use(bodyParser.urlencoded());
app.use(csrf());
app.use(util.csrf);
app.get('/', routes.index);
app.get('/login', routes.login);
app.post('/login', routes.loginProcess);
app.get('/chat', routes.chat);
app.use(errorHandlers.error);
app.use(errorHandlers.notFound);
```

We have now learned all the basic building blocks of using Express. We will now take them and see how to build a functioning site.

 CSRF should be used for any POST endpoint that you make public. Without it, anyone can make POST requests to your server, and it will process them!

Very simple authentication

We want everyone who goes to /chat to be authenticated. We will build a very simple, yet very insecure, authentication system. We will then gut this and put in a real authentication system later, but this exercise will show us how all the pieces we have talked about work together. The first thing is to check if a user is logged in during a request. We will use middleware for this. Open up our utilities.js from the middleware folder, and add two new functions.

The first function is to add an isAuthenticated variable for our templates, which we will use shortly. The following is our function:

```
module.exports.authenticated = function authenticated(req, res, next){
  res.locals.isAuthenticated = req.session.isAuthenticated;
  if (req.session.isAuthenticated) {
    res.locals.user = req.session.user;
  }
  next();
};
```

We will store whether or not someone is authenticated in the session. We are just adding it to the response so that a template can check the isAuthenticated value. We also add a user object if the user is logged in.

Next, we will create middleware to check to see if someone is authenticated. If not, we redirect them to the login page. The following is the function:

```
module.exports.requireAuthentication = function
requireAuthentication(req, res, next){
  if (req.session.isAuthenticated) {
    next();
  }else {
    res.redirect('/login');
  }
};
```

This middleware is pretty straightforward. If you are authenticated, run the next middleware, if not, redirect to /login.

Now, we need to add these to our middleware stack. Add the authenticated function right after our CSRF and before our routes, as you can see in the following code:

```
app.use(util.csrf);
app.use(util.authenticated);
```

Our other middleware is going to go on the chat route. So far, all middleware has been added by using app.use. The app.use function will apply the middleware to every request coming in. For a lot of middleware, this is the correct place. For some though, the middleware should only be executed on certain routes. To do this, add them as the second parameter on a route definition. You can also chain multiple middleware together by using an array. Here is how our chat route looks now:

```
app.get('/chat', [util.requireAuthentication], routes.chat);
```

You can just pass the function by itself as the second parameter, but I wanted to demonstrate this syntax. Each middleware passed in the array will be executed in order.

If you load this up, you will see that you cannot get to http://localhost:3000/chat; it will always redirect you to /login.

We need to build an authentication function so that we can log users in. Open up utilities.js from middleware, and add the following function:

```
module.exports.auth = function auth(username, password, session){
  var isAuth = username === 'joshua' || username === 'brian';
  if (isAuth) {
    session.isAuthenticated = isAuth;
    session.user = {username: username};
  }
  return isAuth;
};
```

This is a very simple username check as it will only authenticate if you enter joshua or brian as the username.

 I will reiterate — do not use anything like this in production. We will cover how to do proper and secure local authentication in *Chapter 3, Authenticating Users*.

We now have to execute this inside our login post route. Open up index.js from routes and edit the loginProcess function:

```
//add a reference to util at the top of the file
var util = require('../middleware/utilities');
//then modify loginProcess
function loginProcess(req, res){
  var isAuth = util.auth(req.body.username, req.body.password, req.
session);
  if (isAuth) {
    res.redirect('/chat');
  }else {
    res.redirect('/login');
  }
};
```

We pass in the username, password, and session so that auth can do its job. Depending on whether the user is authenticated or not, we will send them to /chat or redirect them back to /login. If the authentication was successful, our auth function will set isAuthenticated on the session, which means that our requireAuthentication function will not redirect you. Our little app works, well kind of. It is still a little clunky and missing some polish, and in addition to that, there is no way to log out.

This leads us right into writing a logout function, so in our utilities.js file, add the following function:

```
module.exports.logOut = function logOut(session){
  session.isAuthenticated = false;
  delete session.user;
};
```

A simple `logOut` function for a simple auth system. We have set `isAuthenticated` on the session back to `false` and got rid of the user in the session. Now, we have to put this in a route, so let's add that route in `index.js` present in the `routes` folder.

```
function logOut(req, res){
  util.logOut(req.session);
  res.redirect('/');
};
```

We log the user out, and then redirect to root. Finally, it needs to be added to our `routes`. Open up `app.js`.

```
app.get('/logout', routes.logOut);
```

After logging in, we can log ourselves out by going to `http://localhost:3000/logout`. We are still missing a little polish on our app, so let's add links to log in and out of our app.

We will do this by using partials. We will have a `loggedin` and `loggedout` partial. Create a directory in `views` called `partials`, before adding two files called `user-loggedin.ejs` and `user-loggedout.ejs`. The files should look like the following:

- `user-loggedin.ejs`: Hello <%= user.username %> <a href="/logout">Logout</a>

- `user-loggedout.ejs`: <a href="/login">Login</a>

We can use the `user` object in our templates because of our middleware. We know the logged-in template will only be run when a user has successfully authenticated.

We will now update our layout to use these partials. Remember this functionality is provided by `express-partials` as of Express 3 and 4. Express 2 had this built in, so you can run into issues with code from the Internet. Here is what our `layout.ejs` should look like now:

```
<!DOCTYPE html>
<html>
<head>
    <title><%= title %></title>
    <link rel="stylesheet" href="css/cosmo.min.css">
    <link rel="stylesheet" href="css/style.css">
</head>
<body>
```

```
<div class="container">
  <div class="row">
      <div class="col-sm-4"><h1 class="pull-left">PacktChat</h1></div>
      <div class="col-sm-4 col-sm-offset-4 top-margin">
        <div class="pull-right">
      <% if (isAuthenticated) { %>
        <%- partial('partials/user-loggedin') %>
      <% } else { %>
        <%- partial('partials/user-loggedout') %>
      <% } %>
        </div>
    </div>
  </div>
  <div class="row">
  <%- body %>
  </div>
</div>
</body>
</html>
```

Our authentication middleware sets `req.locals.isAuthenticated`, which means that any request can run a Boolean check on it. It also sets the `req.locals.user` object for the template. The `partial` function will search for the path that is passed to it beginning at the `views` directory. The following is a screenshot of what our site should look like now:

PacktChat   Login

Index

The following screenshot highlights our other partial that uses the logged in user's username and changes the link to **Logout**:

PacktChat   Hello joshua Logout

Chat

The final part of our app that we will add is flash messages. Flash messaging is when we have something to tell the user from one request to the next. It is called flash because we only want to show it once. A great example of this is when someone enters a wrong username or password, which is in fact what we are going to implement. Right now, our app just takes you back to the login page without letting you know why, which is a very bad user experience.

We will use `connect-flash` to let the user know when something has happened. Connect-flash uses the session, so it must be after the session middleware. Let's initialize it and add it to our middleware stack:

```
//variable declarations
Var flash = require('connect-flash');
//middleware stack after session, but before the routes
app.use(flash());
```

This gives us access to `req.flash` to get and set flash messages. The first message we will set is our login failed message. Change the `loginProcess` function in `index.js` present in the `routes` folder to include our message, as follows:

```
function loginProcess(req, res){
  var isAuth = util.auth(req.body.username, req.body.password, req.
session);
  if (isAuth) {
    res.redirect('/chat');
  }else {
    req.flash('error', 'Wrong Username or Password');
    res.redirect('/login');
  }
};
```

The message is now in the session. To display this, we just have to get it out. The act of getting it out will also delete it from the session, so it is time to edit our `login` function in `index.js` present in the `routes` folder.

```
function login(req, res){
  res.render('login', {title: 'Login', message: req.flash('error')});
};
```

The message is now passed to the template, but the template is not ready to display it. Edit `login.ejs`, and add this code right under the form declaration:

```
<form method="post">
<% if (message.length > 0) { %>
    <div class="alert alert-danger"><%= message %></div>
  <% } %>
```

The message will come out in an array. We do a quick check to see if there is at least one message, and then display it. Our users will now see that authentication has failed, as seen in the following screenshot:

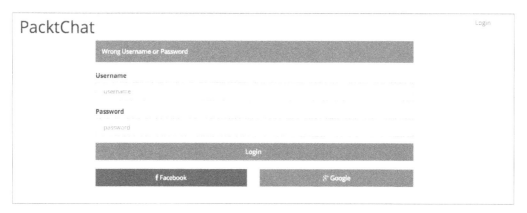

Setting up a config file for our app

Currently, our app runs off of whatever is in the app.js file. If you want to change how the application runs, you will need to edit app.js. This is not very maintainable. As a simple example, what if our cookie secret changes? What happens when we only update one of the references to the cookie secret? Let's say our app grows and the secret is referenced in two other middleware. This will create a lot of pain and waste time tracking down weird bugs in the code. What we need is a config file to store all the application's settings.

The first thing is to create a file named config.js in the root of our app and add this to the file:

```
var config = {
  port: 3000,
  secret: 'secret',
  redisUrl: 'redis://localhost',
  routes: {
    login: '/login',
    logout: '/logout'
  }
};

module.exports = config;
```

We are creating an object and then returning it when this file is required. We have the port, cookie secret, Redis URL, and simple route map in our config. We now have to go find where all of these are used, and then update the code.

Route mapping

A route map allows us to use a programmable name for a specific URL. Our new config does this for login and logout. A quick check of our application shows that we are using the string `'/login'` in four different places. Let's all make it in one place.

We will do this by creating another piece of middleware. Any backend file can get access to this by loading the `config` module with `require()`, but the templates do not have this ability. Also, if they did, we do not want to put a boilerplate requirement at the top of every view template. This is where our new middleware comes in. Add a reference at the top of the `utitlities.js` file present in the `middleware` folder, and create a new function in the file.

```
var config = require('../config');
//the other functions or you could put this at the top
exports.templateRoutes = function templateRoutes(req, res, next){
  res.locals.routes = config.routes;

  next();
};
```

We can see that this just adds the `routes` object from `config` to `res.locals`. Every template will now be able to use the login and logout routes.

Now, add it to the middleware stack. Thinking about our middleware execution order, we know that it just has to go before any templates render. The first middleware that renders is our `app.router`, so it must go before this.

```
app.use(flash());
app.use(util.templateRoutes);
```

Our app now has a config, so we must find all the references to the various settings.

Updating our app to use the config

The first thing to look at is `app.js`. We will need to add this object to the scope, so add this line as the last variable declaration:

```
Var config = require('./config');
```

Now, we must find each reference to the settings in our config. Let's update the secret.

```
app.use(cookieParser(config.secret));
app.use(session({
  secret: config.secret,
```

```
saveUninitialized: true,
resave: true,
store: new RedisStore(
 {url: config.redisUrl})
})
);
```

We fixed the issue that we had initially posed. The only change that we now need to make is in `config.js`, and all the secrets will be set.

We can now set up the route map's routes. We will change three of our routes in `app.js`.

```
app.get(config.routes.login, routes.login);
app.post(config.routes.login, routes.loginProcess);
app.get(config.routes.logout, routes.logOut);
```

The app now uses the route map to determine the actual URL to bind to. However, now we have an issue: if we update the route in the config, we have some functions that have hard coded `'/login'`. This will throw a 404 error. We need to track down all the references to login and logout.

The first reference, `utilites.js`, present in the `middleware` folder, is the `requireAuthentication` function. We will update `isAuthenticated` to redirect back to `config.routes.login`.

```
module.exports.requireAuthentication = function
requireAuthentication(req, res, next){
  if (req.session.isAuthenticated) {
    next();
  }else {
    res.redirect(config.routes.login);
  }
};
```

Next is our `index.js` present in the `routes` folder; it is the `loginProcess` function. We will need to redirect back to login on an auth failure.

```
//add the config reference
var config = require('../config');
//change the function
function loginProcess(req, res){
  var isAuth = util.auth(req.body.username, req.body.password, req.
session);
```

```
    if (isAuth) {
      res.redirect('/chat');
    }else {
      req.flash('error', 'Wrong Username or Password');
      res.redirect(config.routes.login);
    }
};
```

The last two files that we will update are the partials. Each partial file has a hard-coded URL that we will change to use `config.route` as follows:

- The `user-loggedin.ejs` file present in the `views/partials` folder:
  `Hello <%= user.username %> <a href="<%= routes.logout %>">Logout</a>`

- The `user-loggedout.ejs` file present in the `views/partials` folder:
  `<a href="<%= routes.login %>">Login</a>`

Here is where our middleware is valuable. Every template will have a route's object straight from the config. We are only using it for login and logout, but a site-wide URL should be here so that you can easily update it. For example, we can change the `config.routes` login and logout to `'/account/login'` and `'/account/logout'`, and the app will not break.

Finally, we will update the port that the app listens on. This is in `app.js`:

```
app.listen(config.port);
```

Methods to extend an application

One thing you can do to extend an application if you are building a larger site is to build it using **MVC (Model, View, Controller)**. We already have the view part sorted, so let's look at the other pieces. We have some sort of a controller setup with our `routes` directory. The next step will be to create a file for each. For example, we can have `account.js`, which will have the `login`, `logout`, and `createAccount` functions. We haven't really covered adding models to our app. We can create a directory called models, and then add a user model, for which we can find a user, update, and create a user to tie in with our account controller. Note that there are some other frameworks that build on Express in this way (`sails.js` is a good example). We are not using any so that you can see the insides, if you will, of the application.

Another key point from this chapter is to learn how to use middleware. In our app, we had 6 routes and 14 pieces (15, if you include the middleware that only runs on the /chat route) of middleware. There are three great reasons for this. Firstly, middleware allows you to create flexible and reusable code. We built a quick and dirty authentication module in just two pieces of middleware. If we decide to create a profile page, we just create a route like the following:

```
app.get('/profile', [util.requireAuthentication], routes.profile);
```

Then, when we build our profile template, we will know that the user object will be populated with the user's username. No more copying/pasting if statements in our routes check a session whether the user is logged in or not!

Next, there is a great ecosystem of current middleware. Everything we built in this app has a package that can do the same thing. As we covered, Express uses Connect internally, so we can use any of the Connect middleware. Currently, it has 18 bundled middleware (we have used quite a few already, such as csrf, sessions, body parsing, cookies, and static, to name a few). There are also many third-party middleware. We have used two: connect-redis and connect-flash. The Connect website has a list of the most popular third-party middleware on GitHub.

Finally, middleware functions are the perfect size for unit tests. We did not cover them here, but having a set of reusable and unit test-covered functions will make your life as a developer much better. We will cover unit testing with Nodeunit in *Chapter 8*, *JavaScript Best Practices for Application Development*.

Summary

Our app now looks and feels like a real application. We went from little knowledge of Express to actually using it to build a small yet fully functional site. At this point, we now know how to respond to different HTTP methods. We know how to wire up routes in a clean and extendable manner. Our app has 14 different pieces of middleware. This might seem like a lot, but our app is also doing a lot. We can use templates and partials to render our pages easily. Finally, we have a simple authentication system that uses sessions. We laid a very good base for our chat application, all in just over 40 lines, in our app.js.

In our next chapter, we will cover how to add real-time communication between the server and the browser using Socket.io.

2
Extending Our Development with Socket.IO

In the last chapter, we built a simple web application that can serve HTML pages. Let's add some more functionality to our application. We have to build a chat app, so we will need some sort of real-time event framework. Luckily for us, there is Socket.IO, which will provide us with this real-time communication. Socket.IO fits right into the entire evented nature of Node.js. The whole paradigm of Socket.IO is completely different from using a web server. Socket.IO uses WebSockets to create a connection between the server and client. You will need to understand all this to get Socket.IO to do what you want it to. In this chapter, we will cover the following topics:

- Sending and receiving events
- Creating rooms to divide users
- Adding and reading data from sessions
- Authenticating connections
- Integrating Socket.IO with what we have built already

Node package versions

We are going to create three different applications through out this chapter. The first two applications we create will only have the requirement for Socket.IO. The other application will be the application we started in *Chapter 1, Backend Development with Express*. So, the following is the list of packages in addition to everything we have already installed:

- socket.io: 1.0.6
- socket.io-redis: 0.1.3

- connect: 3.0.2
- cookie: 0.1.1
- express-session: 1.6.5

Building a simple Socket.IO app

Before you add Socket.IO to your current PacktChat app, let's first build a couple of very simple apps. This will first allow us to understand what we are doing, and then build on it.

Installing the package

The first thing, of course, is to get the package from npm. We will do this exactly like we did in the last chapter, by adding all the packages to package.json and running npm install.

Socket.IO has quite a few dependencies, so this may take a minute or two. Once that is done, you can create your first app. Create a directory named first app, create an app.js file, and add the following code in it:

```
var io = require('socket.io').listen(4000);

io.sockets.on('connection', function(socket){
  socket.emit('ping');

  socket.on('pong', function(data){
    console.log('pong');
  });
});
```

Since Socket.IO is event driven, we start off by listening for a connection event. Do not think of this in terms of HTTP actions as it does not map to any. While we will run them on the server, HTTP and Socket.IO respond to requests in different ways. This event gives us access to the socket that we will then use to communicate with the client.

When we want to send an event to a client from the server-side socket, we use the emit method. It will send a message over the socket to the client. On the client side, it needs to have a listener with the same event name.

For the opposite actions, we will need to listen for events sent from the client. This is where we use the `on` method. This will allow the client to send a message to the server.

Not much for now. Our app has no one to talk to. We need to build the client side now.

Building the client

Our Socket.IO server needs something to communicate with and that is what we will build now. The server is going to send a `'ping'` event to the client and it will return a `'pong'` event. Just as the server needs the Socket.IO server framework, our client needs the Socket.IO client framework. The Socket.IO client library is at the `node_modules/socket.io/node_modules/socket.io-client` directory. Inside this directory, there are the `socket.io.js` and `socket.io.min.js` files. We will create a symlink to the file by running the following command in the terminal:

```
ln -s node_modules/socket.io/node_modules/socket.io-client/socket.io.js
```

There are also a couple of flash objects. These flash objects are used to give older browsers that lack WebSocket abilities (mainly IE 8 and IE 9) the ability to use Socket.IO. If you are using a newer version of Chrome or Firefox, you can just use the JavaScript file.

We need to create our HTML page for the client to use. Create an `index.html` page alongside your `app.js` and `socket.io.js`. The following code is what the file should be like:

```html
<!DOCTYPE html>
<html>
<head>
  <title>Ping Pong</title>
  <script type="text/javascript" src="socket.io.js"></script>
</head>
<body>
<script>
var socket = io.connect('http://localhost:4000');
socket.on('ping', function(data){
  console.log('ping');
  socket.emit('pong');
});
</script>
</body>
</html>
```

This is a pretty empty page; in fact, there is nothing in it. We are just using it to load our JavaScript. We include the `socket.io.js` file in `head` so we can get access to the `io` variable. The first thing we want to do is connect to our Socket.IO server. We have the server listening on port 4000, so we tell the client to connect to it.

I know I mentioned earlier that Socket.IO is nothing like HTTP, but the connection does use HTTP to start. The initial HTTP request is upgraded to a WebSocket connection.

Now that the socket has been created, we can start listening for events. Exactly like the server side, we use `on` to listen for socket events. We know the server will be sending out a `ping` event, so we will need to listen for that. We will then log that a ping happened and send an event back to the server. Again, this is the exact same method the server uses. We send off a `pong` event with the `emit` method.

When we start our Socket.IO server and load our webpage, we should see the `log` `'ping'` browser to the console and then the `log` `'pong'` server (this will actually happen very quickly). Let's go ahead and try this.

Using Python to serve our site

We have run into an issue. We can't serve our `index.html` page that we made. Python can help us out here. We will use Python later to build our deploy scripts, so hopefully we have it installed. I am using Mac OS X, which comes with Python already installed. This allows me to run a simple Python command to run an HTTP server in whichever directory I am in:

```
$ python -m SimpleHTTPServer
```

You don't have to write any code; just load a module, and it will run right in the console. By default, the server listens on port 8000. If you want to change this, just add the port number as the last parameter, as shown in the following command line:

```
$ python -m SimpleHTTPServer 8080
```

Python is a great glue language. It has a great standard library that allows you to build small scripts that do a lot.

We will just use the default port for now. Point your browser to `http://localhost:8000`, and you should see your blank page.

Ping-Pong

Technically, nothing should happen on the web page. You should see the console of the Node server log pong.

Let's now take a look at the browser. Open your console. I always get to it using Chrome by right-clicking and selecting **Inspect Element**. Then, click on **Console** all the way to the right. You should see the following screenshot:

Creating some interaction

At this point, we have sent an event to the client and responded back. Technically, we could have easily done this with an Ajax call, so let's add some interaction between browsers to highlight what Socket.IO can do. First of all, clean out the `socket.on('connection')` function. We are going to write all new code. The following is what our `app.js` should look like:

```
var io = require('socket.io').listen(4000);

io.sockets.on('connection', function(socket){

socket.on('join', function(data){
    io.sockets.emit('userJoined', data);
    socket.username = data.username;
  });
  socket.on('ping', function(data){

    io.sockets.emit('ping', {username: socket.username});
  });
});
```

Let's look at each new event listener separately. The first listens for an event called `join`. The first thing it does is emit an event called `userJoined`. The `socket.emit` function will just send a message to the client in the connection. You will not have interaction between browsers. `io.sockets.emit` function will send a message to every single socket that is connected. With this, we can send some messages between browsers.

Next, the function saves some information about this socket on its connection. We are expecting an object with a username attribute. We then attach this to the socket object. The other function is listening for a `ping` event, much like our original app. We will pull the username off the socket and send it out with `io.sockets.emit` to ping all the clients.

Adding the browser side

You could restart Node and not much would happen. For every change we make on the server side, we have to make equal and opposite changes on the client side. Open your `index.html` and add jQuery to `head`, as shown in the following code:

```html
<head>
  <title>Ping Pong</title>
  <script type="text/javascript" src="socket.io.js"></script>
  <script type="text/javascript" src="//cdnjs.cloudflare.com/ajax/
libs/jquery/2.1.0/jquery.js"></script>
</head>
```

We are using `cdnjs`, which hosts many of the commonly used JavaScript and CSS libraries on the Internet. It's a great way to include a library quickly, without having to download and drop it in your web server folder.

Now, we need to add some elements to the body, as shown in the following code:

```html
<input type="text" id="username">
<button id="ping">Ping</button>
<ul id="info">
</ul>
```

It's pretty straightforward: a text box, a button, and a blank unordered list. We have given these IDs, as this makes it very easy and efficient to find them in JavaScript. Remember that this must come before our JavaScript code, otherwise the elements will not be available.

Finally, let's add the JavaScript we need. Add all our new elements as variables at the top of our script tag:

```javascript
var socket = io.connect('http://localhost:4000');
var $username = $('#username'),
  $ping = $('#ping'),
  $info = $('#info');
```

If you haven't used jQuery before, the $ is jQuery object. jQuery also has a great selector engine that mimics CSS, so a # is reference to an ID. Each variable should now be connected to each element, respectively.

Now, let's add event handlers. Just like `socket.io`, jQuery allows you to listen for an event by using the `on()` function. We will take these one by one.

First, we will build a small utility function. It is just a quick and dirty way to add a list item to the list:

```
function addLi(message) {
  $info.append('<li>' + message + '</li>');
};
```

Next, our first event listener:

```
$username.on('change', function(){
  socket.emit('join', {username: $username.val()});
});
```

Anytime the username text box changes, we send a `join` event to the server. We will pass in the value of the text box as the username. If you remember, the server will listen for a `join` event and send a `userJoined` event out to everyone with the same data object. This brings us to our next listener:

```
socket.on('userJoined', function(data){
  addLi(data.username + ' has joined');
});
```

We are listening now for the event that comes back from the server when someone joins. We will then add a list item to our list:

```
$ping.on('click', function(){
  socket.emit('ping');
});
```

This is the listener for the click event on the **Ping** button. It just sends the event onto the server. Again, when we look back at the server, we see that it listens for a `ping` event. It then takes that event and sends it to all the socket connections, along with the username that was set for that connection. Here is the browser code that listens for the return ping. It pulls out the username that is passed in the data object and adds it to the list. The following code will replace what is currently in `socket.on('ping')`:

```
socket.on('ping', function(data){
  addLi(data.username + ' has pinged!');
});
```

Open up a browser and add your name to the text box. You should get the message, **Josh has joined**. Click on the **Ping** button and you will get the message, **Josh has pinged!**.

Open another tab and do the same thing (well, use a different name in this tab). Now, go back to the original tab. You will see that another person has joined and pinged. If you split the tabs into separate windows, you can see how quickly the events are sent. It is, for all intents and purposes, instantaneous. Open a few more tabs and see that the events are propagated to all the tabs this way. The following screenshot shows pings between two different tabs:

We have done all this in 14 lines of code on the server and 25 lines on the browser (this includes space between functions and the boilerplate code).

Acknowledgments

Sometimes we want to know if the last action had an error or not. Right now, we are currently working under the assumption that every event will fire off without a hitch. Luckily for us, Socket.IO has an acknowledgement system. On an emit event, we can add an extra function that the server can execute. Let's add this to the server side first in `app.js`. Update the `socket.on('ping')` listener, as shown in the following code:

```
socket.on('ping', function(data, done){
    socket.get('username', function(err, username){
        io.sockets.emit('ping', {username: username});
        done('ack');
    });
});
```

The acknowledgement function comes in as the second parameter in an `on` listener function. We can then execute it at any point we want. We are doing it here after we send the data back to all the other clients. In this example, we are just sending `ack`. We could use it to send back an error. For example, the function can connect to a database and run a query. If there is an error at that point, you can send it back:

```
done({error: 'Something went wrong'});
```

This is the key if you are running a required action. There is no worse user experience than actions failing silently. Users will never trust your app. They will always ask, "is it doing something? Should I click on the button again? Is there something else I should have clicked?"

Now, we will update our client. We are going to add a function that will keep track of how many acknowledged pings we have sent. We will only update our count when the acknowledgement returns. We only have to update the `socket.emit('ping')`, as that is the function we want the acknowledgement on.

In the body, add a div with the sent ID, as shown in the following code:

```
<input type="text" id="username">
<button id="ping">Ping</button>
<div id="sent"></div>
<ul id="info">
</ul>
```

In the script tag, we need to initialize another variable and update the `on` click listener attached to the Ping button:

```
//with the other initialized variables
Var pingSent = 0;
//further down in the script tag
$ping.on('click', function(){
  socket.emit('ping', null, function(message){
    if (message === 'ack')
    {
      pingSent++;
      $sent.html('Pings sent: ' + pingSent);
    }
  });
});
```

We have a third parameter on the `emit` function now. We are not sending data, so we pass `null` as our data object. Our final parameter is the callback (`done()`) that the server runs and then passes back our `'ack'` message. We check this to make sure that `'ack'` was passed, and if so, increment our `pingSent` counter. If not, we will not increment our counter. This is where we would put our error check. In our example, on the server side, we can do this but we won't. This is only a suggestion:

```
socket.emit('importantThing', importantData, function(ack){
  if (ack.error !== undefined){
    alert('Something went wrong');
  }else {
    //continue on
  }
});
```

The following screenshot is what it should look like:

Our app now is still very simple, but you should start to see what you can do with Socket.IO. We have completely real-time events that span multiple browsers. Acknowledgments are even sent on the ping requests. This is all done in 15 lines of code on the server. Guess what? We are not done yet. Let's add some more features to our little Ping-Pong app.

Broadcasting a message

The Ping-Pong app that we built shows all the events, regardless of their source. If someone else pings, it shows in our list. If we ping, it shows on our list. We do not want to do this. We only want the application to show if someone else pings. Showing our own pings isn't necessarily a bad feature to have. What makes it bad is that we send the ping to the server and the server sends it back to us. We can (and will) make it more efficient by only sending the ping to everyone else. How?

Broadcast! This seems to be a misnomer. If you are broadcasting something, you think it goes out to everyone. This is very close to what Socket.IO does. Broadcast will send it out to everyone but you. If there are four clients connected, Socket.IO will send it to the other three. Let's wire it all up.

We will only have to change the server side, as we will use the same event names. We are just changing who they will go to. Inside `app.js` in the `io.sockets.on('connection')`, we will change both the emits, as shown in the following code:

```
socket.on('join', function(data){
    socket.broadcast.emit('userJoined', data);
    socket.username = data.username;
});

socket.on('ping', function(data, done){
    socket.broadcast.emit('ping', {username: socket.username});
    done('ack');
});
```

All we had to do was change `io.sockets` to `socket.broadcast`. We are still using the `emit` method in the same way.

It makes sense why we have to use socket instead of `io.sockets`. Remember that io is tied to the whole Socket.IO server. It is what is returned from `require('socket.io').listen(4000)`. Then, we are getting all the sockets off io. This would be every connected client, including us. Finally, `emit` is called, which sends a message to each one.

The Socket.IO connection object is referenced from the callback when a socket is connected. The socket is in the context of one specific socket connection. `socket.emit` will send our message object back to the connected socket. `socket.broadcast.emit` will then send our message object back to all others, except for the connected socket that initiated the broadcast.

What will happen now is that any event you are sending to the server will not get an event back. The `join` event will return `userJoined` with our username. Now, we only get it when someone else joins. The same is true for our pings. Only other pings will show in our list. We will still get acknowledgements on the pings we send, so our ping counter will still work. Go ahead and load `http://localhost:8000` in a couple of browser tabs and check out what happens.

The following screenshot is how our Socket.IO application should function:

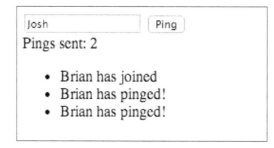

Using the disconnect event

Our app is only capturing connection and joining events. Remember that the connection happens automatically, as we do not check the client at all. As soon as the client's `io.connect()` is called, a connection event is fired. Then, when we change the text input, a `join` event is fired, which goes to all the other clients. Nothing happens when someone leaves.

Socket disconnection events are different than regular HTTP events. Because HTTP is request based, we never really know when someone leaves; we just know what their last request was. Users usually have to take an action to leave, for example, going to the logout page. Socket.IO creates and maintains a persistent connection, so we will know immediately when someone leaves. Let's add it to our application.

We will begin at the backend. Open `app.js` and add a new listener for the disconnect event:

```
socket.on('disconnect', function(){
    socket.broadcast.emit('userDisconnect', {username: socket.
username});
  });
```

There isn't really too much that is new. We know about event listeners, how to get data attached to a socket, and how to broadcast it to everyone but yourself.

Now, we have to go to the client and add the listener there. Add the following to our list of functions:

```
socket.on('userDisconnect', function(data){
    addLi(data.username + ' has left :(');
});
```

This function is similar to the others we have written. It just takes the passed in username and adds a new list item to the list. Connect some users and then refresh the page, and you should get some disconnection events, which are shown in the following screenshot:

Creating namespaces

Socket.IO has another trick up its sleeve. We have been working in only one area so far, but Socket.IO has methods to connect to multiple areas. The first is namespaces. The other is rooms. Both of these ideas are very similar, and we will set both of them up.

We will use the same idea of users being able to ping, but we will add onto this idea. First of all, we will allow users to enter different areas and ping inside those areas. Secondly, we will allow users to send private pings that will only go to one specific user. For this, we will create a new project and start from scratch. We will use namespaces for the first project.

Here is all the boilerplate code that we need to do. Create a directory named second app, files named namespace.js and namespace.html, and a symlink to the socket.io.js client library (remember, it's in the node_modules directory after you install Socket.IO).

We can now build our little app. We will start on the backend. Open up namespace.js and add Socket.IO to our app:

```
var io = require('socket.io').listen(4000);
```

Now, add all your listeners. We will have three: join, ping, and privatePing. Our connection listener should have all three of these functions in it, as shown in the following code:

```
io.sockets.on('connection', function(socket){
  socket.on('join', function(data){
    socket.username = data.username;
```

```
      socket.broadcast.emit('join', {username: data.username, socket:
    socket.id});
      });

      socket.on('ping', function(){
        socket.broadcast.emit('ping', {username: socket.username});
      });

      socket.on('privatePing', function(data){
        io.sockets.connected[data.socket].emit('ping', {username: socket.
    username, priv: true});
      });
    });
```

The `join` and `ping` events are very similar to the functions we built for our first app. The `join` event adds the username to the socket and then does a broadcast emit back. It also broadcasts the client's socket ID to everyone else. We will use this later. The `ping` event does almost the same, except it gets the username and sends that back.

This brings us to our new listener, `privatePing`. It starts off by getting the username, but now it uses `io.sockets.connected[data.socket]`. The `data.socket` JavaScript object contains the socket ID and `io.sockets.connected` has all the connected sockets. Put these together and we get a specific client connection. This is essentially a hash or dictionary of every connection with the socket ID as the key. Earlier, we sent the socket ID to the client, and this is the client sending it back to ping that user. We have a flag that shows this ping event is sent to only one client. So far, we have not really done anything too new and nothing that involves namespaces.

Well, let's add namespaces then. We will need to add another connection listener. The following code is what the file will look like:

```
    io.of('/vip').on('connection', function(socket){
      socket.on('join', function(data){
        socket.username = data.username;
        socket.broadcast.emit('join', {username: data.username, socket:
    socket.id});
      });

      socket.on('ping', function(){
        socket.broadcast.emit('ping', {username: socket.username});});

      socket.on('privatePing', function(data){
        io.of('/vip').connected[data.socket].emit('ping', {username:
    socket.username, priv: true});
      });
    });
```

The first thing you should notice is that it is really similar to the code that doesn't use namespaces. In fact, there are only two lines of code that are different. The first line is where we tie to a namespace. This is done using the `of` method, as follows:

```
io.of('/vip').on('connection', function(socket){});
```

We just pass a string of the namespace. Inside the connection listener, we have the same object and can set up the same events. The socket variable here will only refer to clients that have connected to the `'/vip'` namespace.

The other changed line of code is in the `privatePing` listener. Here, we use the `of` method again. Anytime we use `io.of('/namespace')`, all the methods we use after it will be in the context of that namespace. If we used it the other way (`io.sockets.socket()`), then the response would have been sent back in the default namespace instead of the `'/vip'` namespace. Go ahead, switch them and see what happens.

We have our server side built; now let's build our client side.

Building our namespace client

We know what events the server is listening for, so now we have to create a client that will send them. Open up your `namespace.html` and add the following code:

```
<!DOCTYPE html>
<html>
<head>
  <title>Ping Pong</title>
  <script type="text/javascript" src="socket.io.js"></script>
  <script type="text/javascript" src="//cdnjs.cloudflare.com/ajax/
libs/jquery/2.1.0/jquery.js"></script>
  <style>
    .areas { float: left; width: 50%;}
  </style>
</head>
<body>
  <div>
    <input type="text" id="username">
  </div>
  <div class="areas default">
    Default
    <button class="join">Join</button>
    <button class="ping">Ping</button>
    <div>
      Users
```

```
      <ul class="users">

      </ul>
    </div>
    <div>
      Events
      <ul class="events">      </ul>
    </div>
  </div>
  <div class="areas vip">
    VIP
    <button class="join">Join</button>
    <button class="ping">Ping</button>
    <div>
      Users
      <ul class="users">      </ul>
    </div>
    <div>
      Events
      <ul class="events">      </ul>
    </div>
  </div>
<script>
</script>
</body>
</html>
```

This is a simple HTML structure and `div.areas` are identical. They both have two buttons, `Join` and `Ping`, and two lists, `users` and `events`. This is our skeleton we will use to wire up all our JavaScript muscles. We are using the `socket.io` client (you did remember to link to it from `node_modules`, right?) and jQuery 2.1 from a content delivery network (we will talk about these in *Chapter 8, Javascript Best Practices for Application Development*). All the JavaScript code will go into our script tag at the end of the body (is HTML just one big biology metaphor?).

The first thing to do is to connect to our server. We will create two variables to hold our connections:

```
var socket = io.connect('http://localhost:4000'),
  vip = io.connect('http://localhost:4000/vip');
```

The first connection we have is done already. The second is how we use namespaces. To connect to a namespace, just connect to the server and append the namespace you created. This object is now in the context of a namespace. Any methods we call or any event listeners we attach will only be for events from the `'/vip'` namespace. Let's finish up this app and then test it.

 We will create two connections, but Socket.IO doesn't actually connect twice. It is able to just use one connection for both, including any and all namespace connections.

The next thing we will do is grab our key elements from the page, as follows:

```
var defaultArea = $('.default'),
  vipArea = $('.vip'),
  $username = $('#username');
```

We will create jQuery objects that are tied to `div.default`, `div.vip`, and `input#username`. If you are not familiar with jQuery, it gives us some cross-browser methods and easy selectors. We will cover more jQuery when we build out the frontend.

We now will create a simple utility function, as shown in the following code:

```
function createButton(user){
   return '<li>' + user.username + '<button class="private_ping" data-socket="' + user.socket + '">Ping Me</button></li>';
};
```

We pass in a user object (which we will get from our socket events), and it will return an HTML string for a button with a `private_ping` class.

Finally, we will create the function that will wire everything up:

```
function wireEvents(area, socketio){
  var users = area.find('.users'),
    events = area.find('.events');

  area.on('click', function(e){
    if (e.target.className === 'join') {
      socketio.emit('join', {username: $username.val()});
    }else if (e.target.className === 'ping') {
      socketio.emit('ping');
    }else if (e.target.className === 'private_ping') {
```

```
            socketio.emit('privatePing', {socket: e.target.
    getAttribute('data-socket')});
        }
    });

    socketio.on('join', function(user){
        users.append(createButton(user));
    });

    socketio.on('ping', function(user){

if (user.priv === undefined){
        events.append('<li>Ping from ' + user.username + '</li>');
    }else{
        events.append('<li>Ping from ' + user.username + ' sent directly
    to you!</li>');
    } });
};
```

The `wireEvents` function takes an area and a Socket.IO connection and will attach all the listeners for us.

The first thing we do is find the users list and events list. We will do this with the `find` function of jQuery. It will look in the object we pass in (which will be either `div.default` or `div.vip`) and find all the elements that have users or events in their class list. This gives us the reference to each list.

Next, we add a click listener on the entire area. This is better than adding multiple click handlers for each element that is clicked. We then check the event that is passed in for what element was clicked and what class the element has. With this info, we know what button was clicked, as each button has a specific class attached to it. From there, we pass the event to the server. The `join` and `ping` events are very straightforward. `join` uses the username as input and `ping` just sends the event. `privatePing` uses an attribute attached to the button. This attribute is added from the `createButton` function that uses the socket ID from the `join` event sent from the server. This function will create a button element, as shown in the following screenshot:

```
▼<li>
    "Brian"
    <button class="private_ping" data-socket="rrsfiJYsYYG4Y7ygrSV_">Ping Me</button>
  </li>
```

This is where the socket ID is stored when the server broadcasts the `join` event. We send it back so the server can find that specific socket and send it to only that client.

Next, we add a listener for the `join` events from the server. We just add a list item with the button we just discussed.

Finally, we listen for ping events. If the event does not have the `priv` attribute set, then we know it was broadcast to everyone. If it is set, then we know it was sent to only us. We then append either of these to our events list.

We now have all our events covered. We are listening for clicks, joins, pings, and private pings.

We built this function to be reusable, so we can easily do this for both the `default` and `vip` areas, as shown in the following code:

```
wireEvents(defaultArea, socket);
wireEvents(vipArea, vip);
```

At this point, we can launch Node and our Python HTTP server. Load `http://localhost:8000/namespace.html` in a couple of tabs. Join a couple of areas, ping a few times, and send some private pings. We can see that everything works how we expect it to. All the events will be tied to a specific room. The following screenshot will show the output:

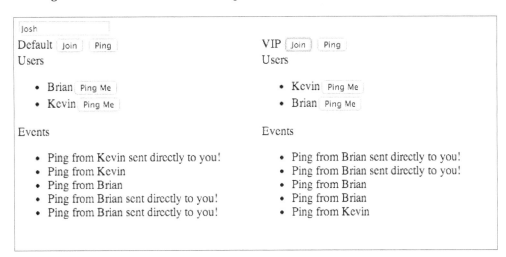

This is not a full-featured app. It is just an example on how to use namespaces in Socket.IO. Let's now modify our little ping app to use rooms instead of namespaces, so we can see what the differences are.

Adding rooms

We will use our current app as the basis since most of it can be reused. Copy `namespaces.js` and `namespace.html` and create `rooms.js` and `rooms.html`. Open up `rooms.js` and get rid of the namespace connection listener, as we are only using rooms here. Then, we will modify the normal connection and add our room-specific elements to it. Your `rooms.js` should look like the following code:

```
var io = require('socket.io').listen(4000);
io.sockets.on('connection', function(socket){
  socket.on('join', function(data){
    socket.username = data.username;
    socket.join(data.room);
    socket.broadcast.to(data.room).emit('join', {username: data.
username, socket: socket.id, room: data.room});
  });
  socket.on('ping', function(data){
    socket.broadcast.to(data.room).emit('ping', {username: socket.
username, room: data.room});
  });
  socket.on('privatePing', function(data){
    io.sockets.connected[data.socket].emit('ping', {username: socket.
username, priv: true, room: data.room});
  });
});
```

So, let's talk about what's new and different. The initial thing to note is that every listener now is expecting data to be sent with it. This is because every event will need to send what room it came from.

On our connection event, we use `socket.join(data.room)`. This is how we join a room. All it takes is a string of the room name. Rooms do not require an additional connection, but they do require us to join. The only exception to this is the default room of `''` (an empty string). Every client on connection is in that room.

This brings us to our next new function: `socket.broadcast.to(data.room).emit()`. When we add `to(room)`, it will only send the emit event to the connections that have joined that room. Because it is not a separate connection such as a namespace, the client does not inherently know what room this event is coming from. That is why we are sending the room back out in the message.

Our ping event changes very much like the connection. We need to pass in the event with the room and then send it back out with the room as an attribute. Other than this, it is the same.

Lastly, our `privatePing` is in the same boat. We need the room, so we can determine where it came from and where it is going. If you compare our `emit` function to `namespace.js`, you will see the only thing that changed is the addition of the `room` attribute.

Our server is ready, so let's update the client. Open `rooms.html` to edit it. We do not have to change any of the head or body, as it can be reused as is.

> HTML should always just be structure. JavaScipt should be behavior. Do not mix them! Do not add `onclick` attributes to your HTML. Our examples here show this. The look of the page stays, so we do not touch HTML. The behavior does change, so we have to modify JavaScript. This same rule applies to CSS. Do not use inline styles. Use CSS that can target and style elements on a page. HTML is structure, JavaScript is behavior, and CSS is style.

Inside the `script` tag, we will modify our JavaScript code. First, remove the reference to the `vip` namespace connection. The only Socket.IO connection we should have is our default connection:

```
var socket = io.connect('http://localhost:4000');
```

We also can leave the element references and the `createButton` utility function alone, as we will need them:

```
var defaultArea = $('.default'),
  vipArea = $('.vip'),
  $username = $('#username');
//some code
function createButton(user){
  return '<li>' + user.username + '<button class="private_ping" data-
socket="' + user.socket + '">Ping Me</button></li>';
};
```

This brings us to the key part we need to change: the `wireEvents` function. The following code is what it should eventually look like:

```
function wireEvents(area, room){
  var users = area.find('.users'),
    events = area.find('.events');

  area.on('click', function(e){
    if (e.target.className === 'join') {
```

```
        socket.emit('join', {username: $username.val(), room: room});
      }else if (e.target.className === 'ping') {
        socket.emit('ping', {room: room});
      }else if (e.target.className === 'private_ping') {
        socket.emit('privatePing', {socket: e.target.getAttribute('data-
socket'), room: room});
      }
    });
  socket.on('join', function(user){
    if (user.room === room)
      users.append(createButton(user));
  });
  socket.on('ping', function(user){
    if (user.room === room){

if (user.priv === undefined){
        events.append('<li>Ping from ' + user.username + '</li>');
      }else{
        events.append('<li>Ping from ' + user.username + ' sent
directly to you!</li>');
      }    }
  });
};
```

It is very similar to our `wireEvents` namespace. In fact, it has all the same listeners as the namespace function.

The parameters coming in are different. In the room version, we pass in the element as the area and a string as the room. We changed the server side to expect a room on any incoming event and send a room on every outgoing event. Really, all we are doing is changing this to match that.

On our click handler, we only have added the room attribute to every event going to the server. We also have changed the socket object to use just the one default connection.

Finally, we have added a room check before doing anything with events sent from the server. This is because we only have one socket connection. A ping from different rooms will look exactly the same except for the room in the data object passed with the event. What we end up doing is adding two event handlers to the ping event and then just checking to see if it is sent to the room we are listening for. If so, then do something with it. If not, do nothing.

The last thing we have to do is run `wireEvents` for our two rooms.

```
wireEvents(defaultArea, '');
wireEvents(vipArea, 'vip');
```

We can launch this and run the same exact type of test we did with namespaces. Launch Node and our Python server and go to `http://localhost:8000` on a couple of tabs and click around.

One thing you may have noticed is that you will not get events in the `vip` room without first joining. This is different than our namespace app because we immediately connect to the `vip` namespace. This will send us all the events in that namespace whether or not we have clicked on **Join**. The room version does not put us in that room until we click on the **Join** button. We will get the default events as everyone is in the `''` room.

Using namespaces or rooms

We have now used both and can see that rooms and namespaces in Socket.IO are really similar. They are both ways of segmenting all the connections into groups. This leads us to the question, when do we use either of them?

Namespaces

JavaScript is a scripted language that executes in essentially one context. If you create a function in a different file (without using any module or closure system), it is created in the global scope. Identically named functions will overwrite each other. If you have used any strongly typed object-oriented language (C#.NET or Java are two examples), you will have seen and used namespaces. Namespaces in those languages allow you to create objects with the same name, but they would be separate as they will live in different namespaces, otherwise known as scopes.

This is the same thought process you should have with Socket.IO namespaces. If you are building a modular Node web application, you will want to namespace out the different modules. If you look back at our namespace code, you will see that we were able to listen for the same exact events in different namespaces. In Socket.IO, the connection event on the default connection and connection event on a `/vip` namespace are different. For example, if you had a chat and comment system on your site and wanted both to be real time, you could namespace each. This allows you to build an entire Socket.IO application that lives only in its own context.

This would also be true if you were building something to be packaged and installed. You cannot know if someone is already using certain events in the default namespace, so you should create your own and listen there. This allows you to not step on the toes of any developer who uses your package.

Finding namespaces

Now that we know how and why we use namespaces, let's look at namespaces so we can see what is going on. The following is the screenshot of the `io.nsps` object from our `namespaces` object:

```
▼ Watch Expressions
▼ io.nsps: Object
  ▶ /: Namespace
  ▼ /vip: Namespace
    ▶ _events: Object
    ▶ acks: Object
    ▶ adapter: Adapter
    ▼ connected: Object
      ▶ iNuUs-o17Moutm7jAAAA: Socket
    ▶ fns: Array[0]
      ids: 0
      name: "/vip"
    ▶ server: Server
    ▶ sockets: Array[1]
```

We can see that each attribute of this object ties to a namespace. There is the default namespace and the `/vip` namespace. I have expanded the `/vip`, so you can see its attributes. The two attributes of note are the name, which is the string that we pass in when we first create it (`io.of('/vip')`), and the other is the connected object. This has all our sockets that are currently connected. The connections are mapped based on their socket ID.

When to use rooms

Namespaces allow us to carve up connections into different contexts. We can compare this to rooms, which allow us to group connections together. Everyone that connects joins the default `' '` (empty string) room by default. We can then have the same connection join other rooms, as well.

Finding rooms

We should think of rooms as hashes of connections because that is exactly what they are! There is a `rooms` object right off of `io.sockets.adapter` that has each room and the clients that are in that room.

```
▼ Watch Expressions
▼ io.sockets.adapter: Adapter
  ▶ encoder: Encoder
  ▶ nsp: Namespace
  ▼ rooms: Object
    ▶ : Array[0]
    ▶ 3tEhBwhj9d34eJU2AAAA: Array[0]
    ▶ ikr3pDEdUpZiGSEXAAAB: Array[0]
    ▼ vip: Array[0]
        3tEhBwhj9d34eJU2AAAA: true
        ikr3pDEdUpZiGSEXAAAB: true
        length: 0
  ▶ sids: Object
```

The objects may look a little weird because they say they are an array of `0`. This is correct, as each socket is attached as a property of the array and not as a member. A little confusing, but it does allow us to use the array like a hash.

Using namespaces and rooms together

We can now discuss the fact that namespaces and rooms are not mutually exclusive. You can use them at the same time. Now that we have discussed how they work, this will make sense. Namespaces allow you to create different contexts for Socket.IO to work in. Rooms allow you to group client connections inside of those contexts.

Namespaces are farther up in the hierarchy so that you can use them together if they come first. As an example, let's say that we built our Ping-Pong app with a namespace of `pingpong` with two rooms, `''` (empty string) and `'vip'`. A lot of code can stay exactly the same because the socket object inside of a connection event is already tied to the namespace. If you were outside of the namespace, though, you still could get a list of clients in a room.

We don't have to view these as an exclusive option. We should view them as options. Most likely, you will need both in any moderately complex project.

Using Socket.IO and Express together

We previously created an Express application. This application is just the foundation. We are going to add features until it is a fully usable app. We currently can serve web pages and respond to HTTP, but now we want to add real-time communication. It's very fortunate that we just spent most of this chapter learning about Socket.IO; it does just that! Let's see how we are going to integrate Socket.IO with an Express application.

We are going to use Express and Socket.IO side by side. As I mentioned before, Socket.IO does not use HTTP like a web application. It is event based, not request based. This means that Socket.IO will not interfere with Express routes that we have set up, and that's a good thing. The bad thing is that we will not have access to all the middleware that we set up for Express in Socket.IO. There are some frameworks that combine these two, but it still has to convert the request from Express into something that Socket.IO can use. I am not trying to knock down these frameworks. They simplify a complex problem and most importantly, they do it well (Sails is a great example of this). Our app, though, is going to keep Socket.IO and Express separated as much as possible with the least number of dependencies. We know that Socket.IO does not need Express, as all our examples have not used Express in any way. This has an added benefit in that we can break off our Socket.IO module and run it as its own application at a future point in time. The other great benefit is that we learn how to do it ourselves.

We need to go into the directory where our Express application is. Make sure that our `pacakage.json` has all the additional packages for this chapter and run `npm.install`. The first thing we need to do is add our configuration settings.

Adding Socket.IO to the config

We will use the same config file that we created for our Express app. Open up `config.js` and change the file to what I have done in the following code:

```
var config = {
  port: 3000,
  secret: 'secret',
  redisPort: 6379,
  redisHost: 'localhost',
  routes: {
    login: '/account/login',
    logout: '/account/logout'
  }
};
module.exports = config;
```

We are adding two new attributes, `redisPort` and `redisHost`. This is because of how the `redis` package configures its clients. We also are removing the `redisUrl` attribute. We can configure all our clients with just these two Redis config options.

Next, create a directory under the root of our project named `socket.io`. Then, create a file called `index.js`. This will be where we initialize Socket.IO and wire up all our event listeners and emitters. We are just going to use one namespace for our application. If we were to add multiple namespaces, I would just add them as files underneath the `socket.io` directory.

Open up `app.js` and change the following lines in it:

```
//variable declarations at the top
Var io = require('./socket.io');
//after all the middleware and routes
var server = app.listen(config.port);
io.startIo(server);
```

We will define the `startIo` function shortly, but let's talk about our `app.listen` change. Previously, we had the `app.listen` execute, and we did not capture it in a variable; now we are. Socket.IO listens using Node's `http.createServer`. It does this automatically if you pass in a number into its `listen` function. When Express executes `app.listen`, it returns an instance of the HTTP server. We capture that, and now we can pass the `http` server to Socket.IO's `listen` function. Let's create that `startIo` function.

Open up `index.js` present in the `socket.io` location and add the following lines of code to it:

```
var io = require('socket.io');
var config = require('../config');

var socketConnection = function socketConnection(socket){
  socket.emit('message', {message: 'Hey!'});
};

exports.startIo = function startIo(server){
  io = io.listen(server);
  var packtchat = io.of('/packtchat');
  packtchat.on('connection', socketConnection);

  return io;
};
```

We are exporting the `startIo` function that expects a server object that goes right into Socket.IO's `listen` function. This should start Socket.IO serving. Next, we get a reference to our namespace and listen on the connection event, sending a message event back to the client. We also are loading our configuration settings.

Let's add some code to the layout and see whether our application has real-time communication.

We will need the Socket.IO client library, so link to it from `node_modules` like you have been doing, and put it in our static directory under a newly created `js` directory. Open `layout.ejs` present in the `packtchat\views` location and add the following lines to it:

```
<!-- put these right before the body end tag -->
<script type="text/javascript" src="/js/socket.io.js"></script>
<script>
var socket = io.connect("http://localhost:3000/packtchat");
socket.on('message', function(d){console.log(d);});
</script>
```

We just listen for a message event and log it to the console. Fire up the node and load your application, `http://localhost:3000`. Check to see whether you get a message in your console. You should see your message logged to the console, as seen in the following screenshot:

```
Object {message: "Hey!"}                                        (index):28
>  |
```

Success! Our application now has real-time communication. We are not done though. We still have to wire up all the events for our app.

Who are you?

There is one glaring issue. How do we know who is making the requests? Express has middleware that parses the session to see if someone has logged in. Socket.IO does not even know about a session. Socket.IO lets anyone connect that knows the URL. We do not want anonymous connections that can listen to all our events and send events to the server. We only want authenticated users to be able to create a WebSocket. We need to get Socket.IO access to our sessions.

Authorization in Socket.IO

We haven't discussed it yet, but Socket.IO has middleware. Before the connection event gets fired, we can execute a function and either allow the connection or deny it. This is exactly what we need.

Using the authorization handler

Authorization can happen at two places, on the default namespace or on a named namespace connection. Both authorizations happen through the handshake. The function's signature is the same either way. It will pass in the socket server, which has some stuff we need such as the connection's headers, for example. For now, we will add a simple authorization function to see how it works with Socket.IO.

Open up `index.js`, present at the `packtchat\socket.io` location, and add a new function that will sit next to the `socketConnection` function, as seen in the following code:

```
var io = require('socket.io');

var socketAuth = function socketAuth(socket, next){
return next();
  return next(new Error('Nothing Defined'));
};

var socketConnection = function socketConnection(socket){
  socket.emit('message', {message: 'Hey!'});
};

exports.startIo = function startIo(server){
  io = io.listen(server);
  var packtchat = io.of('/packtchat');

  packtchat.use(socketAuth);
  packtchat.on('connection', socketConnection);

  return io;
};
```

I know that there are two returns in this function. We are going to comment one out, load the site, and then switch the lines that are commented out. The socket server that is passed in will have a reference to the handshake data that we will use shortly. The next function works just like it does in Express. If we execute it without anything, the middleware chain will continue. If it is executed with an error, it will stop the chain. Let's load up our site and test both by switching which return gets executed.

We can allow or deny connections as we please now, but how do we know who is trying to connect?

Cookies and sessions

We will do it the same way Express does. We will look at the cookies that are passed and see if there is a session. If there is a session, then we will load it up and see what is in it. At this point, we should have the same knowledge about the Socket.IO connection that Express does about a request.

The first thing we need to do is get a cookie parser. We will use a very aptly named package called `cookie`. This should already be installed if you updated your `package.json` and installed all the packages.

Add a reference to this at the top of `index.js` present in the `packtchat\socket.io` location with all the other variable declarations:

```
Var cookie = require('cookie');
```

And now we can parse our cookies. Socket.IO passes in the cookie with the socket object in our middleware. Here is how we parse it. Add the following code in the `socketAuth` function:

```
var handshakeData = socket.request;
var parsedCookie = cookie.parse(handshakeData.headers.cookie);
```

At this point, we will have an object that has our `connect.sid` in it. Remember that this is a signed value. We cannot use it as it is right now to get the session ID. We will need to parse this signed cookie.

This is where cookie-parser comes in. We will now create a reference to it, as follows:

```
Var cookieParser = require('cookie-parser');
```

We can now parse the signed `connect.sid` cookie to get our session ID. Add the following code right after our parsing code:

```
var sid = cookieParser.signedCookie (parsedCookie['connect.sid'],
config.secret);
```

This will take the value from our `parsedCookie` and using our secret passphrase, will return the unsigned value. We will do a quick check to make sure this was a valid signed cookie by comparing the unsigned value to the original. We will do this in the following way:

```
if (parsedCookie['connect.sid'] === sid)
    return next(new Error('Not Authenticated'));
```

This check will make sure we are only using valid signed session IDs.

The following screenshot will show you the values of an example Socket.IO authorization with a cookie:

```
▼ parsedCookie: Object
    connect.sid: "s:f0WO6MohcxtjvlyQI1iZ6AYx.vMqCF23fVF3Tu5EwdgIVcyNb4TP9M8fkIaogE8uCVGw"
    sid: "f0WO6MohcxtjvlyQI1iZ6AYx"
```

Getting the session

We now have a session ID so we can query Redis and get the session out.

If you recall in *Chapter 1, Backend Development with Express,* when we added Redis as our session store, we mentioned that connect-redis extends the default session store object of Express. To use connect-redis, we use the same session package as we did with Express, `express-session`. The following code is used to create all this in `index.js`, present at `packtchat\socket.io`:

```
//at the top with the other variable declarations
var expressSession = require('express-session');
var ConnectRedis = require('connect-redis')(expressSession);
var redisSession = new ConnectRedis({host: config.redisHost, port:
config.redisPort});
```

The final line is creating the object that will connect to Redis and get our session. This is the same command used with Express when setting the store option for the session. We can now get the session from Redis and see what's inside of it. What follows is the entire `socketAuth` function along with all our variable declarations:

```
var io = require('socket.io'),
  connect = require('connect'),
```

```
      cookie = require('cookie'),
      expressSession = require('express-session'),
      ConnectRedis = require('connect-redis')(expressSession),
      redis = require('redis'),
      config = require('../config'),
      redisSession = new ConnectRedis({host: config.redisHost, port:
   config.redisPort});

   var socketAuth = function socketAuth(socket, next){
      var handshakeData = socket.request;
      var parsedCookie = cookie.parse(handshakeData.headers.cookie);
      var sid = connect.utils.parseSignedCookie(parsedCookie['connect.
   sid'], config.secret);

      if (parsedCookie['connect.sid'] === sid)
        return next(new Error('Not Authenticated'));

      redisSession.get(sid, function(err, session){
        if (session.isAuthenticated)
        {
          socket.user = session.user;
          socket.sid = sid;
          return next();
        }
        else
          return next(new Error('Not Authenticated'));
      });
   };
```

We can use `redisSession` and `sid` to get the session out of Redis and
check its attributes. As far as our packages are concerned, we are just another
Express app getting session data. Once we have the session data, we check the
`isAuthenticated` attribute. If it's true, we know the user is logged in. If not,
we do not let them connect yet.

We are adding properties to the socket object to store information from the session.
Later on, after a connection is made, we can get this information. As an example,
we are going to change our `socketConnection` function to send the user object to
the client. The following should be our `socketConnection` function:

```
   var socketConnection = function socketConnection(socket){
      socket.emit('message', {message: 'Hey!'});
      socket.emit('message', socket.user);

   };
```

Now, let's load up our browser and go to `http://localhost:3000`. Log in and then check the browser's console. The following screenshot will show that the client is receiving the messages:

```
Object {message: "Hey!"}                     chat:28
Object {username: "joshua"}                  chat:28
>
```

Adding application-specific events

We have extended our Express application we created in *Chapter 1*, *Backend Development with Express*, to include real-time communications using Socket.IO. The next thing to do is to build out all the real-time events that Socket.IO is going to listen for and respond to. We are just going to create the skeleton for each of these listeners. In *Chapter 7*, *Using Backbone and React for DOM Events*, we will add the code to respond to these events, as they are going to retrieve and add data to Redis.

Open up `index.js`, present in `packtchat\socket.io`, and change the entire `socketConnection` function to the following code:

```
var socketConnection = function socketConnection(socket){
  socket.on('GetMe', function(){});
  socket.on('GetUser', function(room){});
  socket.on('GetChat', function(data){});
  socket.on('AddChat', function(chat){});
  socket.on('GetRoom', function(){});
  socket.on('AddRoom', function(r){});
  socket.on('disconnect', function(){});
};
```

Most of our emit events will happen in response to a listener.

Using Redis as the store for Socket.IO

The final thing we are going to add is to switch Socket.IO's internal communication about room participation. By default, Socket.IO will not let other Socket.IO nodes know about room changes. As we know now, we cannot have an application state that is stored only on one server. We need to store it in Redis. Therefore, we add it to `index.js`, present in `packtchat\socket.io`. Add the following code to the variable declarations:

```
Var redisAdapter = require('socket.io-redis');
```

An application state is a flexible idea. We can store the application state locally. This is done when the state does not need to be shared. A simple example is keeping the path to a local temp file. When the data will be needed by multiple connections, then it must be put into a shared space. Anything with a user's session will need to be shared, for example.

The next thing we need to do is add some code to our `startIo` function. The following code is what our `startIo` function should look like:

```
exports.startIo = function startIo(server){
  io = io.listen(server);

  io.adapter(redisAdapter({host: config.redisHost, port: config.
redisPort}));

  var packtchat = io.of('/packtchat');

  packtchat.use(socketAuth);
  packtchat.on('connection', socketConnection);

  return io;
};
```

The first thing is to start the server listening. We create a new `redisStore` and set all the Redis attributes (`redisPub`, `redisSub`, and `redisClient`) to a new Redis client connection. The Redis client takes a port and the hostname.

Socket.IO inner workings

We are not going to completely dive into everything that Socket.IO does, but we will discuss a few topics.

WebSockets

This is what makes Socket.IO work. All web servers serve HTTP, that is, what makes them web servers. This works great when all you want to do is serve pages. These pages are served based on requests. The browser must ask for information before receiving it. If you want to have real-time connections, though, it is difficult and requires some workaround. HTTP was not designed to have the server initiate the request. This is where WebSockets come in.

WebSockets allow the server and client to create a connection and keep it open. Inside of this connection, either side can send messages back and forth. This is what Socket.IO (technically, Engine.io) leverages to create real-time communication.

Socket.IO even has fallbacks if you are using a browser that does not support WebSockets. The browsers that do support WebSockets at the time of writing include the latest versions of Chrome, Firefox, Safari, Safari on iOS, Opera, and IE 11. This means the browsers that do not support WebSockets are all the older versions of IE. Socket.IO will use different techniques to simulate a WebSocket connection. This involves creating an Ajax request and keeping the connection open for a long time. If data needs to be sent, it will send it in an Ajax request. Eventually, that request will close and the client will immediately create another request.

Socket.IO even has an Adobe Flash implementation if you have to support really old browsers (IE 6, for example). It is not enabled by default.

WebSockets also are a little different when scaling our application. Because each WebSocket creates a persistent connection, we may need more servers to handle Socket.IO traffic then regular HTTP. For example, when someone connects and chats for an hour, there will have only been one or two HTTP requests. In contrast, a WebSocket will have to be open for the entire hour. The way our code base is written, we can easily scale up more Socket.IO servers by themselves.

Ideas to take away from this chapter

The first takeaway is that for every emit, there needs to be an on. This is true whether the sender is the server or the client. It is always best to sit down and map out each event and which direction it is going.

The next idea is that of note, which entails building our app out of loosely coupled modules. Our `app.js` kicks everything that deals with Express off. Then, it fires the `startIo` function. While it does pass over an object, we could easily create one and use that. Socket.IO just wants a basic HTTP server. In fact, you can just pass the port, which is what we used in our first couple of Socket.IO applications (Ping-Pong). If we wanted to create an application layer of Socket.IO servers, we could refactor this code out and have all the Socket.IO servers run on separate servers other than Express.

Summary

At this point, we should feel comfortable about creating and using real-time events in Socket.IO. We should also know how to namespace our io server and create groups of users. We also learned how to authorize socket connections to only allow logged-in users to connect. We did this in the context of our Express application that we created in the previous chapter.

Our next chapter will demonstrate the correct way to authenticate users using Passport.

3
Authenticating Users

We technically have built authentication into our application already, but it is definitely not ready for production. We are going to need an authentication framework that will allow users to sign up using accounts they already have and to create a local user account. Node.js has a great and extensible authentication framework: Passport. It has a foundation package that will easily integrate with Express. In addition to this, it has over 140 strategies (what Passport calls its authentication plugins) to use. If Passport cannot authenticate it, no one is probably using it. We will cover the following topics in this chapter:

- How to register applications for Facebook and Google
- How to authenticate to Facebook
- How to authenticate to Google
- How to authenticate locally

Node package versions

We need to install Passport, and the three strategies we will use: local, Facebook, and Google. We are extending our application that we created in *Chapter 1*, *Backend Development with Express*; so, these are in addition to all the packages we already have installed. The following list details out the versions for each package. We will only be working in our main application, so add them to our current list of packages in `package.json` and run `npm install`:

- passport: 0.2.0
- passport-local: 1.0.0
- passport-facebook: 1.0.3
- passport-google-oauth: 0.1.5
- scmp: 0.0.3

Let's build our authentication

With our packages installed, we now have the basis to build our authentication system. The first thing to do is create a folder named `passport` and create a file named `index.js` in that folder. Inside `index.js`, we will get a reference to Passport and pass it back to the main `app.js`, as shown in the following code:

```
var passport = require('passport');

exports.passport = passport;
```

We could have done this in `app.js`, but we are going to set some things up and add some utility functions to this object. This will help keep our `app.js` file clean and easy to understand. We can now jump over to `app.js` and use our new module. Add the following lines to `app.js`:

```
//at the top with variable declarations
passport = require('./passport');
//in the middleware section
app.use(session({
  secret: config.secret,
  saveUninitialized: true,
  resave: true,
  store: new RedisStore(
    {url: config.redisUrl})
  })
);
app.use(passport.passport.initialize());
app.use(passport.passport.session());
app.use(bodyParser.json());
```

It might seem redundant to have `passport.passport`. This is because we pass the `passport` object back off of `exports`. We are doing this so that we can expose other functions later into the `app.js` scope. We will need to put Passport's session middleware after Express' session middleware. This is because Passport extends Express' session. Before Passport can do that, the session must exist off the request object. Before we can use Passport's session, we will need to initialize it. At this point, we can start our Node server and whether it is working. We are using Passport! It's not doing anything, but we are using it.

Registering a Facebook application

Our next step will be to create a Facebook application. The `passport-facebook` package requires a client ID and a client secret. We cannot just make them up, even for test. We will have to create a valid Facebook application. Let's do that.

The first thing we need to do is go to `https://developers.facebook.com/`. You will need to log in and register as a new developer. Click on `Apps | Create a New App` from the header, as shown in the following screenshot:

 Now would be a good time to note that this may all look different. In the past, Facebook has not been shy about changing the layout and look of their site.

A dialog will appear for **Create a New App**. Fill **Display Name** (what the app is called), **Namespace** (this must be unique in all of Facebook), and choose **Category**. Then, click on **Create App**. The following screenshot shows my choices:

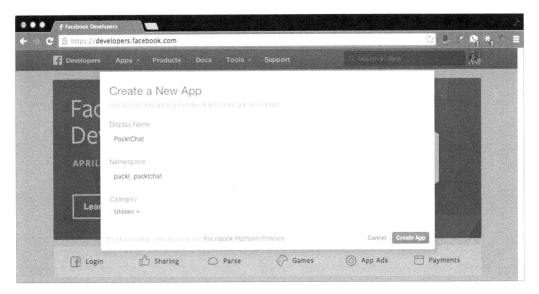

Most likely, you will have to pass a captcha security check next. You will then be taken to your application's dashboard. Here you can see your **App ID** and **App Secret**, as shown in the following screenshot:

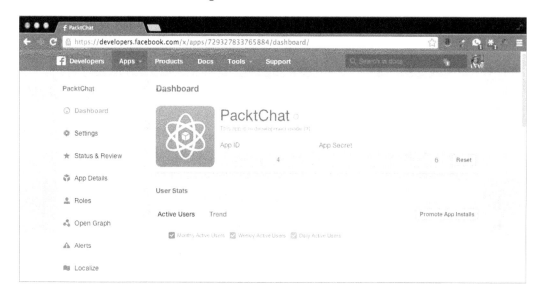

 Do not let your **App ID** and **App Secret** get out! Someone can make calls in the context of your application. I have redacted them here. Our **App ID** is actually public information and is used in our redirect URLs from the client. Your **App Secret** should always be protected. Because anyone can find our **App ID**, our **App Secret** is how we let Facebook, or any other OAuth server, know it is our application.

Before we can use this app, we will have to set it up.

Click on the **Settings** link to the left. Here, you will see your **App ID** and **App Secret** again. This is where we let Facebook know where the authentication requests will be coming from. Click on **Add Platform** and select **Website**, which is shown in the following screenshot:

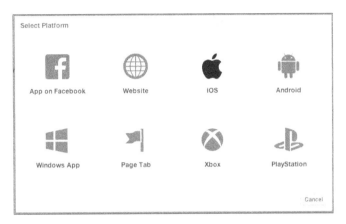

Under **Site URL**, enter our development URL: `http://localhost:3000/`. Finally, click on **Save Changes**. Your **Settings** should look similar to the following screenshot:

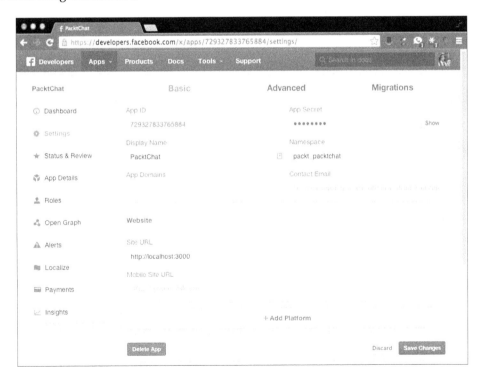

As shown in the following screenshot, you can click on **App Details** and update information about our application. You can set descriptions, why you want certain permissions, any service URLs (for example, terms of service or privacy), a logo, and an icon. This is where you will build a custom dialog box for your app. This is just for test, so we won't do any of this. The following screenshot shows what options are available:

Using Passport to authenticate to Facebook

We are now ready to make Passport work with Facebook. We also are going to do this correctly from the start by adding our configuration to the `config` file from the start. We want our code to be modular. This allows us to replace certain parts and config settings without disturbing other parts. So, let's start there. Open up `config.js` in the root of our folder and add the following lines to it:

```
routes: {
    login: '/account/login',
    logout: '/account/logout',
    chat: '/chat',
    facebookAuth: '/auth/facebook',
    facebookAuthCallback: '/auth/facebook/callback'
},
```

```
host: 'http://localhost:3000',
facebook: {
  appID: 'YOUR_APP_ID',
  appSecret: 'YOUR_APP_SECRET',
}
```

We are adding three more routes, `facebookAuth`, `facebookAuthCallback`, and `chat` as we will need to use these in at least two different places. We want to add any URLs here that need to be definitively defined. Any authentication URL will fit this description. Next, we are adding a host attribute. We need this because Facebook needs a **fully qualified domain name** (**FQDN**) to redirect to after authentication. Finally, we are adding `appID` and `appSecret` in the `config` file.

 We are keeping our secret in the `config` file for ease here, but we should never have this information accessible in a public repo. We will cover where to put this info in *Chapter 8, JavaScript Best Practices for Application Development*.

As a quick aside, we have to change the chat route in two other files. The first is `app.js` and the other is in `index.js` present in the `routes` folder. Both of the files `reference/chat` and we need to update these references to `config.routes.chat`.

We are ready to build out our Passport authentication object now. Open up `index.js` present in the `passport` folder to add the following lines at the top of the file:

```
var passport = require('passport'),
  facebook = require('passport-facebook').Strategy,
  config = require('../config');

passport.use(new facebook({
  clientID: config.facebook.appID,
  clientSecret: config.facebook.appSecret,
  callbackURL: config.host + config.routes.facebookAuthCallback
},
function(accessToken, refreshToken, profile, done){
  done(null, profile);
}));
exports.passport = passport;
```

We start off by getting a reference to all the objects we will need. Then, we tell Passport that we are going to be using Facebook. We configure the Facebook authentication strategy with our `config` object. Here, we can see that we need to use `host` and `route` to build a FQDN for Facebook to redirect back to.

The anonymous function is what Passport will run after a successful authentication request. For Facebook, this will involve some tokens, a user profile object, and a callback. We are not doing anything special here. We just take the user profile and pass it to the next function. If we had a database, we could use it to check whether that Facebook ID existed on a user, and then return that user or create a new user if that Facebook ID was not used. Now, we need to build the functions that takes the user in and out of the session. This is what our done(null, profile) callback will call.

Add the following two functions in index.js present in the passport folder, right before the final exports:

```
passport.serializeUser(function(user, done){
  done(null, user);
});

passport.deserializeUser(function(user, done) {
    done(null, user);
});
exports.passport = passport;
```

We have configured Passport to use a session (in app.js with app.use(passport. passport.session())), so Passport needs to know how to serialize the user to go into the session and how to get it back out. If we have our own database backend, we can just store the user ID that we could have looked up in the callback from the authentication method. In this example, we are just storing the user object as is to the session. I personally think that storing the whole user object is the best way to do this, as I don't want to make a query to look up the user on every request. This is especially true when we have a super-fast backend for our session, such as Redis. We will now have an object at req.session.passport.user when someone authenticates their details. We will use this in just a few paragraphs. Next, we need to build our routes for Facebook.

The last lines we are going to add in index.js present in the passport folder are the routes function and exports, as shown in the following code:

```
var routes = function routes(app){
  app.get(config.routes.facebookAuth, passport.
authenticate('facebook'));
  app.get(config.routes.facebookAuthCallback, passport.
authenticate('facebook',
    {successRedirect: config.routes.chat, failureRedirect: config.
routes.login, failureFlash: true}));
};

exports.passport = passport;
exports.routes = routes;
```

We built our routes in the `config` file, so we just reference them here. The `routes` function will need a reference to Express, so it is passed in as a parameter. We can then use it to tell Express how to respond to these requests. Each function is just a simple Express route with a Passport authentication middleware added. The first route is where we should send the initial Facebook authentication request. It will redirect the user to Facebook to approve the request. Facebook will then send the request back to our second route. This will finalize the authentication. We can configure this middleware by passing in an `options` object as the second parameter. We are doing this with the Facebook callback route and specifying where to redirect on success and failure. In addition to this, we also tell it to use the flash middleware to log for any errors.

To make this work, we need to tell Express about these routes. In `app.js`, after all the other routes have been created, add the following line:

```
passport.routes(app);
```

The `passport.routers` function is executed with app, which is our Express server object. Express now knows about our two Facebook routes.

Because we have updated our authentication process, we will need to update some middleware utilities and views. Let's start with the middleware.

Our old authenticate middleware will not pick up a Passport authentication. Open up `utilities.js` present in the `middleware` folder and change the authenticated function to the following code:

```
Module.exports.authenticated = function authenticated(req, res, next){
  req.session.isAuthenticated = req.session.passport.user !==
undefined;
  res.locals.isAuthenticated = req.session.isAuthenticated;
  if (req.session.isAuthenticated) {
    res.locals.user = req.session.passport.user;
  }
  next();
};
```

Before, we were manually setting the `isAuthenticated` variable in the session in the `auth` function. Now, we will check to see whether there is a passport user in the session. If so, set the `res.locals.user` to that user. Authentication through Passport will now work correctly. If we do not change this function, it will not see a Passport authentication as valid.

Next, we need to change the `logOut` function in the same file, as follows:

```
Module.exports.logOut = function logOut(req){
   req.session.isAuthenticated = false;
   req.logout();
};
```

Passport adds a `logout` function off of the request that will take care of removing the user from the session; we will use this. We did change the function signature of this, so we will need to update any other functions that call this. Luckily, this is just one. Open `index.js` present in the `routes` folder and modify the `logOut` function there, as shown in the following code:

```
exports.logOut = function logOut(req, res){
   util.logOut(req);
   res.redirect('/');
};
```

Now, we can edit the views. Our user object has changed, so our reference in `user-loggedin.ejs` present in the `views/partials` folder is not correct anymore. Open that file and change it to the following:

```
Hello <%= user.displayName %> <a href="<%= routes.logout %>">Logout</
a>
```

Finally, we will make the **Facebook** button on our login form actually take us to Facebook. Open `login.ejs` present in the `views` folder and change the Facebook button to the following:

```
<div class="col-sm-6">
                    <a class="btn btn-block facebook" href="<%= routes.
facebookAuth %>"><i class="fa fa-facebook"></i> Facebook</a>
</div>
```

We changed the button to an anchor tag. We could have left it as a button and tied a click handler to it, but I always try to let the browser execute the default action if possible. We then set the `href` to our `facebookAuth` route. This is a perfect example of why we want a route map. At this point, we should be able to authenticate to Facebook.

Load our app in Node and go to the login page and click on **Facebook**. The following screenshot is what you should see (with your Facebook photo of course!):

If you had added an application icon, it would show up here. This is the first time we will select **Cancel** to see what happens. The following screenshot shows what should happen:

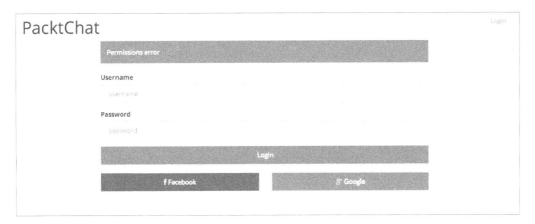

This is exactly what we wanted. It redirects back to the login and has a flash message of what went wrong. Let's do it again, except this time approve the request. Success! We should now see that we are logged in and it displays our name from Facebook. The following screenshot is what it should look like:

PacktChat

Hello Joshua Johanan Logout

Chat

Our middleware are all working together as we designed. Even though we have completely changed how our application authenticates, all our pieces are working as they should.

>
> If you are trying to test your Facebook authentication and you approve the application, you can still remove that approval. Go to `https://www.facebook.com/appcenter/my` and remove the application from your profile. This may change in the future.

Using Google for authentication

We have Facebook working great. Let's authenticate to Google now. The process will be very similar, so this shouldn't be too hard. The first thing we have to do is register an application with Google.

Go to `https://console.developers.google.com/project`. This page will list out all the applications that you have created with Google before. This includes any App Engine or OpenID projects. I have tried a few different services with Google, so I have a few projects here.

We want to click on the **CREATE PROJECT** button shown in the following screenshot:

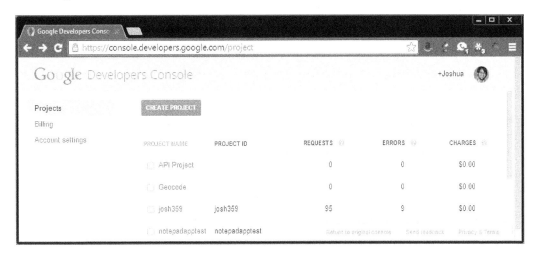

A **New Project** dialog will pop up. Filling this out will be similar to Facebook's process. **Project name** is the name by which we will call the project. **Project ID** is the Google identifier for our application. It defaults to a randomly created name which we will use here. Then, click on the **Create** button. This can be seen in the following screenshot:

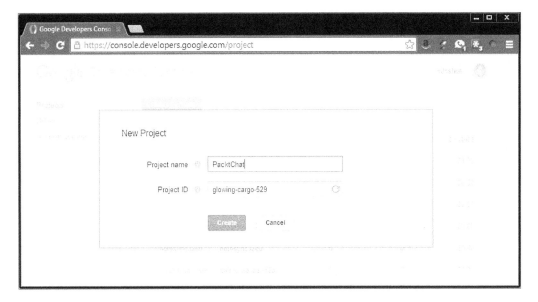

Our newly created application will be on our list now. Click on the application name and you will see a screen that asks us, **Not sure what to do next?** To be honest, it is not really clear what you are supposed to do next. There are a lot of options here. The Google **Developers Console** allows you to create everything from OAuth applications (what we want to do now) to using Google Compute Engine. Our next step is to click on **Apis & auth** and then on **Credentials** from the menu that comes up. You will see **Compute Engine and App Engine** credentials, but we cannot use those. You can see it in the following screenshot:

You need to click on **CREATE NEW CLIENT ID**. This will pop up a new dialog. The application type is **Web application, Authorized JavaScript origins** is `http://localhost:3000`, and **Authorized redirect URI** is `http://localhost:3000/auth/google/callback`. Your dialog should look like the following screenshot:

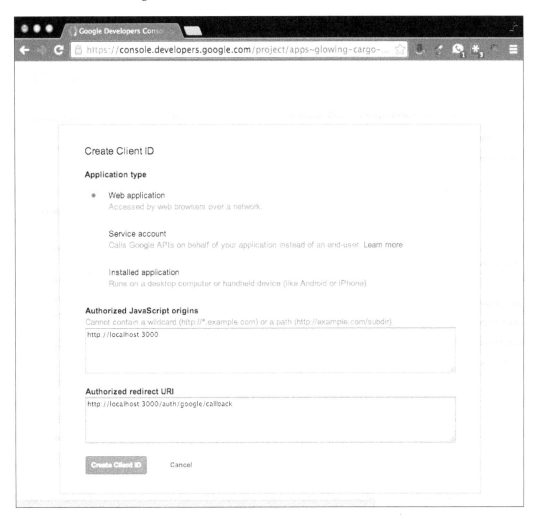

We can now click on **Create Client ID**. Our API **Credentials** list should now have a new **Client ID** and **Client secret** for us. You can see this in the following screenshot:

The last thing we can do is modify **Consent Screen**. This is the page that you will be redirected to to authorize the application. You can add logos, privacy policies, terms of service, and a few other things. The one setting you will want to change is **Product name**. If you don't do so, your application will show up as **Project Default Service Account**, which is not very user friendly.

This process is very similar to Facebook's. We also come out of it with the same exact type of data, a client ID, and secret. Setting up the authentication will be very easy as well.

Adding Google authentication to our application

First, we need to add our Google-specific information to our `config`. Open `config.js` and add the following lines:

```
routes: {
    login: '/account/login',
```

```
      logout: '/account/logout',
      chat: '/chat',    facebookAuth: '/auth/facebook',
      facebookAuthCallback: '/auth/facebook/callback',
      googleAuth: '/auth/google',
      googleAuthCallback: '/auth/google/callback'
   },
   //host and facebook
   google: {
      clientID: 'YOUR_GOOGLE_ID',
      clientSecret: 'YOUR_GOOGLE_SECRET'
   }
```

We haven't added anything different. We just had to create the two Google authentication routes and add the ID and secret.

The package we will use is passport-google-oauth. This should be installed already at this point through npm install. Notice that this is not passport-google. That package is used to authenticate with OpenID, and we want to use OAuth2.

Open index.js present in the passport folder and add a reference to our Google strategy as follows:

```
//other variable declarations
google = require('passport-google-oauth').OAuth2Strategy,
```

The next step is to tell Passport that we want to use Google as an authentication provider. Add this middleware to our auth stack.

```
//right under the Facebook passport.use
passport.use(new google({
    clientID: config.google.clientID,
    clientSecret: config.google.clientSecret,
    callbackURL: config.host + config.routes.googleAuthCallback
},
function(accessToken, refreshToken, profile, done) {
  done(null, profile);
}));
```

If you compare this chunk of code to the Facebook portion, you will see that they are almost exactly the same. This is because we are trying to do the exact same thing. We need to pass in our client ID and client secret. Then, we need to tell Google what URL to use as a callback. The final function is how we would tie this together with a database. We would be able to find or create a user based on their Google ID. Here, we are not doing that; we are just using the profile as is from Passport.

This is important enough to repeat; do not let your client ID and secret get out! With them, other apps can masquerade using your identity.

The next step is to set up routes to start authentication and our authentication callback. Inside `index.js`, present in the `passport` folder, add the following routes to the `routes` function:

```
var routes = function routes(app){
  app.get(config.routes.facebookAuth, passport.
authenticate('facebook'));
  app.get(config.routes.facebookAuthCallback, passport.
authenticate('facebook',
    {successRedirect: config.routes.chat, failureRedirect: config.
routes.login, failureFlash: true}));
  app.get(config.routes.googleAuth, passport.authenticate('google',
    { scope: ['https://www.googleapis.com/auth/userinfo.
profile','https://www.googleapis.com/auth/userinfo.email'] }));
  app.get(config.routes.googleAuthCallback, passport.
authenticate('google',
    {successRedirect: config.routes.chat, failureR edirect: config.
routes.login, failureFlash: true}));
};
```

Again, these lines of code are very similar to our Facebook routes. The main difference here is that our initial Google authentication URL has an extra object passed into it. This is the scope. The scope tells Google what we want to access from the user. Google then shows that to the user, so they can approve or deny the request. Other than that difference, these routes are here to do the same thing the Facebook routes do.

 Facebook also can use scope. If you do not specify a scope, Facebook will use a default scope. Google requires that a scope be explicitly defined.

Finally, we need to add our Google Auth URL to the login view. Open up `login.ejs` present in the `views` folder and change the Google button HTML code to the following:

```
<div class="col-sm-6">
<a class="btn btn-block google" href="<%= routes.googleAuth %>"><i
class="fa fa-google-plus"></i> Google</a>
</div>
```

We can now test Google authentication. Fire up your app with Node and go to `http://localhost:3000/login`. Then, click on the Google **login** button. You should see the following screenshot:

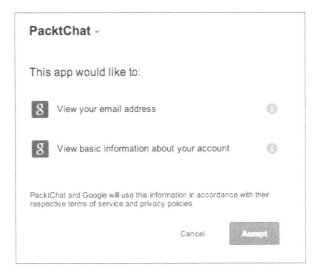

We can see our scope is passed as Google tells us that the application wants our e-mail address and basic profile information. Click on **Accept**, and you should be redirected to `http://localhost:3000/chat` and be logged in. We have wired up Google OAuth and it works!

 If you are testing Google authentication, you may want to remove access to your application. If not, subsequent authentication calls automatically return. Just go to your Google account and then click on the **Security** tab, and then **Account Permissions**. You will see a list of all the applications you have approved from your account.

Adding more OAuth providers

At this point, hopefully, we can see that adding more authentication providers should be easy with Passport. At the time of writing this book, Passport has 140 authentication packages we can use. Many of them are OAuth wrappers because OAuth is a great way to maintain security and give access to third parties. Each new provider that you add will roughly follow the process we have just done. First, you will sign up with the provider and create an application/client. Most likely, you will get an ID and a secret. Plug those into your application config along with your initial route and callback route. Finally, create the routes using Passport's middleware and add the link to a view. Congratulations! You have added a new provider!

Adding secure local authentication

We have Facebook and Google authentication working perfectly. We should be able to sign in and go to `http://localhost:3000/chat` and get an authorized Socket.IO handshake, although we now cannot sign in using our local username and password.

 Technically, the function does come back as authorized, but we do not set the correct variables in the session anymore.

We also want to create a function that is much more secure than just a username check.

The `passport-local` module will work in the `passport.authenticate` middleware, but we will have to write our own logic. This is different than the other modules where the logic is written, and we just have to add our application specific parts. Let's build our authentication logic.

Open your `config.js` file in the root directory. We are going to add some cryptographic settings as follows:

```
crypto: {
    workFactor: 5000,
    keylen: 32,
    randomSize: 256
}
```

We will talk about and use the `workFactor` later. The `keylen` Integer is the size of our hash that comes back and `randomSize` is the size of the `salt`. We will use all of these and discuss what they do later in this chapter.

Now that we have our crypto settings, we will create a file in the passport directory named `password.js`. This will hold all of our password utilities.

The first thing we will do is use a package name `scmp`. This will allow us to do constant time comparisons. We will discuss why this is important later in the chapter.

Add the following code to `password.js` present in the `passport` folder:

```
var crypto = require('crypto'),
    scmp = require('scmp'),
    config = require('../config');

var passwordCreate = function passwordCreate(password, cb){
  crypto.randomBytes(config.crypto.randomSize, function(err, salt){
```

```
    if (err)
      return cb(err, null);
        crypto.pbkdf2(password, salt.toString('base64'), config.
    crypto.workFactor, config.crypto.keylen, function(err, key){
            cb(null, salt.toString('base64'), key.toString('base64'));
        });
    });
};

var passwordCheck = function passwordCheck(password, derivedPassword,
salt, work, cb){
    crypto.pbkdf2(password, salt, work, config.crypto.keylen,
function(err, key){
        cb(null, scmp(key.toString('base64'), derivedPassword));
    });
};

exports.passwordCreate = passwordCreate;
exports.passwordCheck = passwordCheck;
```

`Crypto` is a built-in Node.js module, so we don't have to install anything to use it. Our `passwordCreate` function takes a password and will create a secure hash. The function first uses `randomBytes` that will return 256 random bytes of data. The 256 bytes of data is based on our `config` setting. We then take that as `salt` and the clear text password and send it to **Password-Based Key Derivation Function 2 (PBKDF2)**, which is a function that will create a derived key based on `salt`, our `password`, and a `work` factor. We then return `salt` and the derived key back so that we can store it somewhere (most likely a database).

The `passwordCheck` function will do the opposite of that. It will take a password, a derived password, a `work` factor, and `salt`, and rerun the hashing function. Then, it will compare the values using `scmp` (we will cover why we do this later in the chapter). If they match, then the password was correct, and if not, it was not a valid password. We now have the two basic password functions that any application requires: creation and checking.

We will now create a user object to find and add users to our application. Create a file at `user.js` present in the `passport` folder. We will not be using a database here, but this is where you would pull in your database to look up users. We will just use a simple object to store all of our users, as shown in the following code:

```
var passUtil = require('./password');

var Users = {
```

```
    josh: {
      salt: 'G811JERghovMoUX5+RoasvwT7evsK1QTL33jc5pjG0w=',
          password: 'DAq+sDiEbIR0fHnbzgKQCOJ9siV5CL6FmXKAI6mX7UY=',
          work: 5000,
          displayName: 'Josh',
          id: 'josh',
          provider: 'local',
          username: 'josh'
    }
};
```

This could be the schema for your database. It mimics Passport's profile object with the addition of our password-related fields. The salt is much smaller here than you will get if you run the application. If I used a `salt` for the length we configured, it will take a page or two to display. If you were using a database, you will most likely tie the `Users` object to the users table or schema in your database. Now, let's add our functions as follows:

```
var findByUsername = function findByUsername(username, cb){
  cb(null, Users[username]);
};

var addUser = function addUser(username, password, work, cb){
  if(Users[username] === undefined)
  {
    passUtil.passwordCreate(password, function(err, salt, password){
      Users[username] = {
        salt: salt,
        password: password,
        work: work,
        displayName: username,
        id: username,
        provider: 'local',
        username: username
      };

      return cb(null, Users[username]);
    });
  }else{
    return cb({errorCode: 1, message: 'User exists!'} 'User exists!',
null);
  }
};
```

```
var updatePassword = function(username, password, work){
  passUtil.passwordCreate(password, function(err, salt, password){
    Users[username].salt = salt;
    Users[username].password = password;
    Users[username].work = work;
  });
};

exports.findByUsername = findByUsername;
exports.addUser = addUser;
exports.updatePassword = updatePassword;
```

findByUsername is pretty straightforward. It looks in the object for an attribute of our username and returns that. This is just a simple example. We should never trust data that was sent from the client. This is a perfect example of SQL injection (or object injection in the case here). We could add your SQL here for finding a user with a database or a key lookup in Redis. The next function adds a user. This function uses our passwordCreate function and adds an attribute to our object with their username, password, and salt. Finally, we have an updatePassword function which will update a user's password in the object based on the output of the passwordCreate function. If you were using a database, these last two functions would require an INSERT and UPDATE SQL commands, respectively inside a transaction. Without using a transaction, we can leave the data in an unusable state.

> Because the user list is an object, restarting the server will clear out all the added users. This is also true if you are running multiple web servers. Each one will have their own view of this data. This is not production safe, and we are using it here to demonstrate what will be stored over how to store it.

We can now create our Passport strategy to authenticate local users. In index.js, present in the passport folder, add the following variable declarations:

```
local = require('passport-local').Strategy,
  passwordUtils = require('./password'),
  user = require('./user'),
```

We can now put in our authentication middleware. Add the following line after Facebook and Google:

```
passport.use(new local(function(username, password, done){
  user.findByUsername(username, function(err, profile){
    if(profile)
    {
```

```
        passwordUtils.passwordCheck(password, profile.password, profile.
salt, profile.work, function(err,isAuth){
        if(isAuth)
        {
          if (profile.work < config.crypto.workFactor)
          {
            user.updatePassword(username, password, config.crypto.
workFactor);
          }
          done(null, profile);
        }
        else
        {
          done(null, false, {message: 'Wrong Username or Password'});
        }
      });
    }
    else
    {
      done(null, false, {message: 'Wrong Username or Password'});
    }
  });
}));
```

Passport's local strategy requires us to build our own logic to determine if someone is authorized. If they are, Passport will take care of adding them to the session. The first thing we do is check to see if a user exists; if not, return with the message **Wrong Username or Password**. Remember, you do not want to give attackers information, such as whether or not a username is in use. Next, we use our `passwordCheck` function. It will return a Boolean that states whether or not the password matched what was stored. Again, if it doesn't match, we will send our message back to the user. If the password does match, we perform one last check to see whether the work factor is smaller than our `config`. If so, update the salt, derived password, and work factor. This allows us to update our work factor, and as users authenticate, we will store their password more securely.

 We will cover a little theory after we create all of our new functions and files. First the practical, what you need to know, then we will have the theory.

Finally, return the profile back. At this point, it is handed over to Passport to serialize and store the information in the session.

The last thing we must do to make this work is create the route URL. Inside of the routes function, add these lines:

```
app.post(config.routes.login, passport.authenticate('local',
    {successRedirect: '/chat', failureRedirect: config.routes.login,
failureFlash: true}));
```

This should look like our other routes. Any POST to the login URL will run our local authentication function. It will also process our redirects. Before we test this, we will need to remove our other functions that listen for a POST on the login URL. Open `app.js`, and remove the following line from the routes:

```
app.post(config.routes.login, routes.loginProcess);
```

We can also remove the `loginProcess` function from `index.js` present in the `routes` folder and the `auth` function from `index.js` present in the `middleware` folder, as we will not need them anymore.

Start Node with our application and browse to `http://localhost:3000` and test logging in. The user we have loaded has `josh` as the username and a password of `password`. If you are using the code from Packt Publishing, you will also have two more users: `brian` and `test`. Both of these users have the same password: `password`. If you forget to pass either a username or password, then you will get an alert. This is shown in the following screenshot:

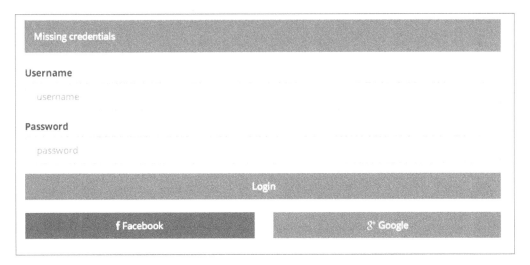

This is built into Passport's local strategy. If you pass in the wrong username or password, you will get our message of **Wrong Username or Password**.

Our authentication now works locally through Facebook and through Google. Unfortunately, we can only authenticate a few users locally.

Adding registration

We have built most of everything we need to enable registrations, so let's do that. We will want to create our registration URL, so open `config.js` and add the following line to the route map:

```
logout: '/account/logout',
register: '/account/register',
facebookAuth: '/auth/facebook',
```

Next, we will create our view. Create a file named `register.ejs` in the `views` directory. The file should have the following HTML code in it:

```html
<div class="row">
    <div class="col-sm-8 col-sm-offset-2">
        <div class="row">
            <div class="col-sm-12">
              <form method="post">
                <% if (message.length > 0) { %>
                  <div class="alert alert-danger"><%= message %></div>
                <% } %>
                <input type="hidden" name="_csrf" value="<%= token %>">
                <div class="form-group">
                    <label for="username">Username</label>
                    <input type="text" class="form-control" id="username" placeholder="username" name="username">
                </div>
                <div class="form-group">
                    <label for="password">Password</label>
                    <input type="password" class="form-control" id="password" placeholder="password" name="password">
                </div>
                <button class="btn btn-primary btn-block">Register</button>
            </div>
          </form>
        </div>
    </div>
</div>
```

This form is actually the `login` form with the **Facebook** and **Google** buttons removed. Now, we need to add a link to this page. Open `user-loggedout.ejs` present in the `views/partials` folder and add the following line to it:

```
<a href="<%= routes.login %>">Login</a> or <a href="<%= routes.
register %>">Register</a>
```

When you are logged out, the upper right of the page will now have links for logging in and registering.

The next step is to create our `route` function to respond to the `routes`. Open `index.js` present in the `routes` folder and add the following variable and two functions to it:

```
//variable declaration
var user = require('../passport/user');
//exports
module.exports.register = register;
module.exports.registerProcess = registerProcess;
//functions
function register(req, res){
  res.render('register', {title: 'Register', message: req.
flash('error')});
};


function register Process (req, res){
  if (req.body.username && req.body.password)
  {
    user.addUser(req.body.username, req.body.password, config.crypto.
workFactor, function(err, profile){
      if (err) {
        req.flash('error', err);
        res.redirect(config.routes.register);
      }else{
        req.login(profile, function(err){
          res.redirect('/chat');
        });
      }
    });
  }else{
    req.flash('error', 'Please fill out all the fields');
    res.redirect(config.routes.register);
  }
};
```

The first `register` function is just a simple render passing in the title and any messages. The next function does all the work of registering. `registerProcess` will be tied to POST action, so we can check the body for values. That is the first thing we do. We make sure both the username and password are filled out. If not, let the user know that they need to fill them both out. Then, we run our `addUser` function passing in the form values and our config's work factor. This function will first check if the user exists, as we don't want to just overwrite any user. If that happens, we set a flash message and redirect them back to the register form. If everything works out, then the user is returned. We then run `req.login` a Passport function that will set all the session variables for a logged-in user. `req.login` does not take a password because it assumes you have already done authentication checks.

Now we can add these functions to our main `app.js`. Open it and add the following routes:

```
app.get(config.routes.register, routes.register);
app.post(config.routes.register, routes.registerProcess);
```

We can now test this. Restart the Node and browse to `http://localhost:3000/account/register`. Create a new user and you will see that you are logged in. Then, log out and you will be able to log in again with the credentials you created. Just remember that this user will not last between server restarts.

Adding a database

If we wanted to add a database, it would be very easy. There are possibly two files we would change. The first file we would have to change is `user.js` present in the `passport` folder. This is the file that stores all our users. We would need to point it to our database. It's not really in the scope of this book to cover all the different types of databases you could use, but you would just have to look up users, add users, and update users. If you used the same schema as the `Users` object does in `user.js` (present in the `passport` folder), you will not need to update any other files. If you use a different schema, you will need to update `index.js` present in the `passport` folder. This file assumes that `salt`, `password`, and the `work` factor are separate columns. If they are not, you will just have to update any functions that look for these columns. Other than that, all the other functions are not dependent on where the data comes from.

Password-storing theory

We did not spend any time on why we chose PBKDF2 as our password-storing function. We will step through different levels of password security and talk about why we did not choose these methods.

First up is clear text passwords. I think this is very clear why this is a bad security practice. If attackers ever get your database, they have every user's username and password without doing any work. Most users reuse passwords, so this could give the attackers access to many people's Facebook, Gmail, and even the users' bank accounts. Never do this, especially when doing it correctly is very easy.

The next step up in storing passwords is using a hash function. A couple of popular functions are MD5 and SHA-256. These functions will take a clear-text password and turn it into a one-way hash of the password. When we check the password, we hash what a user has entered and compare it against what is in the database. If they match, then we know it is the correct password. This seems like it is all we would need to do, but there is one large issue here. There are files called rainbow tables which have thousands, millions, or even billions of password hashes. An attacker can just download an MD5 or SHA-256 rainbow table and then compare the hashes to our database. Not as easy as clear text, but if the hash exists in the rainbow table, that password is compromised.

We can protect against rainbow tables using a salt. This is some value that is used with the password. For example, if our salt was `salt` and the password was `password`, then the value we will hash would be `salt password`. This negates rainbow tables as each password will have a random value added to each password and would not be in the rainbow table. The most effective way for this to work would be to have a different salt for each password. If there is only one salt, then the attacker could create a salted rainbow table. Again, there is a problem here. It is the speed of hashing. MD5 and SHA-256 are designed to be fast. These hashing algorithms were not designed for passwords. Have you ever downloaded an ISO or file and there was an MD5 hash of the file? MD5 is fast so that you can quickly calculate the hash of the file and compare it to see whether there was any corruption. An attacker could go to Amazon Web Services run a few servers that can create 10,000 hashes a second on each CPU and go through every salted password hash in a matter of weeks, maybe even days. As each year goes by and CPUs become more efficient, this will become increasingly easier.

This brings us to what we are doing in this application. You should notice that we are using distinct salts for each password. The concept of salting a password is good; the use of MD5 or SHA-256 was the bad practice. That is where **PBKDF2 (Password-Based Key Derivation Function 2)** comes in. PBKDF2 allows you to add a work factor that will make the algorithm slower to compute. Instead of checking a hash every 1/10000th of a second, we are now talking about every half-second or second. Given enough time, the attacker can still crack each password, but it would take thousands of times longer. Now, we are talking about years or even decades to crack an entire database. In addition to this, the site is set up to allow us to increase the work factor. You will just need to change the value in `config.js`, and as users log in, it will recompute the stored value and a higher work factor. This helps as computers get faster.

The last security best practice we will cover is using `scmp`, which is constant-time comparison package. There are attacks named timing attacks that measure how long our application returns from a password check and uses that to determine what each letter of a password is. If it returns in 1 millisecond compared to 3 milliseconds, then the attack knows that the first few characters are correct. It then continues on down the password. This is done over thousands of calls. The protection for this is to run a constant-time comparison, which will return the same amount of time every time. This stops this type of attack in its tracks.

OAuth process

We are using OAuth for Facebook and Google for our current app. If we add anymore providers, there is a large chance that they will be using OAuth. OAuth has almost become the standard for remote authentication.

OAuth is great in that the user has control over their own permissions, and we do not have to store a password for them. Our application's flow is first, the user decides which service to authenticate with. We then ask for a URL from the provider that we can redirect the user to. This URL will let the provider know which application is asking for permissions. This will involve our application ID, referring domain, and application secret. Once the user logs in and approves our application, the provider will create a redirect back to our servers. We then get a code that we can exchange for a token. That token uniquely identifies our application's access to that specific user. No passwords are exchanged, and the user can later change the access.

 OAuth can be very complex. Depending on how the site is accessed, some of these steps could be different. OAuth is great for users, but can be a pain for developers, as each provider can have small differences. This is where a great library like Passport comes in handy.

Summary

We now have broad and secure authentication. We can check against Facebook and Google, which can account for 100 percent of the users. In addition to this, we can allow users to register and login locally, storing their passwords securely. Because we used Passport, we have access to hundreds of other authentication providers. The Passport site lists them out if you are curious.

In the next chapter, we are going to look at adding message queues to our application using RabbitMQ.

4

RabbitMQ for Message Queuing

We are going to cover a concept that relates to making our application scalable: message queuing. Message queues allow us to break down our application into smaller pieces and hand out these pieces to be worked on. Message queues also help with scalability. We can parcel out the work to many different nodes, increasing our reliability and the handling of burst traffic. We will need a message queuing server to do this. This is where RabbitMQ (`https://www.rabbitmq.com`) comes in. So far, everything has been running on Node.js, and now we are adding another server application. We will cover the following topics in this chapter:

- Installing RabbitMQ
- Creating exchanges
- Creating queues
- Building workers
- Passing messages
- Replying to specific processes
- Adding message queues to our app

Node package versions

We are again adding to our current application, so all the previous Node packages are going to use the same version. We are also creating a couple of example applications that will use their own `package.json`. Each new example application will need `npm install` executed. We are only adding two packages here.

The first package is amqp. This package was not designed specifically for RabbitMQ, but it implements a protocol that RabbitMQ can understand. The other package is q, which gives us promises. Promises allow us to use asynchronous objects synchronously. The following are the new packages that we will be using in this chapter:

- amqp: 0.2.0
- q: 1.0.1

As always, add these two packages to your main application's package.json file and run npm install.

Getting RabbitMQ

RabbitMQ is one of the leading message queuing servers today. It runs on every OS and has clients in almost every programming language you can think of. It also can use many different queuing protocols. The main protocol we are concerned with is **Advanced Message Queuing Protocol (AMQP)**. Let's get started by installing RabbitMQ so we can build something with it.

Installing on Mac OS X

I have noted earlier that most of my development for this book is being done on Mac OS X, so that is where we are going to start. RabbitMQ has an installation page that details each of these installations. RabbitMQ's page will always have the latest versions and instructions, and I recommend you check it to ensure you get the most up-to-date information.

We are going to use Homebrew (http://brew.sh/), which is a package manager for Mac OS X. It allows you to easily install applications with only one line, which is what we are going to do now. In your terminal application, type the following command:

```
brew install rabbitmq
```

If everything went smoothly, you should see something similar to the following screenshot. The version may vary depending on when you run the command:

```
joshuas-mini:~ jjohanan$ brew install rabbitmq
==> Downloading http://www.rabbitmq.com/releases/rabbitmq-server/v3.2.3/rabbitmq
Already downloaded: /Library/Caches/Homebrew/rabbitmq-3.2.3.tar.gz
==> /usr/bin/unzip -qq -j /usr/local/Cellar/rabbitmq/3.2.3/plugins/rabbitmq_mana
==> Caveats
Management Plugin enabled by default at http://localhost:15672

Bash completion has been installed to:
  /usr/local/etc/bash_completion.d

To have launchd start rabbitmq at login:
    ln -sfv /usr/local/opt/rabbitmq/*.plist ~/Library/LaunchAgents
Then to load rabbitmq now:
    launchctl load ~/Library/LaunchAgents/homebrew.mxcl.rabbitmq.plist
Or, if you don't want/need launchctl, you can just run:
    rabbitmq-server
==> Summary
🍺  /usr/local/Cellar/rabbitmq/3.2.3: 1038 files, 25M, built in 5 seconds
```

It installs in `/usr/local/sbin/`, so you can either add this to your path or prepend it to all your commands. Let's start up our RabbitMQ server by typing the following command:

`/usr/local/sbin/rabbitmq-server`

You should see the server start with a little ASCII rabbit, as shown in the following screenshot:

```
            RabbitMQ 3.2.3. Copyright (C) 2007-2013 GoPivotal, Inc.
  ##  ##    Licensed under the MPL.  See http://www.rabbitmq.com/
  ##  ##
  ##########    Logs: /usr/local/var/log/rabbitmq/rabbit@localhost.log
  ######  ##          /usr/local/var/log/rabbitmq/rabbit@localhost-sasl.log
  ##########
            Starting broker... completed with 10 plugins.
```

The RabbitMQ management plugin

You can also connect to the RabbitMQ management plugin by browsing to
`http://localhost:15672`. The default username and password are `guest`.
For now, we are not going to worry about the configuration, as this is just going to be
our development server. It should only have connections coming from the localhost.

 This is a very insecure setup. Do not run RabbitMQ in this manner on the open Internet.

Installing on Linux

I am going to use Xubuntu 13.10 as my Linux distribution. Covering how to
install RabbitMQ across many different distributions is outside the scope of this
book. RabbitMQ does have instructions for a few other distributions on its web
site (`https://www.rabbitmq.com/download.html`).

The version of RabbitMQ in the repository is 3.1.3. This version is a little too
old, so we will use RabbitMQ's packaged version. If you browse to RabbitMQ's
Debian/Ubuntu Installation page, it will have a link to a `.deb` package of the
current version. At the time of writing this book, it is 3.3.0. It is a little newer than our
Mac OS X installation, but that's all right. Click on the link for the package and install
it. Technically, this is all you have to do. The server should be running at this point.
The Mac OS X version has the management plugin turned on by default; if you want
to enable the management web server, you can run the following commands:

```
sudo rabbitmq-plugins enable rabbitmq_management
sudo service rabbitmq-server restart
```

These commands will start the management server and then restart RabbitMQ,
as the change does not take effect until after a restart. In our Linux install, we can
now browse to `http://localhost:15672/` and log in with `guest` as the username
and password.

There is also a command-line application, `rabbitmqadmin`, which you can download
from the management server at `http://localhost:15672/cli/`. You can use this to
view information about the RabbitMQ server from the terminal. In Mac OS X, this is
already installed and ready.

We will cover the other ways of installing RabbitMQ using Linux in *Chapter 9,
Deployment and Scalability*. Right now, we just want a test server close to the version
we will be using for production.

Installing on Windows

The Windows install is going to be very similar to the other installs, except for one thing. We will need to install Erlang first. You can still go to the installation page, as the Windows executable will kick you over to the Erlang download page if you don't have it installed. Download and install the version that matches your OS (32-bit or 64-bit). Once Erlang is installed, you can install RabbitMQ. You can just click on **Next** in the main installation screen, as shown in the following screenshot:

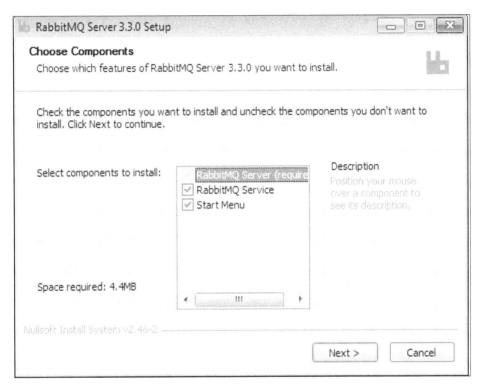

You will now have a `RabbitMQ Server` folder in your Start menu. Open up this menu, click on **RabbitMQ Command Prompt**, and enter the following command:

```
rabbitmq-plugins.bat enable rabbitmq_management
```

Then, use the Start menu to find **RabbitMQ Service - stop** and **RabbitMQ Service - start**. The menu is shown in the following screenshot:

You can also use the Services Management Console to restart RabbitMQ. After this, you can go to `http://localhost:15672` and see the management interface. The username and password is...yep, you guessed it right: `guest`. You should have a working RabbitMQ server on almost any operating system you are running.

The RabbitMQ servers we installed will be for local, initial development only. We will cover production and testing environments fully when we get to them.

Our first message queue

Now that we have a working RabbitMQ server, let's use it to build something. We will create a simple web server that will add a message to a queue on each request. We will also have a worker script that will work the queue.

First, create a new directory named `rabbit_first`. Create a `package.json` file and add the following code to it:

```
{
  "dependencies": {
    "amqp": "0.2.0"
  }
}
```

Then, run `npm install`. After this command finishes, create the `app.js` file and add the following code to it:

```
var http = require('http'),
    amqp = require('amqp');
```

```
var rabbit = amqp.createConnection();

rabbit.on('ready', function(){
  rabbit.exchange('my-first-exchange', {type: 'direct', autoDelete:
false}, function(ex){
    startServer(ex);
  });
});

function startServer(ex)
{
  var server = http.createServer(function(req, res){
    console.log(req.url);
    ex.publish('first-queue', {message: req.url});

    res.writeHead(200, {'Content-Type': 'text/html'});
    res.end('<h1>Simple HTTP Server in Node.js!</h1>');
  });

  server.listen(8001);
}
```

Here we create a connection to our RabbitMQ server (make sure it is running).
By default, it will try to connect to the localhost on port 5672, which is great because
this is what our server is running on. Next, we listen for the ready event, as the
connection is asynchronous. When the connection is ready, we create an exchange.
An exchange is essentially a router. We will give it jobs, and the exchange will figure
out which queues get the jobs. The job can be sent to one or many exchanges based
on the type of exchange and configuration. Possible types of exchanges are direct,
fanout, topic, and headers. We will explore direct and topic types in this chapter.
Note that the publisher (here, the HTTP server) does not have any knowledge nor
should it care about who/what actually does the job. We create the exchange to be
direct, which means that it's the exchange that maps one message to one queue. We
also turn the autodelete off. This will keep the exchange alive if we disconnect for
any reason. This call takes a callback when the exchange is created and connected.
At this point, we have configured the exchange and it is ready. We take the exchange
reference and pass it to our HTTP server, which we have wrapped in a function.
Now, on every request, we will log which URL was requested in our console
and pass the same information to the exchange. We do this by using the publish
command and a routing key of 'first-queue'.

Similar to the previous chapter, we will create the code first and then cover the whys of the code at the end of the chapter. We will cover all the different types of exchanges and routing and why you will use them.

Let's open up our management interface by going to `http://localhost:15672`. Then, start up the Node and load the page a few times. If you jump back to the RabbitMQ management page, you will see that you have one connection, one channel, and some activity. If you do not see this, you may have to reload the page. It should look similar to the following screenshot:

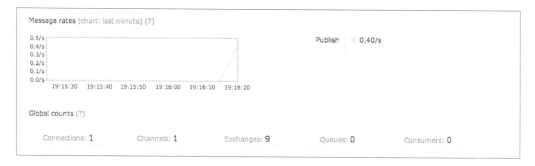

We don't have anything to work the queue, so let's fix this. Create a file named `worker.js` and add the following code to it:

```javascript
var amqp = require('amqp');

var rabbit = amqp.createConnection();

rabbit.on('ready', function(){
  rabbit.queue('first-queue-name', {autoDelete: false}, function(q){
    q.bind('my-first-exchange', 'first-queue');
    q.subscribe(function(message, headers, deliveryInfo,
messageObject){
      console.log(message);
      console.log(headers);
      console.log(deliveryInfo);
      console.log(messageObject);
    });
  });
});
```

This code starts off in a very similar way to our HTTP server code. We will need a reference to `amqp` and will also need to wait for the connection to be ready. After this, we create a queue, passing in the option to turn off `autoDelete`. Auto delete does the same thing here as it did with the exchange—if we get disconnected, the queue will still exist. We have named this queue `first-queue-name`. This method uses a callback to ensure that the queue gets created and is ready. We then bind the queue to an exchange using the exchange's name and a routing key. Our routing key here is `first-queue`, which is what our HTTP server was sending the jobs with. We now have an exchange and a queue for the jobs to route to. Finally, we subscribe to the queue to get any of the messages that are routed through the queue. In this example, our worker will log every object passed to it from the queue so that we can see what is sent. We can now start our worker by running `node worker.js`.

Using the management interface

Before we send any messages, we will check out the management interface. Click on **Exchanges** from the header menu and then click on our exchange, **my-first-exchange**. Then, go to the **Bindings** tab. You should see that our queue (`first-queue-name`) is bound to this exchange. This is shown in the following screenshot:

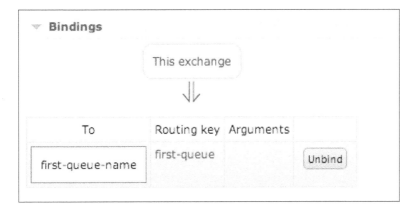

Next, click on **Queues** from the header, click on your queue, **first-queue-name**, and then go to **Bindings**. You should now see the same information, but from the queue's perspective. This is shown in the following screenshot:

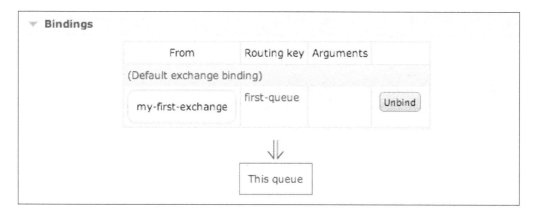

We can see that any message sent to **my-first-exchange** with the routing key of **first-queue** will be put in the **first-queue-name** queue. Our HTTP server is configured to add these exact messages, and our worker is subscribed to this queue.

Sending messages

Open another console tab or window and launch Node with `worker.js`. You should now have two Node processes running, `app.js` and `worker.js`. When you turned on your worker, did you expect to see some messages come through? We did create some from the HTTP server. Unfortunately, if an exchange does not have a queue to put in messages, they are lost, which is what happened to our first few messages.

Let's now load `http://localhost:8001` a few times. Upon logging in your console, you should see where the worker is running. Most likely, each request will create two messages (one for the `root/` and one for the `favicon/favicon.ico`). The first object logged should be your JSON object from the HTTP server. The next blank object is `headers`. Then comes the `deliveryInfo` object. Finally, the last large object is `messageObject`. We will need to use all of these at different times. Each time we load the web page a message is sent.

Queuing messages

Let's clean up our worker by commenting out everything but the message. Our subscribe callback should have the following code as the body:

```
console.log(message);
      //console.log(headers);
      //console.log(deliveryInfo);
      //console.log(messageObject);
```

Next, we will kill our worker, but don't restart it right away. We are going to run some quick tests. Our queue should still exist because it should not have auto deleted and there should be no RabbitMQ message consumers. We can easily verify this by going to the RabbitMQ management interface and checking the queue by clicking on **Queues** from the tabs in the header. We should see that the queue is present and after going into details, we can also see that there are no consumers.

Now, let's load our page a few times to add some messages. If we check the queues page again by clicking on **Queues**, we should see that the queue has some messages queued up! This is exactly what we wanted and expected. Let's add one more message.

Using the management interface, click on **Exchanges** and select **my-first-exchange**. Near the bottom of the page, there is a **Publish message** heading. Create a message with the only key piece of data being the routing key, which must be **first-queue**. We should have something similar to the following screenshot:

Click on **Publish message**. We should get a confirmation that it was published. We can then check out the queue again, by clicking on the **Queues** tab, and see whether it was added. The following screenshot is how it should look; the count of queued messages will depend on how many times you loaded the page:

Name		Overview				Messages				Message rates	
	Exclusive	Parameters	Policy	Status	Ready	Unacked	Total	incoming	deliver / get	ack
first-queue-name				Idle	9	0	9	0.00/s	0.00/s	

We can now start our worker. The worker should pull out every message from the queue and log it to the console. The following are all the messages that we just looked at in the queue:

```
{ message: '/' }
{ message: '/favicon.ico' }
{ message: '/' }
{ message: '/favicon.ico' }
{ message: '/' }
{ message: '/favicon.ico' }
{ message: '/' }
{ message: '/favicon.ico' }
{ data: <Buffer 4f 4b>, contentType: undefined }
```

We can see that our HTTP server created JSON objects and our manual message created a data buffer. Our worker then cleaned up the queue. We can verify this by checking the queue in the management interface.

Adding another worker

We can test what will happen if we add another worker. This should be extremely easy as we already have the code ready in worker.js; we do not need to make any code changes. Launch another Node process running worker.js. Then, load your web page a few times. You will see that each worker will work the queue in a round-robin fashion. We can connect as many workers as we want to this queue. We are able to see each connection in the **Connections** tab of the management interface and also under the **Queues** tab as consumers of **first-queue-name**.

This test application has demonstrated horizontal scalability perfectly. If we are able to break down tasks that our application needs to get done, we can then package them and pass them around in queues. When the queues start to get backed up, we can then bring on more workers, which is what horizontal scaling means. Depending on what the work is and if there are any patterns to the workload, we can even schedule workers to come up when needed and then go down when not needed.

This idea of having reusable jobs allows you to decouple tasks in separate applications. The main service of what we are building is to serve web pages. We should build an application that serves web pages very efficiently and does not worry about anything else. In addition to this, our application will most likely need to do other things, as well, such as logging, transaction e-mails, computing statistics, and many other things. We can then create small applications that can do these jobs. This allows you to control how the task should be implemented and also how many workers perform the task.

Sending messages back

Our first application that we built in this chapter is very simple. It had one queue, where the publisher did not care what happened to the job and the worker did not have to let the publisher know the job was done. We will cover one more example of message queues. We are now going to create an application where the publisher needs to know when the worker is done. A great example of this is charging a credit card. We are not going to build out an entire charging application, but we will mimic one. Let's build it! Create another folder named rabbit_second, and create a package.json file with the following code (remember to run npm install in order to get all the packages):

```
{
  "dependencies": {
    "amqp": "0.2.0",
    "socket.io": "1.0.6"
  }
}
```

We are going to use Express to give us easy static file serving, and routing, and Socket.IO for the real-time charging of credit cards (we will build the structure, but we will not actually charge any cards). We can now create an app.js file and get a reference to all our packages. Start app.js with the following code:

```
var express = require('express'),
  amqp = require('amqp'),
  io = require('socket.io');

var app = express();

app.use(express.static(__dirname));

var rabbit = amqp.createConnection();
```

We have previously discussed everything in the preceding code. This code is just initializing our application.

We have configured Express to serve static files out of the root, so let's create the static file we need, index.html. Add the following code to it:

```
<!DOCTYPE html>
<html>
<body>
  <h1>Simple Reply Message Application</h1>
  <a href="/credit_charge">Charge my Card</a>
  <button id="socket_credit">Charge my Card</button>
  <script src="/socket.io/socket.io.js"></script>
  <script>
    var socket = io.connect('http://localhost:8002');
    socket.on('charged', function(){alert('Charged!');});
    document.getElementById('socket_credit').addEventListener('click',
function(){
      socket.emit('charge');
    });
  </script>
</body>
</html>
```

The first thing we are doing here is creating a link to /credit_charge so that we can see a request-based message queue reply. We also have a real-time message queue reply with Socket.IO. The client-side Socket.IO code is very simple. We connect to the server and then listen for a charged event, which will create an alert and listen for a button click event to tell the server to charge the credit card. Let's go back to the server side to set this up.

Open up app.js and add the following code:

```
rabbit.on('ready', function(){
  rabbit.exchange('credit_charge', {autoDelete: false}, function(ex){
    rabbit.queue('charge', {autoDelete: false}, function(q){
      q.bind('credit_charge', q.name);
      q.close();
      startServer(ex);
    });
  });
});
```

This code creates the exchange and queue that we need. We will have an exchange named `credit_charge` and a queue named `charge` that is bound to our exchange. Both will not auto delete on disconnect. Because we don't need the queue now, we close our connection. Without doing this, we will keep resources open on both the Node.js server and the RabbitMQ server. We then start everything off using the `startServer` function, passing in a reference to the exchange.

Creating StartServer

Create the `startServer` function with this code. First, we will create the code that responds to the `/credit_charge` GET request, as shown in the following code:

```
function startServer(ex){
app.get('/credit_charge', function(req, res){
    rabbit.queue('', {exclusive: true, autoDelete: true}, function(q){
      q.bind('credit_charge', q.name);
      ex.publish('charge', {card: 'details'}, {replyTo: q.name});
      q.subscribe(function(message){
        console.log(message);
        q.destroy();
        q.close();
        res.send('Charged! Thanks!');
      });
    });
  });

var server = app.listen(8002);
};
```

This is a simple Express route. The first thing we do is create a queue for our worker to respond to our request. We do this by passing in a blank routing key in queue creation. This will give us a random, unique queue name. Even if we tried to do this with random numbers or time in milliseconds, we could create duplicates with enough clients connecting. The next new thing we do is create the queue as exclusive. This means, as you've probably guessed, that only the client that created it can connect and get messages from it. Then we bind it to our exchange name, `credit_charge`, even though we did not give an explicit name to the queue. The queue name is in the object that is returned in our callback. We now have a uniquely named queue from which only this specific response can pull messages out.

Now, we need to tell our worker to process a credit card. This is done by publishing a message to the charge queue. The message you pass here will contain the details of the card so that the processor can charge the card. We also are passing in an `options` object with the `replyTo` attribute set to our queue name. This is how we let the worker know which queue to put its response back in to.

The last thing that this code does is subscribe to our personal queue. We log the message and then destroy the queue and close our connection. We need to do this as each request will get its own specific queue. If we do not destroy and close our connection, we will end up with a RabbitMQ server that has thousands of open queues and Node keeping a connection with all of them. This will use resources, so it can be costly on a large scale. At last, we can send a response to the browser. If there were any errors, we could add checks in this function. Because this is just a test application, we know there will be no errors.

Building the worker

We don't have anything to actually charge our credit cards. We are just going to act as if the worker charges the card. Let's build the worker. Create a file named `worker.js` and add the following code:

```
var amqp = require('amqp');

var rabbit = amqp.createConnection();

rabbit.on('ready', function(){
  rabbit.exchange('credit_charge', {autoDelete: false}, function(ex){
    rabbit.queue('charge', {autoDelete: false}, function(q){
      q.bind('credit_charge', 'charge');
      q.subscribe(function(message, headers, deliveryInfo,
messageObject){
        setTimeout(function(){
          console.log(message);
          console.log(headers);
          console.log(deliveryInfo);
          ex.publish(deliveryInfo.replyTo, {message: 'done'},
{headers: headers});
        }, 1500);
      });
    });
  });
});
```

This is similar to previous workers. We first need to connect to RabbitMQ and the exchange we are going to use. We initialized the queues in our app.js file and when we connect to these queues here, we need to pass in the same options or we will not connect to the exchange. Here, we are passing the autoDelete option as false; if we pass it in as true, we will not connect to the exchange. This is also true for connecting to our queue. We need to pass in the same name and options. We also bind it to the exchange. If we started app.js, the queue should be bound, but if worker.js starts first, we will bind it here. Remember that a queue will not start getting messages until it is bound. Both app.js and worker.js are making sure the exchanges and queues are created and bound so messages will not fall through the cracks.

Next, we subscribe to the queue so we can process it. We are logging everything so we can see what each object holds. We then put a message back in the queue that was sent in the replyTo attribute. This would be the queue that our request created. We also pass back the headers, which for now are blank. This is all wrapped in setTimeout, which will wait 1500 milliseconds to fire. This simulates charging the card. What should happen now is that when we go to /credit_charge, the request should wait 1.5 seconds and then respond. Let's try this out.

Start Node in two different terminals: one with app.js and the other with worker.js. Browse to http://localhost:8002 and click on the **Charge my Card** link. The server should respond with **Charged! Thanks!**. We can check out our terminals to see all the objects that have been logged. We just put a message in a generic queue for a worker to process and then responded to a specific request. This is not that impressive with only one request, but this will scale to quite a few requests.

Charging cards in real time

Now, we will do the same thing except that we will use Socket.IO. Remember that Socket.IO is not request-driven like HTTP, so we will need to set it up differently, although the same pieces will be present. Inside the startServer function in app.js, add the following code right after the Express code:

```
io = io.listen(server);

  io.on('connection', function(socket){
    rabbit.queue(socket.id, {exclusive: true, autoDelete: true},
function(q){
      q.bind('credit_charge', q.name);

      q.subscribe(function(message, headers, delivery){
        socket.emit(headers.emitEvent);
      });
```

```
        socket.on('charge', function(data){
            ex.publish('charge', {card: 'details'}, {replyTo: q.name,
    headers: {emitEvent: 'charged'}});
        });

        socket.on('disconnect', function(){
            q.destroy();
            q.close();
        });

    });
});
```

After a socket creates a connection, we create a queue that uses the socket ID as its name. We could have passed in a blank name, but this will allow us to see socket-based queues in the management interface, as they will have different naming conventions. Exactly like the request's queue, we want it to be exclusive and to auto delete on disconnect. We then bind the queue to our exchange.

> Using the socket ID is fine for a single server, but it can create issues when there are multiple Socket.IO servers. In this case, we could create a UUID (using the node-uuid package) and concatenate it with the Socket ID to create a truly unique name.

Next, we subscribe to the queue to process the messages that come back from our worker. What this does is emit an event that is defined in the headers. Then, we listen for the charge socket event and add a message to the charge queue with the card details. We also add our queue name as the queue to reply back to along with the emitEvent header we want to use in the subscribe function. If we look at the worker again, we will see that the worker just takes the headers from the message and puts them in the next message going out.

Finally, on the socket disconnect event, we close down the queue and our connection to it.

We can test this by loading http://localhost:8002 and clicking on the **Charge my Card** button. It should take about 1.5 seconds, and we will get an alert that lets us know our card was charged. If we check the console, we should see our message logged.

This example also demonstrates the power of workers. We only have one worker, but we can add messages from multiple places. The worker will process these messages and then send them back to the specific client waiting for the response.

The following diagram demonstrates the flow of messages:

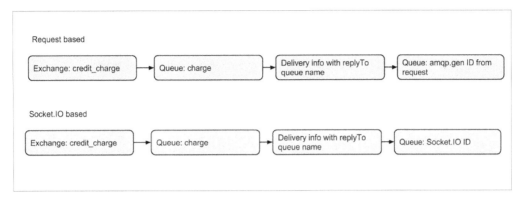

We can see that both versions start the same way. This is important to remember, as we want a reusable exchange and queue to start this process. Once the credit card has been charged, we divert, as each one will respond to different queues. This allows us to have one worker but many unique response queues.

Adding message queues to PacktChat

We can now add message queues to the application we are building. Our application does not need credit card processing or transaction e-mails, but we will add logging through RabbitMQ. We will create a logging exchange and two queues, `debug.log` and `error.log`. The `debug.log` queue will log everything that comes through the exchange (including errors), and `error.log` will only log errors.
We will do this by using a topic exchange.

Topic exchange

Our test applications have used a direct exchange. What this means is that the queue must use the same exact routing key that the message was published with. Topic exchanges allow pattern matching in the routing key. In our example, we will bind the `debug.log` queue with a routing key of `*.log`. This will match any messages that are `debug.log` or `error.log`. The `error.log` queue will bind using `error.log`, so it will work exactly like a direct exchange. The exchange will put an `error.log` message in both the error and debug logs. This is how we know the debug queue will log all messages. Let's get started.

The first thing is to create a copy of our application from the last chapter. At this point, we should have Express, Socket.IO, and Passport all working together. Our `package.json` file should have `amqp` and `q` in the dependencies, and we can run `npm install`.

Then, open up `config.js` and add the following code to the file after our `crypto` object:

```
rabbitMQ: {
    URL: 'amqp://guest:guest@localhost:5672',
    exchange: 'packtchat.log'
}
```

This is just explicitly defining our URL and exchange to use. We will use this when connecting to RabbitMQ, which brings us to our next file. We will need to create a new directory named `queue` and add a `rabbit.js` file. Add the following code to the file:

```
var amqp = require('amqp'),
  config = require('../config'),
  q = require('q');

module.exports = q.Promise(function(resolve, reject, notify){
  var rabbit = amqp.createConnection(config.rabbitMQ.URL);
  rabbit.on('ready', function(){
    resolve(rabbit);
  });
});
```

The first three lines are setting up our variables. We are exporting a `Promise` object with the next line. Promise objects allow us to react to asynchronous events without worrying about when the events occur. In our example, our asynchronous event is a connection to RabbitMQ. When the connection is made, we resolve this promise so that the `rabbit` object can be used. When we require this file, it will send this object back synchronously. This can happen before we are sure that a connection has been made. What might happen if we were not using promises is that we could try to use the connection before it is ready and create an error. Promises allow us to send a promise back so that other objects can do something when the connection is ready.

Now, we will create a file named index.js, which will create our queues and exchange. Put the following code in index.js:

```
var rabbitPromise = require('./rabbit'),
  config = require('../config'),
  q = require('q');

function queueSetup(rabbit){
  rabbit.queue('debug.log', {autoDelete: false}, function(q){
    q.bind(config.rabbitMQ.exchange, '*.log');
    q.close();
  });

  rabbit.queue('error.log', {autoDelete: false}, function(q){
    q.bind(config.rabbitMQ.exchange, 'error.log');
    q.close();
  });
}

module.exports = q.Promise(function(resolve, reject, notify){
  rabbitPromise.done(function(rabbit){
    rabbit.exchange(config.rabbitMQ.exchange, {type: 'topic',
autoDelete: false}, function(ex){
      queueSetup(rabbit);
      resolve(ex);
    });
  });
});
```

Here, we can see promises in action. Once the connection is ready, Promise is resolved and the done function can execute with a reference to the rabbit connection. Any other object that has a promise for this will be able to get a reference to this object in its connected state. We then create an exchange using the name defined in our config. The exchange is created as a type of topic and is not be auto deleted. We then run a function that will create two queues and bind them to our exchange. In this function, we can see that we bind debug.log to our exchange using *.log as the routing key. We also set up the error.log queue. At this point, we have our exchange setup and both the queues created and bound. Any message that is published will have somewhere to go. We then resolve our other promise with a reference to a connected exchange. The Promise for our exchange is then exposed.

It does not matter whether we are connected to RabbitMQ or our exchange or not. Promises can be returned immediately after creating them. Now, let's use these promises. The first place we will add them is in `log.js`, in the `packtchat\middleware` location. Right now, it is just middleware that is logging any request URL to the console. We will change it to add this information to the queue. Replace the contents of the file with the following code:

```
var exchange = require('../queue');

function debug(message){
  exchange.done(function(ex){
    ex.publish('debug.log', message);
  });
};

function error(message){
  exchange.done(function(ex){
    ex.publish('error.log', message);
  });
}
```

The first thing we do here is get a reference to the exchange object we just created. The exchange promise will resolve with a reference to our exchange. We can see this in the first function, `debug`. It takes this promise and adds `done` to the promise. It will then take the exchange that is passed in and publish the message that is passed to it. The `done` function will execute when the connection is created, or if the connection is already created, it will fire right away. Either way we do not have to worry about when the connection is finished; we have a promise that our code will run when that event happens. We do the same for our `error` function. Next, replace the current `exports.logger`, as shown in the following code:

```
exports.logger = function logger(req, res, next){
  debug({url: req.url, ts: Date.now()});
  next();
};

exports.debug = debug;
exports.error = error;
```

We updated our `logger` middleware to use our new `debug` function. We pass in the URL as we did before, as well as a timestamp of the current time. This is important because this message could be queued for a period of time before being processed and we want to know when it was first created. The last thing we do is export the debug and error functions so they can be used elsewhere.

We will now use these functions in our `passport` object. We will log each incorrect login. Open up `index.js` from the `passport` folder and add this code inside `passport.use(new local())` around each call to `done` that returns a failed attempt. Each call to `done` that passes `Wrong Username or Password` should look as shown in the following code:

```
//add a reference to the log file
Var log = require('../middleware/log');
//replace inside of the local authentication function
//would be lines 43 and 44
log.debug({message: 'Wrong Username or Password', username:
username});
done(null, false, {message: 'Wrong Username or Password'});
```

Next, we will add logging to the error handler. Open up `errorhandlers.js` from the `middleware` folder and replace or add the following lines to the file:

```
var log = require('./log');

exports.notFound = function notFound(req, res, next){
  res.status(404).render('404', {title: 'Wrong Turn'});
};

exports.error = function error(err, req, res, next){
  log.error({error: err.message, ts: Date.now()});
  res.status(500).render('500', {title: 'Mistakes Were Made'});
};
```

At this point, we can load our app and create some messages. Start Node and browse to `http://localhost:3000` and `http://localhost:3000/error`. After this, load our RabbitMQ management website at `http://localhost:15672`. Click on **Queues** to view what is currently queued. We should see something similar to the following screenshot:

| | Overview | | | | Messages | | | Message rates | | |
Name	Exclusive	Parameters	Policy	Status	Ready	Unacked	Total	incoming	deliver / get	ack
debug.log				Idle	7	0	7	0.00/s	0.00/s	
error.log				Idle	1	0	1	0.00/s	0.00/s	

If both our queues have messages in them, then we know that our message-queue-based logging is working.

Building the worker

We have messages queued up, but nothing to work them. Create a directory named `workers` and a file named `log.js` under this directory. Add the following code to the file:

```
var rabbitPromise = require('../queue/rabbit'),
  config = require('../config');


rabbitPromise.done(function(rabbit){
  rabbit.queue('debug.log', {autoDelete: false}, function(q){
    q.bind(config.rabbitMQ.exchange, '*.log');
    q.subscribe({ ack: true, prefetchCount: 1 }, function(message,
headers, delivery, messageObject){
      console.log('Debug-Routing:' + delivery.routingKey + JSON.
stringify(message));
      messageObject.acknowledge();
      //setTimeout(function(){messageObject.reject(true);}, 2000);
    });
  });

  rabbit.queue('error.log', {autoDelete: false}, function(q){
    q.bind(config.rabbitMQ.exchange, 'error.log');
    q.subscribe({ ack: true, prefetchCount: 1 }, function(message,
headers, delivery, messageObject){
      console.log('Error-Routing:' + delivery.routingKey + JSON.
stringify(message));
      messageObject.acknowledge();
    });
  });

});
```

This file starts off by getting a reference to the rabbit promises and the configuration. We then call on the rabbit promise to give us our rabbit connection. Once we have our connection, we create our queues. We do this so the queues will be created regardless of whether the worker or the web server starts up first. Then, we subscribe to the queue to get the messages. We then use `console.log` and add in the logger, routing key, and message that was passed in. We can finally start this worker with Node in another terminal.

The output should be similar to the following screenshot:

```
Debug-Routing:debug.log{"url":"/css/style.css","ts":1397101112047}
Debug-Routing:debug.log{"url":"/","ts":1397103518502}
Debug-Routing:debug.log{"url":"/css/cosmo.min.css","ts":1397103518634}
Debug-Routing:debug.log{"url":"/css/style.css","ts":1397103518634}
Error-Routing:error.log{"error":"A contrived error","ts":1397101111988}
```

Note that this subscribe event passes in an `options` object. In this object, we tell the package that we will acknowledge the message and that we want one message at a time. In our code, we run the `acknowledge` function after logging to the console. The next line after this is commented out. This line will wait for two seconds and then reject the message. The true value sent through the `reject` function will requeue the message. When something happens and a worker cannot finish the work for a message, we should requeue it so that another worker can attempt it. Comment out line 9 of `log.js`, uncomment the `setTimeout` line, and run the worker. We can see that the worker will pull out one message, wait for two seconds, and then requeue it. This is not productive, but it should demonstrate what is possible. After this, delete the `setTimeout` line and uncomment our acknowledge line.

Our example is still just logging to the console, but we could easily expand this. We could use the great `Winston` package and log to the console, file, and database, and send an e-mail, Amazon notifications, and possibly more by the time you are reading this. The great part about this is that the web server doesn't need to know how you are logging this information. It will just keep on publishing messages.

Message queuing in RabbitMQ

At this point, we have already covered a few of the exchange types, but we will cover all of them here. The first and simplest exchange type is direct. It works by matching the routing key to the routing key that the queue used when binding. If they match, the queue gets the message. The next type is topic. We used this in our PacktChat application. The routing key can be pattern based. This allows workers to select a broad range of messages easily. If you have designed your routing keys to be hierarchical, then you can easily create queues that are inclusive or exclusive. Our logging exchange is an example of this. The debug queue will get any message put in the queue that matches `*.log`. The error queue only gets messages that are specifically `error.log`. If we create a warn queue that matches `warn.log`, debug will still have all the messages. The next type is fanout. This type works as a broadcaster. Every queue that is bound to this exchange will get a message no matter what the routing key is. If you need to get information across to many different clients at the same time, fanout can work for you.

Finally, the last type is headers. Instead of using the routing key to determine which queue to send the message to, it will use the message's headers. This allows you to get around the requirement that a routing key has to be a string. You can now route on anything you can add to the header.

RabbitMQ exchanges and queues can be configured to be more error-resistant. In our application, we use acknowledgments to let RabbitMQ know that the message has been successfully processed and that it can delete the message. If you do not do this, RabbitMQ will delete the message after sending it. This will protect you against a worker going down while processing a task. In addition to this, we can set up a dead letter exchange. This is kind of like a message graveyard. If a message is rejected, timed out, or the queue has too many messages in it, we can configure another queue to receive those messages. Finally, another thing we can do is create our queues as durable. This means that the queue will not be emptied out on a server restart. Each of these will help to keep RabbitMQ from losing messages.

Message queues allow you to build applications by composition. This means building parts of our application that are not tightly coupled. For example, we could add transaction e-mails to our application. Every time someone signs up and after they take a certain action (purchase something), we will send them an e-mail. If we have the application just drop a message in a queue, we can easily update that portion of our application without affecting other parts. We could completely change our e-mail provider and the web server would never even know. This also lends itself to scalability. If our e-mail queue always has messages in it, then we can just create another worker.

Another benefit is that you do not have to do expensive operations during a request. Sending an e-mail, charging a credit card, or doing image manipulations can all take several hundred milliseconds or longer. If this is done during the request, the user will have to wait for our web server to respond. If these tasks are moved out of the request into a message queue, the web server can respond immediately. You will then have workers, which will do all the expensive operations. You could even have the workers e-mail the user when an expensive task is done.

Finally, message queues allow you to utilize already written code, even if that code is in a different language. If you have a credit card processor written in Java, you can use this instead of rewriting one to be used in Node. Depending on your code infrastructure, you can build an app quickly doing this.

Summary

We just covered message queues, which will help us build more maintainable and scalable applications. We also talked about using promises to make asynchronous actions easier to deal with.

In the next chapter, we will learn how to install Redis and use it in our application.

5
Adopting Redis for Application Data

We are now going to look at using Redis to store the current state of our application. Redis is a simple key-value store that uses the system memory. This means that it is fast. There are very short lookup times for values. Redis, being a key-value store, means that our data is stored very differently than in a **relational database management system (RDBMS)**. Redis also allows connections either locally or remotely. This will allow us to scale our application as more web servers come online to utilize the data stored in Redis. Redis also has a simple message queue system that we will explore as well.

We will cover the following topics in this chapter:

- Installing Redis
- Using data structures in Redis
- Using Redis in Node.js
- Using Redis's publish/subscribe
- Integrating Redis into our application

Node package versions

We will use the Redis client that we installed in an earlier chapter. In addition to this, we are going to use one new package named `flow-maintained`. `Flow-maintained` is a small framework that will help us manage the number of callbacks we will have to write. It makes asynchronous code run seemingly synchronous. It also includes a synchronous `forEach` loop that we will use.

These are the packages to add before running `npm install`.

- redis: 0.10.1
- flow-maintained: 0.2.3

Our `dependencies` in our main `package.json` file should now look like the following code:

```
"dependencies": {
    "body-parser": "1.4.3",
    "connect": "3.0.2",
    "connect-flash": "0.1.1",
    "connect-redis": "2.0.0",
    "cookie-parser": "1.3.2",
    "csurf": "1.3.0",
    "ejs": "0.8.5",
    "express": "4.6.1",
    "express-partials": "0.2.0",
    "express-session": "1.6.5",
    "redis": "0.10.1",
    "cookie": "0.1.1",
    "socket.io": "1.0.6",
    "socket.io-redis": "0.1.3",
    "passport": "0.2.0",
    "passport-local": "1.0.0",
    "passport-facebook": "1.0.3",
    "passport-google-oauth": "0.1.5",
    "scmp": "0.0.3",
    "amqp": "0.2.0",
    "q": "1.0.1"
    }
```

Installing Redis

Technically, at this point, we are already using Redis to store some of our application state. Express/Connect is using Redis as its session store, although if you came from an earlier chapter because you do not have Redis installed, we will cover how to do it in this chapter.

Installing on Mac OS X

We will start with Mac OS X. We are going to use brew again as it makes installing software incredibly easy. In a terminal, type the following command:

```
brew install redis
```

You should then see something similar to the following screenshot:

```
joshuas-mini:finalChapters jjohanan$ brew install redis
==> Downloading https://downloads.sf.net/project/machomebrew/Bottles/redis-2.8.5
Already downloaded: /Library/Caches/Homebrew/redis-2.8.5.mavericks.bottle.tar.gz
==> Pouring redis-2.8.5.mavericks.bottle.tar.gz
==> Caveats
To have launchd start redis at login:
    ln -sfv /usr/local/opt/redis/*.plist ~/Library/LaunchAgents
Then to load redis now:
    launchctl load ~/Library/LaunchAgents/homebrew.mxcl.redis.plist
Or, if you don't want/need launchctl, you can just run:
    redis-server /usr/local/etc/redis.conf
==> Summary
🍺  /usr/local/Cellar/redis/2.8.5: 10 files, 1.2M
joshuas-mini:finalChapters jjohanan$
```

At the time of writing, Redis 2.8.8 was the newest stable version and brew installed Version 2.8.5. This is close, and we will not worry about the difference.

Homebrew installs Redis to `/usr/local/Cellar/redis/2.8.5`. Homebrew also puts this directory into our path. This will allow us to launch the server and command-line interface from our terminal. We should now launch the server to make sure that it works. In the terminal, type the following command:

```
redis-server
```

You should see something very similar to the following screenshot:

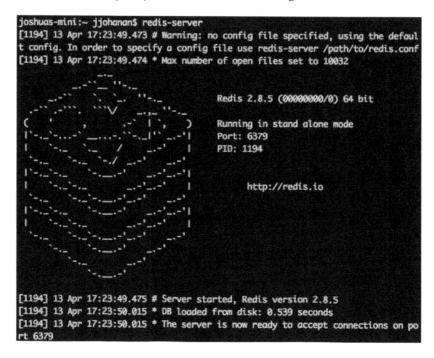

If you have jumped to this chapter to see how to install Redis, you can jump back to the chapter you came from as Redis is installed and working. Every time we launch our Node.js application, we will have to first launch Redis, unless we follow the commands Homebrew gives us to run this as a service. If Redis is not launched, sessions will not work. Of course, if you are not using Mac OS X, jump to the OS that you are running.

Installing on Linux

We are going to use Xubuntu 13.10, the current version of Ubuntu at the time of writing. Ubuntu uses the super simple and easy software package tool named `apt-get`. Let's install Redis on Linux using the following command:

```
sudo apt-get install redis-server
```

This should download Redis from the repository and install it. Redis will already be running in the background after the install. Let's stop it and launch it ourselves. Run the following command in a terminal:

```
sudo service redis-server stop
redis-server
```

We should see Redis start, which looks very similar to Mac OS X, except for one thing, the version is 2.6.13. We want to be running at least something in the 2.8 Version range. We are going to have to use a **Personal Package Archive** (**PPA**). PPAs allow you to install newer software than what is in the current Ubuntu repository. Many of the PPAs are run by Canonical (the company behind Ubuntu) or the software vendor. What is nice about PPAs is that they are a targeted upgrade. In our example, we can just use the Redis PPA, and the only packages that will be updated will be `redis-server` and its requirements. Open up a terminal and enter the following commands:

```
sudo add-apt-repository ppa:chris-lea/redis-server
sudo apt-get update
sudo apt-get install redis-server
```

The first command adds the PPA to our repository list. The command should ask you to press *Enter* to continue or *Ctrl* + *C* to cancel. We, of course, want to install it. Then, we update our sources. This checks all our repositories for new versions of packages. When we run the install command, we have already installed it, so this is an update, and `apt-get` will see that there is a new version.

We can verify that we have a new version by using the Redis command-line tool, `redis-cli`. In our terminal, enter the following command:

```
redis-cli
127.0.0.1:6379>info
```

We should see a lot of information scroll across the screen. The first bit should be `redis_version`. The version I have installed is 2.8.8. This is a better version to build our development machine on, because we will be using 2.8.x on the production server.

PPAs are great for allowing you to run newer software packages on older distributions. Just remember that you still want a relatively new distribution or you may run into dependency problems.

Installing on Windows

First, let me state that running Redis on Windows is not supported. It is designed to work on Unix/Linux systems. That being said, you can get Redis to run on Windows.

Microsoft's Open Tech team maintains a Git repository of Redis that is ported to Windows. It is currently at `https://github.com/MSOpenTech/redis`.

You can pull down the source and then build Redis yourself using Visual Studio (you can use the free Express version if needed). Another option is to use the precompiled binaries that are already present in the repository. In each branch, there is a `bin/release` folder that has a ZIP file of the compiled binaries. You can then unzip it and use them. The following is the screenshot of Redis running on Windows using the precompiled binaries:

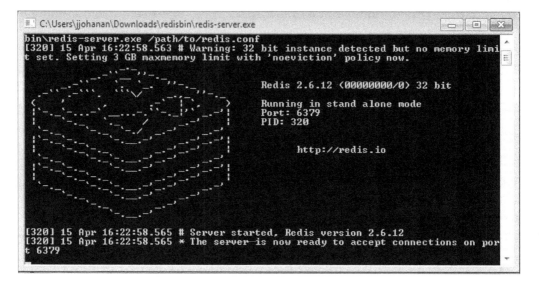

I definitely recommend that you run Redis on Mac OS X or a distribution of Linux. If you are developing on Windows, you can use the MS Open Tech project as a stop gap. You could also install VirtualBox (`https://www.virtualbox.org`) and install a local virtual machine of Linux with Redis installed. You would just have to update any configurations that connect to localhost to then connect to your virtual machine.

Using Redis data structures

Before we build anything, we will cover what data structures Redis supports. We can then discuss what we are building from these structures. Redis is not a database, so it does not have the familiar VARCHAR, INT, DATETIME, or anything like that. Redis is a key-value store. You have a key and you can look up the value of what is stored there. Redis supports a few low-level data types. The first type that we are going to discuss is a string.

Strings are the most basic type and are often the type that we are going to use. Usually, we can serialize almost any data type to a string. If we recall when we used Connect to move the sessions to Redis, we will see that Connect just serializes JSON and stores it as a string. This is always an option. The string type also doubles as an integer. There is no specific integer type, so integers are stored as strings.

The next data type is a hash. This type allows us to store information in fields in the hash. For example, a user hash could have a username and a display name. We can then pull out the entire hash or each field separately.

Lists are the next data type. This is just a simple linked list. You can easily add another element on to the right or left side of the array. It is also very quick in selecting multiple elements in a row starting from a specific index. Lists can only store strings though.

Sets are another data type. They are very similar to lists, but with one important difference; they only store distinct values. If a value already exists, another member will not be created in the set. This is a small and powerful difference from a list.

Another related type is the sorted set. It keeps the restriction of distinct members, but it can be ordered by a score. The score is used when adding a member and can be used to filter or order the members. This may not seem that useful at first glance, but this is a great feature. The score can be used to track timestamps, and then, we can filter the set to only show users who were here within the last 30 minutes.

The descriptions should give us a good idea of what and how to store data in Redis, although they are not fully comprehensive. Let's start using them in a small application.

Building a simple Redis application

Our first adventure in using Redis will involve creating an application where users can leave messages. To keep things simple, we will not do authentication. The user and message will be stored in Redis and will be retrieved for each request.

The first thing we will do is create a directory named `redis_first_app` to store this application. After that, we will create a new file named `app.js` in the root. We are going to install Express and EJS to give us routing and templating. Create a `package.json` file with the following code as the contents:

```
{
  "dependencies": {
    "body-parser": "1.4.3",
    "ejs": "0.8.5",
    "express": "4.6.1",
    "flow-maintained": "0.2.3",
    "redis": "0.10.3"
  }
}
```

As always, do not forget `npm install`.

When this is done, add the following code to `app.js`:

```
var express = require('express'),
  app = express(),
  bodyParser = require('body-parser');
app.set('view engine', 'ejs');
app.use(bodyParser.urlencoded({extended: false}));

app.get('/', function(req, res){
  res.render('index');
});

app.post('/', function(req, res){
  console.log(req.body);
  res.redirect('/');
});
app.listen(8003);
```

There is nothing new here. We just created a simple Express app that renders a template and processes a form. Any questions about this code can be answered in *Chapter 1, Backend Development with Express*.

Now, create a `views` directory and add the `index.ejs` file. The following code is what should be in `index.ejs`:

```
<html>
<body>
<form method="POST">
  <div>
  Username:
  <input type="text" name="username"/>
  </div>
  <div>
  Name:
  <input type="text" name="name"/>
  </div>
  <div>
  Message:
  <textarea name="message"></textarea>
  </div>
  <button>Send Message</button>
</form>
</body>
</html>
```

We can make sure everything works by starting Node and opening our browser to `http://localhost:8003`. We should be able to load the form and submit it.

We can now add some Redis interactions. At the top of `app.js`, add the following lines:

```
app = express(),
  redis = require('redis'),
  client = redis.createClient(),
flow = require('flow-maintained');
```

We do not pass anything into `createClient` because we are going to use the default settings. One great thing about this library is that we do not have to worry about when the connection returns. The library will cache all of the commands before it connects and then execute them right after connecting. This is essentially a promise. Of course, after the connection is established, the commands will not be cached.

Another great feature of this library is that each command has the same name as that of the method. For example, the GET command is `get()` and SET is `set()`. If you know all the commands that you can use in Redis, you can use this library.

Next, we are going to change the GET route for `'/'`. Modify it to look similar to the following code:

```
app.get('/', function(req, res){
  client.incr("test", function(err, counter){
    res.render('index', {redis: counter});
  });
});
```

We have some new code! We are using our client connection to execute the INCR command. This will increment the value at the key specified. If there is nothing at that key, it will return 1. We are using this as a simple counter. Each request will increment this up by one. We then pass it to the template, which means we have to add the template variable to the template. Open up index.ejs and add the following line to it:

```
<html>
<body>
<%= redis %>
<form method="POST">
```

Now, every time you reload the page, the counter will go up. We have stored an application state in Redis. Let's go to redis-cli and check out what is happening. Open up a terminal and type the following command:

redis-cli

Then GET the value of test.

127.0.0.1:6379> GET "test"

"5"

The value returned should be the last value on our page.

Let's use this base and build something that is a little more advanced. Open up index.ejs and remove our Redis template variable. Add the following code after the form:

```
</form>
<% messages.forEach(function(el, index){ %>
<div>
<%= messages[index].message %>
<br/>
  - <%= messages[index].name %>
</div>
<% }) %>
</body>
```

We now have to pass in a `messages` array to our template that has a message and name in each object. This data will be stored in Redis. We are going to use most of the data types we covered earlier when updating our small application. We will also use `flow` to flatten our callback structure. The first thing we need to do is store a reference to the user that creates a message. Add the following function to `app.js`:

```
function CreateUser(username, name, cb){
  client.incr('next:user:id', function(err, userid){
    flow.exec(
      function(){
        var user_string = 'user:' + userid;
        client.set('user:' + username, userid, this.MULTI());
        client.hset(user_string, 'name', name, this.MULTI());
        client.hset(user_string, 'username', username, this.MULTI());
      },function(args){
        cb(userid);
      }
    );
  });
};
```

We will start by discussing flow. Flow will allow us to avoid using nested callbacks. To kick off flow, we run `flow.exec` and add a function. In our example, this is the `INCR` command to get our next `userid`. We use `flow` to help us run our next functions in the order we want. It still runs asynchronously, but we can create our callback chain so that the code appears to run synchronously. We have three functions that we want to finish performing before we move to the callback, so we use `this.MULTI()` in place of the callback. The `this.MULTI()` function will stop `flow` from moving to the next step until they all have been called. The final function passes our `userid` back to the callback. Now, let's talk about what is happening in Redis.

The first INCR will get us a unique ID. We are not worried about authentication here. We then use the ID to create a key with the username that stores the `userid`. If we want to find out what `userid` a username is, we can run `GET "user:username"`. We can then set a hash with the field's name and username. The hash's key will be the `userid`. We can look up a user by their username or ID and get the `userid`, `username`, and `name`.

Now, we will build a function that either gets a `userid` or creates one and returns that. Add this function to `app.js`.

```
function GetUserID(username, name, cb){
  client.get('user:' + username, function(err, userid){
    if(userid){
```

```
      cb(userid);
    }else{
      CreateUser(username, name, function(new_user){
        cb(new_user);
      });
    }
  });
};
```

This function is not using `flow`, so we can see the difference when using callbacks. `GetUserID` is passed in a username and we take that username and check Redis by using `GET` for `"user:username"`. If that key exists, it will return that username's `userid`. If not, it will return null. We can then either send the `userid` back in the callback or run our `CreateUser` function to create a user and return the `userid` from that.

The next thing we need to build is a function that will add the message that this user has sent. This will be again in `app.js`.

```
function AddMessage(message, userid, cb){
  client.incr('next:message:id', function(err, id){
    flow.exec(
      function(){
        var mess_id = 'message:' + id;
        client.set(mess_id, message, this.MULTI());
        client.set(mess_id + ':user', userid, this.MULTI());
        client.lpush('messages', id, this.MULTI());
      },function(){
        cb(id);
      }
    );
  });
};
```

`AddMessage` uses flow in a way that is similar to `CreateUser`. We have three functions that need to run before the callback, but we do not care in what order they execute. We use `this.MULTI()` to do this. First, we get our next message ID. Once we have that, we create the key `"message:messageid"` that has the text of the message as its value. We also store the `userid` in `"message:messageid:user"`. Next, we add the ID of the message at the end of a list that stores all the messages. After these have all returned, we can send the callback.

One thing you may have noticed about Redis is that data gets split up. It is not like a row in a database. Usually, when you retrieve a row from a database, you will have all the data you need. In Redis, you will have to pick out all the data you need from multiple keys. We will do that now as we need a function to get all the data about a message. Add the following function to `app.js`:

```
function FetchMessage(id, cb){
  client.get('message:' + id, function(err, message){
    client.get('message:' + id + ':user', function(err, userid){
      client.hget('user:' + userid, 'name', function(err, name){
        cb({message: message, name: name});
      });
    });
  });
};
```

Here, we run three commands, each inside the previous command's callback. The first is to get the text of the `message`. Next, we have to get the `userid` of the user that created the message. This information is not stored in the value of our message, so we have to look up another key, the message user. This will give us a `userid`. Now, we have to look up the user hash and pull out the name field. We now have all the information we need to create an object with a message and the user that created the message. You can see that our code is slowly stair stepping to the right because of all the callbacks. This is called callback hell. This is a mild example, but imagine what our code would look like if we had to look up six or seven keys. This is where libraries like flow or using promises can help flatten our code and stay out of callback hell. How would you rewrite this function using flow or promises?

We can now build our final function and use them in our application. Again, use `app.js`.

```
function GetMessages(cb){
  flow.exec(
    function(){
      client.lrange('messages', 0, -1, this);
    },function(err, messages){
      //an async foreach
      var final_messages = [];
      flow.serialForEach(messages, function(el){
        FetchMessage(el, this);
      },function(mess){
```

```
        final_messages.push(mess);
      },function(){
        cb(final_messages);
      });
    }
  );
};
```

This will get all of our messages and send them back in an array. The first thing we do is get all of the messages out of our list. We do this by using the LRANGE command. It takes the list, start index, and stop index. 0 is the first item in the list and -1 is the last item. This means that LRANGE 'messages' 0 -1 tells Redis to give us everything in the list. We can step through the list and paginate by using the offsets. For example, we could grab the first ten by using LRANGE 'messages' 0 9, and the next ten using would LRANGE 'messages' 10 19. You can even do this from the other end of the list. This would be LRANGE 'messages' -10 -1, then LRANGE -20 -11, and so on. LRANGE will never throw an error if we ask it for out-of-range indexes. It will either return the indexes that are within our range or nothing. This allows us to know we have grabbed the last page when the amount of elements is under our paging amount or 0.

Once we have an array of message IDs, we can fetch each one and add it to our return array. Flow helps out here. Flow comes with an asynchronous forEach loop. This is important in an asynchronous environment. If we did not do this and just used the forEach normally, our callback would be executed before some or most likely any of the functions would be called. Flow calls their asynchronous forEach function, serialForEach. We pass in the array and the function to be called on each element. It then works in a similar way to Flow.exec, in that when there is a callback, we can use this in the callback's place. We do that here with FetchMessage, which returns an object with the message and user. We then push that object into our array. Flow.serialForEach will then wait for each forEach to execute before it executes the final function in the chain.

We have now built all the functions to create, get, or fetch data out of Redis. We can put them into our routes now. Replace the current index GET routes with the following code:

```
app.get('/', function(req, res){
  GetMessages(function(messages){
    res.render('index', {messages: messages});
  });
});
```

This is pretty straightforward. We get an array of messages and pass them to our template, which is expecting them. Now, let's update the POST route.

```
app.post('/', function(req, res){
  var username = req.body.username;
  var name = req.body.name;
  GetUserID(username, name, function(userid){
    AddMessage(req.body.message, userid, function(messid){
      console.log('Added message: ' + messid);
      res.redirect('/');
    });
  });
});
```

This is a little more complex. We first get `userid`. Then, with that `userid`, we create a message as that user. Finally, we redirect back to the index.

Neither of these routes is doing anything difficult as we have abstracted all the Redis implementation details out of our functions. We can fire up Node and test our site.

Load `http://localhost:8003` in our browser and fill out the form. The console should log each time a message is added to Redis. Our web page will have the newly-created message in it as well. We can use `redis-cli` and use the following command to see everything that has been added:

`KEYS *`

You will see something similar to the following screenshot:

Redis schema

We have used Redis and a few of the data types, so let's now talk about building a Redis schema. I keep making references about how Redis is not a database system, but I feel it is a good shared perspective to discuss building a schema. Databases keep data in rows with multiple columns for each row. In addition to this, you can normalize the data and keep a reference to another row that relates keeping data separate. The end result is the same though; whether or not the database is normalized, the data is a row with multiple columns that store values. We have seen from our example application that you cannot store data this way with Redis. We will now cover some ways to build a Redis schema. The example schema we will build is for the purpose of storing users.

We want to store a user's id, username, password, and last login time. We also have the added constraint of looking up each user by their ID or username. Let's now map out the columns we will need for each user to Redis keys. For each user that we will build, use three keys that have the user's ID in them. This is done by systematically adding to the key. The following are our keys:

- `user:userid:username`: string
- `user:userid:password`: string
- `user:userid:lastLogin`: string (although it will hold a timestamp)

This schema allows us to easily look up all the information about a user if we know the `userid`. What if we do not know the user ID? For example, when someone first logs in, they usually only give us their username and password.

We would add one more key.

- `user:username`: string (stores the `userid`)

Now, we can look up the username and find the `userid`. From there, we can find the rest of the data. Often, it will be tempting to store additional data as JSON in a key, but most of the time, it is not the best way. Redis actually has a built-in data type for storing many different types of data in one key, which brings us to hashes.

Using a hash

We can store data in another way. There are hash types that allow us to store multiple fields per key. This will allow us to flatten our keys. Now, we will have the following keys:

- `user:userid:hash`: a hash with the field's password, username, and last login

- `user:username`: a string with `userid`

From a high level, using a hash is very similar to using a database. We have a row, the hash, which has all the fields we need. We also have indexes, the username string key, which allow us to quickly and easily find a specific row out of thousands, millions, or even billions of keys.

 Remember not to use this in production. Using Redis to store your usernames and passwords is not a very good practice. *Chapter 3, Authenticating Users,* covers a secure way to hash and authenticate local passwords.

Keys in Redis

One thing you may have picked up on is that any Redis schema will involve a lot of keys. The comparison to databases is having many rows in a table. As the rows increase, indexes increase in size and lookups can be slow. In fact, you can lock up a lot of resources on a database server if you run a query that does not use an index on a huge table.

This is where Redis excels. All key lookups (using GET for example) will be an O(1) operation. Without getting into the big O notation (definitely out of scope for this book) and gross oversimplification, what O(1) means is that each operation is constant time. This means irrespective of whether Redis has 1 key or 1 million keys, a GET operation will take the same amount of time, and with Redis, this amount of time is small. We are talking about a few milliseconds.

What this means is that you can be generous with creating keys. If you need a piece of information, create a key for it.

Redis persistence

Our example application has one big caveat. Every key that is added will not be removed. If we released something like this to the public, eventually Redis will fill up all the memory allotted to it. We can test this by connecting to Redis with redis-cli and running KEYS *. We will see that all of our users and messages are still in Redis. This will be true if we shut down the Redis server and bring it back up. Go ahead and restart Redis and then run KEYS * again. We still see the keys are there. Even though Redis is an in-memory key-value store, it persists data to the disk. We can see this happen. Redis will log in to the console when it saves to the disk. This will look like the following screenshot:

```
[1351] 19 Apr 16:16:43.079 * 1 changes in 3600 seconds. Saving...
[1351] 19 Apr 16:16:43.079 * Background saving started by pid 1523
[1523] 19 Apr 16:16:43.080 * DB saved on disk
[1351] 19 Apr 16:16:43.180 * Background saving terminated with success
```

Then, when you launch Redis, it will load data from persistence to create keys on launch. We will see a message like the following one:

```
[1351] 19 Apr 15:16:42.209 # Server started, Redis version 2.8.5
[1351] 19 Apr 15:16:42.216 * DB loaded from disk: 0.007 seconds
[1351] 19 Apr 15:16:42.216 * The server is now ready to accept connections on po
rt 6379
```

Removing Redis keys

Now that we established that Redis keys persist, let's discuss some methods of removing Redis keys. The first method is simple and dangerous. It will remove all keys no matter what state they are in and how long they have existed. It is the FLUSHDB command. This command is destructive and cannot be undone. It is not recommended for use in production Redis stores, although we could use it for our current example application. Connect with redis-cli and run the following commands (if it is alright to delete all Redis keys):

```
127.0.0.1:6379> KEYS *

//all the keys that exist in your Redis instance

127.0.0.1:6379> FLUSHDB

127.0.0.1:6379> KEYS *

(empty list or set)
```

To reiterate the point, this method is really only useful in development. Usually when developing, we want to start with a fresh state and build it up from scratch, so deleting all the keys before each server restart is not an issue. In production, for example, every user will lose their session, meaning every user will have to relogin, and any data in the session will be gone. We definitely need another method for deleting keys from Redis.

The next method we will discuss involves keeping track of each key and then deleting them when they reach a certain age. In doing this, we will uncover another data type, sets!

Sets are collections, like lists, except they are non-repeating. This means if you add a key multiple times, it will only be in the set once. Sets also allow you to do set operations such as intersection, union, or difference. Our current task will not require these, but they are useful.

We can build a set that stores all the keys we have added to Redis. This is important as many different applications can add keys to Redis, and they are all in the same namespace. In our application, Express and Socket.IO both can add keys to Redis. We can then go through the set and delete our keys from Redis when we are done. We can build on this idea and only delete certain keys that we do not need anymore. We can implement this using sorted sets.

Sorted sets are exactly like sets, except that we can add a score to each key. This allows us to pull the data out in an orderly manner. We can set each key and the score equal to the current timestamp. If the key already exists, the command will just update the score; if it does not exist, the command will add it to the set. This will give us a sorted set from the oldest to the newest keys that we have created. Sorted sets also allow us to grab a range of elements that match a range of scores. This is perfect for us as we can calculate what 24 hours before now was and request for all keys that have a score lower than that. We can then take the result of that and delete each key out of Redis.

 We will use sorted set commands later in this chapter, when we add Redis to PacktChat.

The final method we are going to cover is expiration. In Redis, you can mark a key to be expired after a set number of seconds. What is nice about this method is that we do not have to track what keys have been added. There are two ways we could do this.

The first is to set the key and value normally using the SET command. We can then use the EXPIRE command to set an expiration. After the amount of time has passed, the key will have been removed. We can also check the amount of time left with the TTL command. The following is a short example using redis-cli:

```
127.0.0.1:6379> SET test "Expire!"
OK
127.0.0.1:6379> EXPIRE test 60
(integer) 1
127.0.0.1:6379> GET test
"Expire!"
127.0.0.1:6379> TTL test
(integer) 50
//after 60 seconds have passed
127.0.0.1:6379> GET test
(nil)
```

We can easily abstract this out and create a set function that would also expire any keys that we create. There is one caveat with this. If the key is updated with SET again, the expiration is removed. We will have to use EXPIRE on every creation and update. This caveat is only needed when the key is changed. This includes commands such as INCR and HSET. The following is an example of resetting the expiration:

```
127.0.0.1:6379> SET test "Expire"
OK
127.0.0.1:6379> EXPIRE test 60
(integer) 1
127.0.0.1:6379> TTL test
(integer) 57
127.0.0.1:6379> SET test "No-expire"
OK
127.0.0.1:6379> TTL test
(integer) -1
```

There is an even easier way of expiring keys if you are using Redis 2.0.0 or above (which we are!). This is the SETEX command. It combines the two commands we just discussed, SET and EXPIRE, into one. All we have to do is pass in the key, value, and expiration in seconds. The following is our example rewritten using SETEX:

```
127.0.0.1:6379> SETEX test 60 "Expire"
OK
127.0.0.1:6379> TTL test
(integer) 56
127.0.0.1:6379> SETEX test 100 "Higher!"
OK
127.0.0.1:6379> TTL test
(integer) 98
127.0.0.1:6379> SETEX test 2 "Expire"
OK
127.0.0.1:6379> GET test
(nil)
```

Tracking what keys we have added is an important task when using Redis. If we do not know what keys we have added, or more importantly, what keys are currently being used, we will not know what keys can be deleted from Redis when we are done using them. For example, our session storage library connect-redis uses SETEX to expire every key it adds to Redis.

Using Redis as a message queue

In addition to being a super-fast data store, Redis also does message queuing! We just spent the previous chapter covering message queues, so we don't have to cover the reason as to why we should use them. We will only cover how Redis uses them.

Redis's message queuing is much simpler than RabbitMQ. RabbitMQ has many different types of exchanges, queues, protocols, and many other features that Redis does not try to match. Redis is super simple message sending. The method we are using here is publish/subscribe. Redis can also do simple message queuing like RabbitMQ, using RPOPLPUSH. Redis Pub/Sub broadcasts published messages with anyone that is currently subscribed. It does not actually queue the messages. This is an important point to keep in mind. When we built our RabbitMQ workers, we would create persistent exchanges and queues so that any message sent would have somewhere to go.

Even if there were no workers, eventually every message in a RabbitMQ queue would be worked on. When you send a message to be published, Redis will reply with a count of clients that received the message. When there are no clients, we should get a response of 0. Open up a terminal and run `redis-cli` (anytime we run `redis-cli`, the assumption is that redis-server needs to be running as well). The following command will publish a message to `testpubsub`:

```
127.0.0.1:6379> PUBLISH "testpubsub" "message"
(integer) 0
```

If the message is ephemeral in nature, then this is not an issue. If not, then this can be a deal breaker.

Let's build a small little example application that demonstrates how to use Redis Pub/Sub. Create a directory named `redis_second_app` that will serve as the root of our application. The first thing we are going to do is install Express, Socket.IO, and a Redis client using `package.json` and then running `npm install`.

```json
{
  "dependencies": {
    "express": "4.6.1",
    "redis": "0.10.3",
    "socket.io": "1.0.6"
  }
}
```

Create `app.js` and add the following code to it:

```js
var express = require('express'),
  io = require('socket.io'),
  redis = require('redis');

var app = express(),
  redisClient = redis.createClient();

app.use(express.static(__dirname + '/static'));
var server = app.listen(8004);
```

We will initialize all our libraries and then use them. We are connecting to Redis using the default settings (localhost:6379) by not passing anything into `createClient`. We are also using Express' static middleware to serve a static `index.html`. Let's create that now. The following code is what `index.html` present at `redis_second_app\static` should look like:

```html
<!DOCTYPE html>
<html>
<body>
```

```
<h1>Pub/Sub</h1>
<ul id="ul">
<ul>
<script src="/socket.io/socket.io.js"></script>
<script>
  var ul = document.getElementById('ul');
  var socket = io.connect('http://localhost:3000');
  socket.on('pubsub', function(message){
    var li = document.createElement('li');
    li.innerHTML = JSON.stringify(message);
    ul.appendChild(li);
  });
</script>
</body>
</html>
```

We have a UL with `id` so that we can easily create a reference to it. We then connect using Socket.IO. Socket.IO will listen for the `pubsub` event and add a list item to the UL with the value of the JSON object that is the message.

We can now go back to `app.js` and add our Redis and Socket.IO connections. Add the following code to the bottom of `app.js`:

```
var server = app.listen(8004);

//setup pub/sub
redisClient.subscribe('testpubsub');

io = io.listen(server);

io.on('connection', function(socket){
  redisClient.on('message', function(channel, message){
    socket.emit('pubsub', {channel: channel, message: message});
  });
});
```

We have `redisClient`, which is currently connected to our local Redis server. We then use the subscribe method with the name of the channel. This puts the client in a subscriber mode. Any calls made now will be in the context of being subscribed to a channel. We are not using this connection to do anything else, but if we need to run `GET`, `SET`, or anything else, we will just have to create another connection and use that. A good practice would be to have a client for running commands and then a client for each channel that you need to subscribe to.

Next, Socket.IO is set up to listen. Our Redis client then listens for a message. Notice how simple it is to set up Redis Pub/Sub. We have only used two functions, subscribe and the listener for messages. When we get a message, we immediately send it to the client using Socket.IO with the `pubsub` event. That is great because we have configured the client to listen for the `pubsub` event!

Just like all of our other example applications, now is the time to play around with our example application. Start-up Node serving `app.js`. Also, we can connect to Redis using `redis-cli` or using a currently open connection. Arrange your terminal and browser so that you can type in the terminal and still see the browser window. The first thing we will look at is the channels that are currently in Redis. Type the following command into redis-cli. This is only available with Redis 2.8.0 and above:

```
127.0.0.1:6379> PUBSUB CHANNELS
1) "testpubsub"
```

The channel that we subscribed to is displayed. Now, let's see how many subscribers are currently connected. Use the PUBSUB command with the NUMSUB subcommand as follows:

```
127.0.0.1:6379> PUBSUB NUMSUB "testpubsub"
1) "testpubsub"
2) "1"
```

The one connection is our Node process. Finally, let's actually publish a message on the channel. This is done with the PUBLISH command as follows:

```
127.0.0.1:6379> PUBLISH "testpubsub" "Hey!"
(integer) 1
127.0.0.1:6379> PUBLISH "testpubsub" "Another message"
(integer) 1
```

We should have noticed our web page update and immediately add a list item for each message. It should look similar to the following screenshot:

Pub/Sub

- {"channel":"testpubsub","message":"Hey!"}
- {"channel":"testpubsub","message":"Another message"}

Let's do one more experiment. We will use Node's **Read Evaluate Print Loop** (**REPL**) to connect to Redis and publish a message. Open a terminal and just type in `node`. We can now enter commands. Run the following three commands in the Node REPL:

```
> var redis = require('redis');
undefined
> var client = redis.createClient();
undefined
> client.publish('testpubsub', 'From Node REPL');
true
```

Our browser should show the new message.

This is really all the code we would need in order to use Pub/Sub in Redis. As we discussed earlier, it is extremely simple with almost no setup. It definitely does not try to match all the features of RabbitMQ, but that also makes it simpler to use.

Adding Redis to PacktChat

Technically, we are already using Redis in our application. This is only because we have frameworks that are using Redis. However, we want to explicitly use it. We are going to build all the functions our application will need to store the users, rooms, and chats. The first thing is to define what we are going to store.

Defining the Redis structures

All of the objects will be stored in different Redis structures. The reason for this is two-fold. First, we can quickly look up data. Second, every web server will have access to the same data as the others. The following is the list of keys and types of data we will store in Redis:

- `rooms`: a sorted set of all the room names created so far
- `rooms:RoomName:chats`: a sorted set of all the chats sent in this room
- `rooms:RoomName`: a sorted set of all the users in this room
- `users`: a sorted set of all the user IDs that have logged in
- `user:UserID`: a hash of the user's name and type
- `user:UserID:room`: a simple string that holds the current room this user is in

These six simple keys will allow us to track every user, room, and chat. One thing to note is that most of these are sorted sets. This will let us see when the last action had occurred and clean up the set or get rid of the set altogether.

Creating our Redis functions

We will now create all the functions that will add and read data from the structures we just defined. There are no new packages, so we do not need to change the `package.json` file.

The first thing we need to do is create a folder called `redis` and add a filename `index.js`. Add the following code to it:

```
var redis = require('redis'),
  config = require('../config');
var client = redis.createClient(config.redisPort, config.redisHost);
exports.client = client;
```

We will create a Redis connection and then export it. We do this because we need only one connection for most of our Redis commands. As long as we do not put this connection in the subscriber mode, we can run commands in different files using just this connection.

The next thing we need to do is create a type for `User`, `Room`, and `Chat`. JavaScript is a dynamic scripting language, and this can create problems. Every object can be created and modified on the fly, adding or removing properties and methods. This can create issues unless we create a singular creation method. We will do that with a new file named `models.js` in `redis`. The following is what should be in that file:

```
var User = function User(id, name, type){
  if(arguments.length < 3 ) return new Error('Not enough args!');
  return {id: id, user: name, type: type};
};
var Chat = function Chat(message, room, user){
  if(arguments.length < 3 ) return new Error('Not enough args!');
  if(typeof user !== 'object') return new Error('User must be an
object!');
  return {id: user.id + (new Date).getTime().toString(),
  message: message, room: room, ts: (new Date).getTime(), user: user};
};
var Room = function Room(name){
  if(arguments.length < 1)  return new Error('Room needs a name!');
  return {id: name, name: name};
}
exports.User = User;
exports.Chat = Chat;
exports.Room = Room;
```

Each of these functions run very simple parameter checks and then return a JavaScript object. This will help us discover bugs earlier. If we do not pass enough parameters to these functions, they will throw an error when they are called. This is much easier to track down than an error message five function calls later, when it states a property is undefined. The other benefit is that each object that comes out will be the same. If, for some reason, we need another field on User, we can just update the User function and be done with it.

Now that the models are defined, we will create the functions that will read and write these models to Redis. Create the file chat.js in redis and start it off with the following code.

```
var client = require('./index').client,
  q = require('q'),
  models = require('./models');

exports.addUser = function addUser(user, name, type){
  client.multi()
  .hset('user:' + user, 'name', name)
  .hset('user:' + user, 'type', type)
  .zadd('users', Date.now(), user)
  .exec();
};
```

The first few lines require the Redis client, q for promises, and the models we just created. The addUser function is the first of the eight functions that we will use to add data to Redis. This function will add the userid to a sorted set with the current timestamp as the score. The users' sorted set will let us track the users that are currently active. The hash at user:userid stores the display name and the type of user. We will need these two bits of information when we get the list of users in a room. We are doing two hash sets and zadd wrapped with multi. The multi function makes the entire operation atomic. This essentially means that these three actions will be viewed as one action, and either all will execute or none will. Each multi group needs exec at the end to execute. The exec can take a callback with the familiar function(err, reply) structure.

The following code shows the next two functions that deal with rooms:

```
exports.addRoom = function addRoom(room){
  if (room !== '') client.zadd('rooms', Date.now(), room);
};

exports.getRooms = function getRooms(cb){
```

```
        client.zrevrangebyscore('rooms', '+inf', '-inf', function(err, data)
    {
        return cb(data);
    });
};
```

addRoom is very simple. If the room is not an empty string, add it to the room's sorted set with a current timestamp. The zadd function adds to a sorted set with a score. Here, we are adding the name of the room to the sorted set rooms with the score of a current timestamp. The first time, a room will be added. The next time, the room's score will be updated to a current timestamp. We will use this often as this is a powerful pattern.

getRooms uses zrevrangebyscore, which gets a reverse sorted array by score of elements. The score min and max of +inf and -inf will return all the elements. This will return the newest joined room first and the oldest last. Now, let's take a look at the chat functions, shown in the following code:

```
exports.addChat = function addChat(chat){
  client.multi()
  .zadd('rooms:' + chat.room + ':chats', Date.now(), JSON.
stringify(chat))
  .zadd('users', Date.now(), chat.user.id)
  .zadd('rooms', Date.now(), chat.room)
  .exec();
};

exports.getChat = function getChat(room, cb){
  client.zrange('rooms:' + room + ':chats', 0, -1, function(err,
chats){
    cb(chats);
  });
};
```

The first function, addChat, is adding elements to three different sorted sets. The first key is rooms:RoomName:chats, which holds all the chat messages. We are storing these as serialized objects for ease of fetching later. Next, we add the user and room to their respective sorted sets. Sets do not keep duplicate keys, so this action will actually update the timestamp. This allows us to keep track of the most active rooms and users. All of this is wrapped in a multi function.

getChat will just return all the chat messages in a room. This is the ease factor I was talking about. Now, let's see the next two functions, shown in the following code:

```
exports.addUserToRoom = function addUserToRoom(user, room){
  client.multi()
  .zadd('rooms:' + room, Date.now(), user)
  .zadd('users', Date.now(), user)
  .zadd('rooms', Date.now(), room)
  .set('user:' + user + ':room', room)
  .exec();
}

exports.removeUserFromRoom = function removeUserFromRoom(user, room){
  client.multi()
  .zrem('rooms:' + room, user)
  .del('user:' + user + ':room')
  .exec();
};
```

We have a list of rooms and chats in a room, but how do we know who is in a room? That's where these two functions come in. addUserToRoom uses a sorted set to track all the users in a certain room. The users and rooms' sorted sets are updated again in this function. We want to update these anytime something of note happens, like entering a room or adding a chat. The last step for addUserToRoom is to set a key with the user's current room. This will allow us to find all the old users and remove them from the room in the removeUserFromRoom function.

The removeUserFromRoom function simply uses the sorted set's remove command to drop the user out of the set. It also deletes the key that held the user's room.

Finally, let's take a look at our last Redis function. This one is more complex than the others.

```
exports.getUsersinRoom = function getUsersinRoom(room){
  return q.Promise(function(resolve, reject, notify){
    client.zrange('rooms:' + room, 0, -1, function(err, data){
      var users = [];
      var loopsleft = data.length;
      data.forEach(function(u){
        client.hgetall('user:' + u, function(err, userHash){
          users.push(models.User(u, userHash.name, userHash.type));
          loopsleft--;
```

```
        if(loopsleft === 0) resolve(users);
      });
    });
  });
});
};
```

This function is more complex because we need to get more information from Redis for every user in the room. We want to be able to display the user's name and an image. This data is not in the sorted set for all the users in a room. We will use promises in this function, so we immediately return the promise from this function. The first bit of data we need is a list of all the user IDs in a room. Once we have this, we need to loop over every user ID and pull their name and type from the user hash we created earlier. Remember that a forEach loop is not asynchronous. If we just kicked it off, it would return an empty array. We need to make it asynchronous. One way to do this is to get a count of how many rooms that zrange returned, decrement the count on each loop, and when the counter is 0, return our data.

That is exactly what our new forEach loop does. Instead of returning or using a callback, this function resolves the promise we created earlier.

Those were all our Redis functions. Notice that we do not have any update or delete actions. We are not going to give the users the ability to do this. A worker will go through all of the sorted sets and trim off the oldest elements. This is why almost every key is a sorted set. It allows us to put the elements in each set in order.

We are now done building our Redis functions. We will build the pieces that use these functions in the next couple of chapters.

Redis is for application state

Redis is most useful when it is used to keep track of a temporary application state. A perfect example of this is a session. It is only needed when a user is logged in. We store it in Redis, so that it can be easily retrieved and accessible to multiple processes on multiple machines. Redis helps us follow the rule of scalability of never keeping application state locally. Any data that will be needed in multiple requests should be kept in Redis.

Another thing to keep in mind about Redis is that it is only for short term data. Anything that is needed to be stored for a long time should be in a database. Your user table, every time a user logs in, and all tracking information are things that you would keep in a database instead of Redis.

Our application is now ready to store our state in Redis. We have built all the functions that we will use to interact with Redis. All of this interaction is going to happen through Socket.IO. We will be building this part of the application shortly as it will tie the frontend to the backend. We will also build a worker to clean up Redis.

There are many other great things you can do with Redis, but we only focused on using it for scalability.

Summary

You should now have a great understanding of Redis and how to use it to store the application state. Another great feature of Redis is its simple Pub/Sub model, which can pass non-persistent messages between different processes on different machines. Finally, we added Redis to store application state to our PacktChat application.

In the next chapter, we will start the transition where we will focus on the frontend. We will tie up loose ends with the backend and start discussing the tools we will use to build our user interface.

6

Using Bower to Manage Our Frontend Dependencies

We have now built most of our backend, and we are going to switch gears to start focusing on the frontend now. Our application is in a state of transition. We have a lot of functionality at the backend but none on the frontend. There is no way to really interact with our application. We now need to lay the foundation of our frontend. We will introduce new tools to help us track our frontend dependencies. We will also introduce and use two frameworks that will create our HTML elements, handle events, and communicate with our backend. There are a lot of concepts to cover, so let's get started.

We will cover the following topics in this chapter:

- Installing and using Bower
- What is React and why we use React
- What is Backbone and why we use Backbone

As you can see, we will touch upon a lot of different subjects in this chapter. Let's get started.

Node package versions

We will be using one new package in this chapter, Bower. Bower is a package manager that is a lot like npm, except it is for frontend libraries. It allows us to grab versions of jQuery, Backbone, and React and keep them up to date. Most importantly, it allows us to explicitly define the version of each library, for example, bower 1.3.8. It is an npm package like all the others we have installed so far.

Installing and using Bower

Bower is a package manager for frontend libraries. We will be using it to install the libraries needed. A bower.json file will be created at the root of the project. This file will have a list of all dependencies, including the version. This is much better than downloading a JavaScript file and dropping it in a project.

Bower runs on Node, so it is installed using npm. Launch a terminal and type in the following command:

```
npm install -g bower
```

We want to install Bower globally so we can easily use Bower's two most important utilities, bower init and bower install. These commands should seem familiar as they are very similar to the npm commands of the same name. The bower init command will initialize our application directory by asking us some questions about our project and creating a bower.json file. The bower install command will install a package. Exactly like npm, we can use the --save or --save-dev flags that will tell Bower to add the dependency to bower.json.

Bower creates a bower_components directory that holds our packages. Again, this is very similar to npm's node_modules. Each package will have its own directory. Inside of this directory will be all the files that are usually at the library's source. This means there will be the full source in addition to minified versions. Essentially, the Bower package will point to the project's Git URL (usually GitHub) and download the files from there.

In addition to tracking explicitly defined packages, Bower will install all the dependencies of the packages. This is something that has been missing from frontend development for a long time. Bower is a tool that should be in each of our projects that use a fronted library—which will be most of them.

Bower is very similar to npm. They aim to solve the same problem, but have different targets. We will now use Bower for our first frontend library, React.

Introducing React

We only have one chapter on building the frontend. Because of this, we will spend some time on introducing the libraries we will use to build the frontend in this chapter. This will allow us to jump right into writing code.

First up is React (http://facebook.github.io/react/). React is a library that was built by Facebook and Instagram. The entirety of Instagram's interface and Facebook's comments are built using React. It is designed to only be used for user interfaces. It does not make any assumptions about how or where you get data. This makes it easy to interoperate with other libraries.

React uses a virtual **Document Object Model (DOM)**. The DOM is all the elements that are on a page. A virtual DOM allows the library to only render the differences. Anytime a lot of elements render, the browser must take time to figure out what an insertion or deletion of an element will do to the page. Doing this takes time. React is able to keep rendering to a minimum, making it fast.

One more great feature of React is that it has synthetic events. What this means is that when you add an event listener to a component, the listener is not actually tied to that component. This is useful because it gets around the most prolific way of creating memory leaks. Memory leaks are created when an element is removed from the DOM, but an event listener is still attached. When a garbage collection is fired, the element can still be mapped back, which means the element's memory will not be freed. For example, if we render a button and add a click listener, then when we re-render the button again with a click listener, we have created a memory leak.

Cleaning up our events becomes especially hard when anonymous functions are used. This is because we need to use a reference to the function to remove the listener, which we do not have with an anonymous function. This is where synthetic events come in handy. In React, there is only one listener that sits all the way at the top of the component chain. When an event listener is adding to a component lower in the chain, it is registered with the top-level listener. Then, when an event matches the definition (a click on a button, for example), it will bubble up to the top level and get handled. When a component is removed, it can be garbage collected because there are no event handlers tied to that element.

React can use an XML-like syntax called JSX. I will say that this is the most controversial thing about React. It is not required, and in fact, you must transform JSX into JavaScript to use it. We can transform JSX to JavaScript on the fly at load time, but Facebook does recommend to statically transform all JSX beforehand. We are going to build our elements using straight JavaScript, but I recommend everyone at least go out and try JSX. You may like it!

Let's build a simple application to demonstrate what can be done with React. First, create a directory named react. Inside this directory, create a file named bower.json and add the following code to it:

```
{
    "name": "react",
```

```
    "version": "0.0.0",
    "license": "MIT",
    "dependencies": {
      "react": "0.11.1",
      "postal.js": "0.10.1"
    }
  }
```

Then, we just have to run `bower install`. This will install our packages and all the dependencies needed.

React is component-based, so let's build our first component. Create a file named `index.html` inside the `react` directory. Add the following code to it:

```
<!DOCTYPE HTML>
<html>
<head>
  <title>React</title>
  <script src="/bower_components/react/react.js"></script>
</head>
<body>
  <h1>React!</h1>
  <div id="react-root"></div>
</body>
<script>
var Hello = React.createClass({
  handleClick: function(){
    alert(this.props.name);
  },
  render: function(){
    return React.DOM.li({className: "name", onClick: this.
handleClick},
      "Hello There, " + this.props.name + "!");
  }
});

var root = React.renderComponent(Hello({name: "Josh"}), document.
getElementById('react-root'));
</script>
</html>
```

Components are created with the `React.createClass` method. It takes an object as a parameter. This object will at least need a `render` attribute that will render our component. The next step is where React is different than almost all other view renders. We do not add HTML elements or a string that can be turned into HTML. We create `React.DOM` elements. `React.DOM` has almost any element we will need. Here, we are using a list item. The first parameter is a list of attributes to put on `li`. Because `class` is a reserved word in JavaScript, `className` is used to add CSS classes. We also place any event handlers in this object, as well.

The next parameter in the `React.DOM` element is the content that should go in the element. In this example, we are only adding text, but we can add other components. This component is also dynamic. Properties (props) can be passed in and used later in the component. In this example, we pass in a name and use it while rendering. Finally, we render the component into the `div#react-root` HTML element. We can run this using Python with the following command in the root of our project directory:

```
python -m SimpleHTTPServer
```

 React requires the `render` function to return only one element, not a list of elements. If a list is required, then it will need to be wrapped with `div` or `ul` if it is a literal list.

Let's add the list to hold our new list item component. Add the new `HelloList` function and replace the `root` variable:

```
//add this after Hello
var HelloList = React.createClass({
  render: function(){
    return React.DOM.ul({className: "name-ul"},
      Hello({name: "Josh"}),
      Hello({name: "Brian"})
    );
  }
});

//replace the current root
var root = React.renderComponent(HelloList(), document.
getElementById('react-root'));
```

Now we are building `HelloList`, which will render the `Hello` list items inside of it. All we have to do to render a component is call it inside another component. This is a perfect example of reusing a component to build more complex components. We can also keep adding components in a `React.DOM` element after the first parameter. Our page should now have a list with two items that will alert the name passed into it when clicked.

This example demonstrates the ability to compose React components. Each component can encapsulate all the logic, events, and rendering of itself and then be used to build larger components that do the same.

Now, we will get fancy and add a form to add names and removal buttons for each name. We will do this using `postal.js`. Because `postal.js` was in our `bower.json` file, it should already be in our project for use. `postal.js` also has two dependencies, Conduit and lodash. Both of these will be in our `bower_components` directory.

`postal.js` gives us a global message bus where objects can publish messages to other objects that are listening. This is very much like RabbitMQ and Redis Pub/Sub.

We now have to update the head in our `index.html` file with our new libraries:

```
<script src="bower_components/react/react.js"></script>
<script src="/bower_components/lodash/dist/lodash.js"></script>
  <script src="/bower_components/conduitjs/src/conduit.js"></script>

  <script src="bower_components/postal.js/lib/postal.js"></script>
```

First, let's update the `Hello` list item, as shown in the following code:

```
var Hello = React.createClass({
  componentWillMount: function(){
    this.channel = postal.channel();
  },
  removeClick: function(){
    this.channel.publish("Name.Remove", {name: this.props.name});
  },
  render: function(){
    return React.DOM.li({className: "name"},
      "Hello There, " + this.props.name + "!",
      React.DOM.button({onClick: this.removeClick},
      "Remove Me")
    );}
});
```

There is a new `componentWillMount` attribute. This runs right before the component is rendered, giving us a perfect place to run any onetime setup code. We connect to the default channel and add it to the object so we can use it later. Next, we define the `removeClick` function, which will publish a `"Name.Remove"` message that will pass the current name. In render, we have removed the `onClick` alert and added a button that will fire off the `removeClick` function. It is important to note this component does not remove itself. It will let another component know that it needs to be removed.

We need a form, so let's add a React form, as shown in the following code:

```
var AddNameForm = React.createClass({
  componentWillMount: function(){
    this.channel = postal.channel();
  },
  handleSubmit: function(e){
    e.preventDefault();
    var newName = this.refs.name.getDOMNode().value.trim();
    this.channel.publish('Name.Add', {name: newName});
    this.refs.name.getDOMNode().value = '';
  },
  render: function(){
    return React.DOM.form({onSubmit: this.handleSubmit},
      React.DOM.input({type:'text', placeholder: 'Name', ref:
'name'}),
      React.DOM.button(null, 'Submit')
    )}
});
```

Just like the `Hello` component, the first thing we do is set up a channel, so we can let another component know what was submitted in the form. Next is the submit event handler. First, we prevent the form from reloading the page when submitted. Then, we get the value from the text input. The `refs` object has each element that we have added a ref attribute to; here, it is on the input element. We can then easily grab them in functions. The `getDOMNode` function will return the HTML element. Once we have the element, we can run regular JavaScript to get the value of text input. We then publish an event with the name that was entered. The last thing to do is to blank out the value on the input, so it doesn't keep the value between submits.

The final component we will update is `HelloList`. The following code is what the component will look like:

```
var HelloList = React.createClass({
  componentWillMount: function(){
    var channel = postal.channel();
    this.addSub = channel.subscribe('Name.Add', this.addName);
    this.removeSub = channel.subscribe('Name.Remove', this.
removeName);
  },
  getInitialState: function(){
    //async loading
    setTimeout(function(){
      //treat state as immutable
      var copy = this.state.namesList.slice();
      copy.push("Test");
      this.setState({namesList: copy});
    }.bind(this), 3000);
    return { namesList: ["Josh", "Brian"]};
  },
addName: function(data){
    var copy = this.state.namesList.slice();
    copy.push(data.name);
    this.setState({namesList: copy});
  },
  removeName: function(data){
    var copy = this.state.namesList.slice();
    copy.splice(copy.indexOf(data.name), 1);
    this.setState({namesList: copy});
  },
render: function(){
    return React.DOM.ul({className: "name-ul"},
      this.state.namesList.map(function(name){
        return Hello({name: name});
      }),
      AddNameForm());
  },
  componentWillUnmount: function(){
    this.addSub.unsubscribe();
    this.removeSub.unsubscribe();}
});
```

The first `componentWillMount` function sets up the subscriptions so we get the events from other components. We will get to the handlers that are referenced in the `subscribe` function shortly.

There is a new idea introduced with this component—state. Previously, we covered props as a way of getting data into a component. State is another way to store data. The difference between them is that state can and will change over the lifetime of a component and a prop will not. A good example of this is the name prop in our first component, `Hello`. The name will not change; it is just rendered. In the `HelloList` component we are building here, the state is going to change. The initial state is an array of two names. A function is set to update the state after 3 seconds. It will make a copy of the current state and then add a new name to it. Then, the function will run `setState` which will tell the component to re-render itself and any children.

React does not care where state comes from. It could be from an Ajax call, Socket.IO event, or even a Backbone model. React only worries about rendering and handling the DOM and events.

We should always treat state as immutable. What this means is that we should not change it in place. Make a copy of the current state and then change that. This allows React to figure out the difference in the new state.

Next are the handlers to add and remove names. These functions are similar. They both make a copy of the state with `slice()`. Then, an element is either pushed in or spliced out and the state is updated.

Now that we have some state, we can finally render the component. This brings us to the last two functions, `render` and `componentWillUnmount`. The `render` function is actually really simple. React will render other React components, so we can compose our view. The function takes the state and maps each item in the array to a `Hello` component, passing in the name as a prop, and finally adding the form at the end.

In the final function, we unsubscribe from both of the subscriptions we set up in the beginning.

The last thing to do is to render `HelloList` to `div#react-root`. This code has not changed since the last time we updated. React allows us to build a complex application and then render it into any element on a page. Our little application could just be one part of a much larger application and it would be completely self-contained. Any changes here would not affect other components:

```
var root = React.renderComponent(HelloList(), document.
getElementById('react-root'));
```

Load `http://localhost:8000` in your browser. Initially, the page should have two items in the list. Then, after 3 seconds, another item will be added. We can add elements by using the form and remove them using the button in each item. In 80 lines of JavaScript, we have built an interactive list.

It is a best practice to have as few stateful components as possible. In our example, only `HelloList` had state. All the other components used props. Props can easily flow down the component chain. The top-level component, or parent, will be the component that knows what is going on. All the child components will get their data from the element above them. This keeps everything from becoming dependent on each other, and allows any component to be used anywhere else in our application.

React allows us to break down a page's user interface into self-contained components. This means each component is responsible for rendering itself and tracking any events that happen to it. This makes the components composable, and in turn means we define each element separately and then reuse and assemble all the elements to create the whole.

Introducing Backbone

Backbone is a JavaScript library that allows us to define models, collections, and views. It helps to organize keeping track of what is happening on a web page in JavaScript. Like React, it is not a fully-featured library. Backbone does more than React, but a lot less than Angular or Ember.js. This is not better or worse, it is just different. Everything we are building in this application can easily be implemented in any other JavaScript framework.

We just covered how React can render views and track events. Backbone has these same capabilities, but we will not be utilizing them. In my opinion, React's DOM manipulations are better, and eliminates the need to have a view teardown step, where we unattached each event listener. We discussed how React uses synthetic events to only bind event handlers inside of the component. Backbone assigns event handlers without using synthetic events. This can lead to memory leaks if we are not careful when we need to remove a view. Backbone also does not use a virtual DOM to track changes. This means any update in a view will cause multiple elements to render again. React gives us powerful view functions, so we are using those over Backbone's view functions.

We will not do a complete Backbone and React integration in this chapter. We will just cover the parts of Backbone we will use, and the next chapter shows how all of this works together.

Using Backbone models

Backbone has a great way of tracking application data—the model. A Backbone model will fire off some events and keep the data in sync between a server and the page. Backbone can easily map a model to REST API and CRUD data. For our example here, we will only be using the event features.

Models are technically just JavaScript objects with some useful functionalities built in. They can have attributes and methods that utilize the attributes.

Let's create some models. First, we will create a directory named Backbone. Then, create a file named `bower.json` and add the following code to it:

```json
{
  "name": "backbone",
  "version": "0.0.0",
  "license": "MIT",
  "dependencies": {
    "backbone": "1.1.2"
  }
}
```

Next, run `bower install`.

Then, create an HTML page named `models.html` and add the following code to it:

```html
<!DOCTYPE HTML>
<html>
<head>
  <title>Backbone</title>
  <script src="/bower_components/underscore/underscore.js"></script>
  <script src="/bower_components/backbone/backbone.js"></script>
</head>
<body>
  <h1>Backbone!</h1>
  <div id="backbone-root"></div>
</body>
</html>
```

This page loads `backbone` with its dependency underscore. Bower will have installed underscore automatically.

Create a script tag at the end of the body and use the following JavaScript code:

```
var root = document.getElementById('backbone-root');
var Chat = Backbone.Model.extend({});
var chat = new Chat({message: 'Hey'});
chat.on('change', function(model){
  console.log(model);
});

chat.on('change:message', function(model, value){
  console.log(model);
  alert(value);
});
chat.set({message: 'Hey Again'});
```

Backbone uses extend to create different types of objects. Here, we extend `Backbone.Model`. We then create an instance of the model passing in the attributes we want it to have. Models will emit two events when an attribute changes. The first is a `change` event which will pass in the model. The other is a `change:<attributeName>` event. This event will pass the model and the new value of the attribute. In our example, we wire up both events. Both event listeners will log the model that changed. The attribute specific listener will also alert the new value.

Finally, we change the value of the attribute. We do not directly change the attribute. We have to use the `set` function, which will make sure the proper events get fired off. This can be verified by loading `http://localhost:8000/models.html`. An alert should be fired that says `'Hey Again'`. Also, there should be two objects logged to the console.

Although we are not using all the features of a Backbone model, it is still useful. Backbone models allow us to listen for any changes on a model.

Using Backbone collections

Backbone collections are a collection of models. Just like models are basically extended objects, collections are basically extended arrays. Let's jump right in and create a collection. We can make a copy of `models.html` and name it `collections.html`. The only change we need to make is to empty the script tag and add the following code to it:

```
var Chat = Backbone.Model.extend({});
var ChatCollection = Backbone.Collection.extend({
  model: Chat
```

```
    });
    var chat = new Chat({message: 'Hey'});

    var collection = new ChatCollection([
        chat
    ]);

    collection.on('add change remove', function(model, value){
        console.log(model);
    });

    chat.set({message: 'Hey again'});
    var added = collection.add({message: "Another chat"});
    collection.add(chat);
    collection.remove(added);
```

Creating collections involves extending `Backbone.Collection`. Here, we pass in what type of model is in this collection. This allows us to pass in a basic JavaScript object, which will be converted to the type defined here. Collections can be initialized with an array of objects or models. Here, we pass in one model. We then attach listeners to the add, change, and remove events. These events are fired off when a model is added to the collection, when a model in the collection is changed, or when a model is removed, respectively.

The next few lines test different scenarios. The first line changes the chat object we included in the collection. This will fire off a change event. Next, we add a new object to the collection. This addition will fire the add event. Next, we try to add an object that is already in the collection. This will not do anything. Collections are intelligent and know when an object is already in the collection. Finally, we remove a model from the collection.

Backbone models and collections will give us an interface to watch for and react to changes in our data. We will have to create server-side syncing ourselves, as Backbone does not have anything built in for Socket.IO. In addition to this, we will then need to wire up some code to let React know when a model changes. We can create some separation of concerns here. Backbone will only worry about making sure the collections it has are synced properly to the server. React will worry about rendering those collections. `postal.js` will then create an event bus through which we can let different objects know that something has happened without creating a dependency on that specific object.

Summary

In this chapter, we learned how to manage our frontend dependencies. This is done through Bower. Bower is very similar to npm in the way it stores our dependencies (`bower.json` and `bower_components`) and its execution (`install` and `init`). Next, we introduced React, which will serve as our JavaScript view engine in the browser. We covered the reasons why we chose this framework. Then, we covered Backbone models that will emit events when changed. This gives us the ability to decouple changing a collection and then rendering the changed collection. This is important, as we are using two separate frameworks for watching our data and rendering our views. We now have the tools and background to add Bower, React, and Backbone to our application.

In the next chapter, we will make all the code additions and changes that will be required to have a functional chat application.

7
Using Backbone and React for DOM Events

This chapter is going to be the finishing touches on our application. We have built the backend, but this is not very useful unless we have a way of interacting with it. There will be a lot of code being removed, added, and updated. I will try to keep the code changes as localized as possible. I don't want to jump between 13 different files, making small changes. On the other hand, I want to make sure that all code changes happen in a logical order. The following is what we are going to cover in this chapter:

- Finishing our Socket.IO events that get and add data to Redis
- Creating all our view components with React
- Tying our Backbone models to Socket.IO and the components

Bower package versions

Usually we list out the new npm packages we will use, but the application finally has all the npm packages it needs. We will need a few Bower packages to finalize development, though. The following is the inclusive list of packages:

- react: 0.11.1
- backbone: 1.1.2
- postal.js: 0.10.3
- jquery: 2.1.1
- momentjs: 2.8.1

We have covered React, Backbone, Postal.js, and jQuery already. Moment.js will be used to turn time spans into human readable formats. We can now create a `bower.json` file in the root of our `packtchat` directory and add the following code to it:

```
{
  "name": "nodechat",
  "dependencies": {
    "react": "0.11.1",
    "backbone": "1.1.2",
    "postal.js": "0.10.3",
    "jquery": "2.1.1",
    "momentjs": "2.8.1"
  }
}
```

We now run `bower install` and all the frontend dependencies will be downloaded and added to `bower_components`.

> Note that the site has only been tested in Chrome, Safari, and Firefox. It might work in IE 11, but I would not hold out much hope for previous versions. It is out of the scope of this book to discuss cross-browser fixes.

Finishing Socket.IO

We have built many little Socket.IO demonstration applications, and now is the time to create the Socket.IO we are going to use. We only need to update the authorization and connection functions. Let's get started. Open up `index.js` present in the `socket.io` folder and make the following changes to the require statements at the top:

```
var io = require('socket.io'),
  cookie = require('cookie'),
  cookieParser = require('cookie-parser'),
  expressSession = require('express-session'),
  ConnectRedis = require('connect-redis')(expressSession),
  redisAdapter = require('socket.io-redis'),
  redis = require('redis'),
  config = require('../config'),
  redisSession = new ConnectRedis({host: config.redisHost, port:
config.redisPort}),
  redisChat = require('../redis/chat'),
  models = require('../redis/models'),
  log = require('../middleware/log');
```

Here, we are just pulling in the Redis functions we created and the model creation functions.

The next addition is adding a few lines in the authorization function. The `socketAuth` function should look similar to the following code:

```
var socketAuth = function socketAuth(socket, next){
  var handshakeData = socket.request;
  var parsedCookie = cookie.parse(handshakeData.headers.cookie);
  var sid = cookieParser.signedCookie(parsedCookie['connect.sid'],
config.secret);

  if (parsedCookie['connect.sid'] === sid)
    return next(new Error('Not Authenticated'));

  redisSession.get(sid, function(err, session){
    if (session.isAuthenticated)
    {
      socket.request.user = session.passport.user;
      socket.request.sid = sid;
      redisChat.addUser(session.passport.user.id, session.passport.
user.displayName, session.passport.user.provider);
      return next();
    }
    else
      return next(new Error('Not Authenticated'));
  });
};
```

This is the first use of the Redis functions we just created. It will add the current user to Redis when Socket.IO is authorized.

We need to add two utility functions that the event listeners will use. They are as follows:

```
var removeFromRoom = function removeFromRoom(socket, room){
  socket.leave(room);
  redisChat.removeUserFromRoom(socket.request.user.id, room);
  socket.broadcast.to(room).emit('RemoveUser',
    models.User(socket.request.user.id, socket.request.user.
displayName, socket.request.user.provider));
};
var removeAllRooms = function removeAllRooms(socket, cb){
  var current = socket.rooms;
  var len = Object.keys(current).length;
```

```
  var i = 0;
  for(var r in current)
  {
    if (current[r] !== socket.id)
    {
      removeFromRoom(socket, current[r]);
    }
    i++;
    if (i === len) cb();

  }
};
```

The removeFromRoom function is a utility that will be used by other functions. The first step is to remove the socket connection from the room being passed in. The next step is to remove them from Redis, which is keeping its own sorted set of users in each room. Finally, a message is sent out to all the other sockets in that room to remove this user.

The next function, removeAllRooms, will take the current connection out of all the rooms it is currently in. This is done through socket.rooms, which has all the rooms the current socket connection is in. We then loop over each of the rooms. To leave the room, we must pass the room name to socket.leave(). We check to see whether the room is the same as the socket ID and we skip removing the connection from that room. When the function has gone through all the rooms, it will run the callback function, allowing the execution to continue.

This brings us to the main portion of Socket.IO, the connection function. Inside the connection function is where we will add all the event listeners. Right now, it should be just a basic skeleton of listeners that do nothing. We will change that now. The following are the first couple of things to add inside socketConnection.

Let's build our first listener, GetMe, as shown in the following code:

```
socket.on('GetMe', function(){
    socket.emit('GetMe', models.User(socket.request.user.id, socket.
request.user.displayName, socket.request.user.provider));
  });
```

It is a simple function, but there are two important things to note. The first thing to note is that the Socket.IO event name, `GetMe`, is also the name of the event that is emitted to the client. This will make tracking the events much easier. The client will listen for the same event it just sent. If we had different names for each event, `GetMe` coming to the server and `Me` going to the client, we would have double the events. The other thing to note is using the request data. During authorization, `socketAuth`, we grabbed the Passport user object from the session and added it user off the passed-in data object. This data object is now accessible off the socket as a handshake. As long as this connection is open,
we can grab this information, which we will do many more times.

Now, let's look at the two chat listeners:

```
socket.on('GetChat', function(data){
    redisChat.getChat(data.room, function(chats){
      var retArray = [];
      var len = chats.length;
      chats.forEach(function(c){
        try{
          retArray.push(JSON.parse(c));
        }catch(e){
          log.error(e.message);
        }
        len--;
        if (len === 0) socket.emit('GetChat', retArray);
      });
    });
  });

  socket.on('AddChat''AddChat''AddChat', function(chat){
    var newChat = models.Chat(chat.message, chat.room,
      models.User(socket.handshake.user.id, socket.handshake.user.
displayName, socket.handshake.user.provider));
    redisChat.addChat(newChat);
    socket.broadcast.to(chat.room).emit('AddChat', newChat);
    socket.emit('AddChat', newChat);
  });
```

`GetChat` is passed in a data object that has the room set as a property. We use our new Redis `getChat` function to return an array of chats. There is one small issue; each `chat` object is serialized, so we parse it back to a JavaScript object. We do this inside an asynchronous `forEach`, eventually sending the chat array back to the client.

AddChat creates two new models. One is the `chat` object and the other is a `user` object that will go into the `chat` object. These model functions are nice because they create a quasi-interface between functions. The called function has a good idea of which properties the new object will have. Then, the new chat is added to Redis. Lastly, we broadcast the new chat message to everyone in the room. Next up are room functions, as shown in the following code:

```
socket.on('GetRoom', function(){
    redisChat.getRooms(function(rooms){
      var retArray = [];
      var len = rooms.length;
      rooms.forEach(function(r){
        retArray.push(models.Room(r));
        len--;
        if(len === 0) socket.emit('GetRoom', retArray);
      });
    });
});

socket.on('AddRoom''AddRoom''AddRoom', function(r){
    var room = r.name;
    removeAllRooms(socket, function(){
      if (room !== '')
      {
        socket.join(room);
        redisChat.addRoom(room);
        socket.broadcast.emit('AddRoom', models.Room(room));
        socket.broadcast.to(room).emit('AddUser',
            models.User(socket.handshake.user.id, socket.handshake.user.
displayName, socket.handshake.user.provider));
        redisChat.addUserToRoom(socket.handshake.user.id, room);
      }
    });
});
```

The GetRoom function will get all the rooms that are in Redis, create an array of room objects, and return them. AddRoom will run removeAllRooms so the new room will be the only room the connection is in. The rest of the function is inside the callback, so it will run after all the other rooms have been removed. Now that we have removed the connection from all other rooms, we will join the room being added. We will use the AddRoom event to create new rooms and also when users join existing rooms.

After joining the room and letting Redis know there is a new room (remember this is stored in a sorted set, so it will just update the timestamp), the function will emit two events. The first is AddRoom. What will happen is that as and when rooms are created, all other users will have the list of rooms automatically updated in real time. Next, an event to the room is sent that a user has joined. In much the same way, all the users in the room will see the user list dynamically updated when someone joins. Lastly, we let Redis know the user is in the room.

The final listener is added to the disconnect event. It is as follows:

```
socket.on('disconnect', function(){
    removeAllRooms(socket, function(){});
});
```

Socket.IO should clean up the rooms the connection is in automatically, but we are running this to emit the RemoveUser events. If we did not do this, rooms will have users in them that are not actively in the room. The only way they will be removed is when the user entered a different room, which is not guaranteed to happen if they have been disconnected.

Socket.IO is now ready. We have created all the listeners that will be needed by the frontend. It is always a good idea to create some structure when designing a real-time interface. It is easy to just keep creating different event names for every little event, but this becomes difficult to keep track of. A great comparison would be to REST. The **representational state transfer** (**REST**) methods have an HTTP verb and a resource. We have followed this structure by having a verb and a noun, for example, chat. There is GetChat and AddChat. If we were to build out more actions, we would use UpdateChat and RemoveChat. This makes our Socket.IO interface predictable, which is good. These actions map to the common **Create Read Update Delete** (**CRUD**) methods. In addition to this, these actions are the same as the REST methods. REST is a great way to map these functions to URLs.

Creating React components

React was introduced in the last chapter, along with some simple examples. React will perform all of DOM manipulation and DOM event listening.

We will do a quick review of the life cycle events we are going to utilize in various components. The first is componentWillMount. This is fired right before the component is rendered to the DOM. Next is componentWillUnmount. Use this to clean up all the objects we initialized earlier. These first two functions we covered will only fire once in the life cycle. The componentDidUpdate function is executed after the component renders any changes. This can be executed multiple times.

Let's get started. We will be creating this as a static JavaScript file. Create a new folder under `static` named `js`. Then, create a file named `components.js`. The first component we will create is a room form. We need this so that after a user logs in, they can enter the name of a room or join a previously created room. Paste the following code in `components.js`:

```
var RoomForm = React.createClass({
  componentWillMount: function(){
    this.channel = postal.channel();
    this._boundForceUpdate = this.forceUpdate.bind(this, null);
    this.props.rooms.on('add change remove', this._boundForceUpdate,
this);
  },
  componentWillUnmount: function() {
      this.props.rooms.off("add change remove", this._
boundForceUpdate);
    },
  joinRoomHandler: function(){
    this.channel.publish('Room.Join', {roomName: this.refs.roomName.
getDOMNode().value});
  },
  render: function(){
    return React.DOM.div({className: 'col-sm-8 col-sm-offset-2'},
      React.DOM.h2(null, 'Please Select a Room'),
      React.DOM.input({type: 'text', placeholder: 'Room Name',
className: 'form-control', ref: 'roomName'}, null),
      React.DOM.button({className: 'btn btn-primary btn-block top-
margin', onClick: this.joinRoomHandler}, 'Join Room'),
      React.DOM.ul(null,
        this.props.rooms.map(function(r){
          return React.DOM.li({className: 'list-unstyled'}, React.
DOM.a({href: '#room/' + r.get('name')}, r.get('name'))
          );
        })
    )); }
});
```

There is a lot going on here, but it should be easy to follow if we break it up.

The first thing we need to clear up is how we are handling data. In our examples in the last chapter, we used `props` and `state` to track when to update. Here, we are using a Backbone collection that is passed in as prop named `rooms`. The component then registers listeners on the `add`, `change`, and `remove` events on the rooms collection. The function it calls is the component's `forceUpdate`.

We create a reference to `forceUpdate` that is bound using the component as the context. It is important to keep the reference so we can remove the function when the component is being `unmounted`. If we don't do this, a memory leak would be created. This would cause our component to automatically render when any new elements are added, changed, or removed from the rooms collection.

We use Postal.js as a global bus, connecting to it so we can later add an event to it.

This brings us to our click handler for this component, `joinRoomHandler`. It creates an event in postal.js named `Room.Join` with the value from our input text element.

Using a global event bus allows us to decouple the handling of an event with the event's creation. Does the `RoomForm` component care what happens when a room is joined? No. This component will just create the event and send it on to whichever object cares about it. This makes components reusable, as they are not tied to another specific component to work properly.

This brings us to render. Remember `React.DOM` has every HTML element we will need to create. This means this will return a `div` element that has an `h2`, text input, button, and unsorted list in it. The button has a click listener on it and the unsorted list is composed of the rooms from the collection passed in.

This component is demonstrative of all the other components we will build. It sets up, tears down, handles any events, and renders. When viewed in that context, this is a very simple component.

The following screenshot is of this component rendered:

The next component we will look at is `UserView`. It is as follows:

```
var UserView = React.createClass({
  render: function(){
    var name = this.props.useName ? this.props.user.get('user') :
null;
```

```
      return React.DOM.div(null,
        React.DOM.img({src: this.props.user.image(this.props.size),
  className: 'img-circle', title: this.props.user.get('user')}),
        name
      )}
});
```

This view only renders. It does require two properties, though. It will need size
and a Backbone user model (we will get to the models shortly). This view also has an
optional property, useName. If it is true, then the view will add the name of the user,
and if it is false or not passed in, it will not add the name. This demonstrates how
to render a view differently based on the state or properties. Using an if statement
in the middle of a React.DOM element is not allowed, so we have to create a holding
variable and set it before we get to the element. The following screenshot is how this
view will look:

React components are reusable and can be composed. Let's do this with the UserView
and put it into UserList:

```
var UserList = React.createClass({
  render: function(){
    var me = this.props.me;
    return React.DOM.ul({className: 'list-unstyled'},
      this.props.collection.map(function(user){
        if (me.id !== user.get('id'))
          return React.DOM.li(null, UserView({user: user, size: 50,
  useName: true}))
      }) ) }
});
```

This component uses two properties to render correctly: me and collection.
The me property should be the user model of the currently logged in user. If we
are in a room, we do not need to render our name in the list. The other property,
collection, is a Backbone collection of user models. Backbone collections have
the map function available, and we use this to loop over each user in the collection.

The next component that uses `UserView` is `ChatMessage`. Let's build this next:

```
var ChatMessage = React.createClass({
  render: function(){
    var pull;
    if (this.props.me.id === this.props.chat.get('user').id)
      pull = 'pull-right';
    else
      pull = 'pull-left';

    var timeAgo = moment(this.props.chat.get('ts')).fromNow();
    return React.DOM.li(null,
      React.DOM.div({className: 'bg-primary chat-message ' + pull},
this.props.chat.get('message')),
      React.DOM.div({className: 'clearfix'}, null),
      React.DOM.div({className: pull},
        UserView({user: this.props.chat.get('user'), size: 20,
useName: true}), React.DOM.small(null, timeAgo)),
      React.DOM.div({className: 'clearfix'}, null)
    )
  }
});
```

This component has a little more complex render logic. First of all, it should have two properties, me and chat. We already know what me should be, and chat will be a Backbone chat object that has a message, timestamp, and the user that created it. The first thing the component needs to do is determine whether we created the message. If it is us, float this to the right, and if not, float it to the left. Next, we use Moment.js to give us a rough estimate of when the chat was added. We can render the elements now that we have our pull and timeAgo strings prepared. I will admit that building nested elements can become cumbersome in React, like in this component. We want to return a list item that has four different divs in it. The first div is the message, next is a float clear div, then UserView and how long ago, and finally, a last float clear div.

The following is a screenshot of a chat message that was just added:

The ChatMessage component leads us right into the next component, ChatList:

```
var ChatList = React.createClass({
  render: function(){
    var me = this.props.me;
    return React.DOM.ul({className: 'list-unstyled'},
      this.props.chats.map(function(chat){
        return  ChatMessage({chat: chat, me: me});
      }))}
});
```

There is not much new going on here. This is almost exactly the same as UserList. The component returns an unordered list of another component. The component will look similar to the following screenshot when rendered:

How do we add a new chat message? With ChatForm, of course! The following is the code for that component:

```
var ChatForm = React.createClass({
  componentWillMount: function(){
    this.channel = postal.channel();
  },
  formSubmit: function(e){
    e.preventDefault();
    var message = this.refs.message.getDOMNode().value;
    if (message !== '')
    {
      this.channel.publish('Chat.Add', {message: message});
      this.refs.message.getDOMNode().value = '';
      this.refs.message.getDOMNode().placeholder = '';
    }else{
      this.refs.message.getDOMNode().placeholder = 'Please enter a
message';
    }
  },
  render: function(){
```

```
    return React.DOM.div({className: "row"},
      React.DOM.form({onSubmit: this.formSubmit},
        React.DOM.div({className: "col-sm-2"},
          UserView({user: this.props.me, size: 50, useName: true})),
        React.DOM.div({className: "col-sm-8"},
          React.DOM.input({type: "text", className: "form-control",
ref: "message"}, null)),
        React.DOM.div({className: "col-sm-2"},
          React.DOM.button({className: "btn btn-primary"}, 'Send'))
      ))}
  });
```

This form works much like `RoomForm`. We will capture the `submit` event and pass the data through a postal.js channel. Initially, we have to stop the form from refreshing the page, so we use `e.preventDefault()`. Then, we check the value of the text input. If it is a blank string, we do not send a message through the channel, and we change the placeholder to let the user know they need to enter something. This is a nice, subtle alert that is not very distracting. If there is something entered, we send a message through postal.js. Finally, we blank out the text input and the placeholder. We have to blank out the placeholder; otherwise, anytime the input was blank, the place holder message would display, and we only want it to show when the user tries to submit a blank message.

The `render` function is pretty straightforward. It returns a div with a form. It also leverages `UserView` to display the current user. The following screenshot is the look of the form rendered:

We are now at our final component. This component will tie all the other chat components together. It is as follows:

```
var ChatView = React.createClass({
  componentWillMount: function(){
    var channel = postal.channel();
    this._boundForceUpdate = this.forceUpdate.bind(this, null);
    this.props.chats.on('add change remove', this._boundForceUpdate,
this);
    this.props.users.on('add change remove', this._boundForceUpdate,
this);
    this.chatSub = channel.subscribe('Chat.Add', this.chatAdd);
  },
  componentWillUnmount: function() {
```

```
      this.props.chats.off("add change remove", this._boundForceUpdate);
      this.props.users.off("add change remove", this._boundForceUpdate);
      this.chatSub.unsubscribe();
    },
  componentDidUpdate: function(){
      var chatList = this.refs.chatList.getDOMNode();
      chatList.scrollTop = chatList.scrollHeight;
    },
  chatAdd: function(data){
      this.props.chats.sync('create', {message: data.message, room:
this.props.room});
    },
  render: function(){
      return React.DOM.div({className: "row"},
        React.DOM.div({className: 'row'},
          React.DOM.div({className: "col-sm-2"}, UserList({collection:
this.props.users, me: this.props.me}) ),
          React.DOM.div({className: "col-sm-8 chat-list", ref:
'chatList'},
            ChatList({chats: this.props.chats, me: this.props.me})
          )
        ),
        ChatForm({me: this.props.me})
      );
    }
});
```

First up is `componentWillMount`. This is similar to `RoomForm`, in that it connects to the postal channel and adds listeners to the Backbone collections passed in. The only difference is that in this component, it subscribes to the `Chat.Add` messages. These are the messages that will be sent from the `ChatForm`.

Next is `componentWillUnmount`. Here, we are just unregistering the collection listeners and unsubscribing from the postal.js subscription.

The `componentDidUpdate` function runs every time the component renders. In this function, we just make sure the div holding the list of chats is always scrolled to the bottom as messages are added.

The `chatAdd` function is executed from the postal subscription to `Chat.Add`. It will tell the chat Backbone collection to add a new message. As we are listening for any add events on this collection, it will re-render this component.

Finally, we are at the `render` function. There is not really much here. We have already built almost all the elements needed in other components. We render `UserList`, `ChatList`, and `ChatForm`, passing in the required properties.

React summary

These components should demonstrate how to build a user interface with React. There is one more idea I would like to highlight before moving on. If you break down the components, you will notice there are two main ones, `RoomForm` and `ChatView`. They are the only two components that listen for changes off of Backbone collections. The Backbone collections are standing in as React's state, as these two components are listening for changes instead of using React's built-in state. When there is a state change, the components pass properties down to the subcomponents. This makes each component reusable and easy to use. For example, `UserView` does not care whether the user is the current user or a user in the room. `ChatList` also does not care whether a message was added or which room it is in. Its only function is to render an array of chats that was passed to it.

Backbone models

We have just built all the views and a few of them referenced models and collections, which is why we will create all the required objects right now. The first thing we need to do is create a file named `models.js` under `static/js/`. This will be the file that holds all the definitions for our models, collections, and router.

Syncing the models with Socket.IO

Backbone models and collections are built to work within a REST framework. Each Backbone model and collection has a sync method that maps the four CRUD operations (Create, Read, Update, and Delete) to a URL that we would pass in. Our application does not use REST to transfer data from the server to client; it uses Socket. IO. There is no built-in adapter, so we must roll our own. We will break down this object into a couple of pieces. The following code is the first piece:

```
var SocketListener = function SocketListener(noun, collection, socket)
{
  var addModels = function addModels(models){
      collection.add(collection.parse(models));
  };
  var removeModels = function removeModels(models){
```

```
        collection.remove(collection.parse(models));
    };

    socket.on('Add' + noun, addModels);
    socket.on('Get' + noun, addModels);
    socket.on('Remove' + noun, removeModels);

    var destroy = function destroy(){
        socket.removeListener('Add' + noun, addModels);
        socket.removeListener('Get' + noun, addModels);
        socket.removeListener('Remove' + noun, removeModels);
    };
    return {destroy: destroy};
};
```

In `SocketListener`, we will need to pass in a noun, a collection, and a socket instance. The noun will be what we want to sync, for example, chat. The function needs a reference to the collection because we are syncing asynchronously. When syncing through a REST API, all the sync operations are request-based. The collection asks for new models and the server responds with new models. This is different from using Socket.IO. We will set up listeners and then use these functions to add or remove models from the collection. Each function is simple. It first parses the model and then the function either adds it or removes it from the collection.

This last step will trigger our views to render. Our components have listeners for any add, change, or remove events on the collection. After these functions run, an event will be emitted that the component will receive.

Next, we will create the listeners. Here, we can see why we have a noun as a parameter. If the noun was Chat, we would now have listeners for `AddChat`, `GetChat`, and `RemoveChat`. These listeners will call our `add` and `remove` functions.

The final function is `destroy`. This function just removes all the listeners from Socket.IO. An object is returned with a reference to the `destroy` function, so it can be called.

`SocketListener` listens for Socket.IO events, but what will trigger the events? This responsibility comes down to `SocketSync`. `SocketSync` will be used in place of Backbone's default sync method. The following code is SocketSync:

```
var SocketSync = function SocketSync(method, model, options){
    var socket = Backbone.socket;

    var create = function create(model, options, noun){
```

```
      socket.emit('Add' + noun, model);
   };

   var read = function read(model, options, noun){
      socket.emit('Get' + noun, options);
   };

   switch(method){
      case 'create':
         create(model, options, this.noun);
         break;
      case 'read':
         read(model, options, this.noun);
         break;
   }
};
```

The function definition for Backbone sync takes `method`, `model`, and `options`, which are the methods that will be used to map directly to CRUD. As none of our collections will update or delete, we only have to implement `create` and `read`. The `create` and `read` functions are very simple. They emit Socket.IO events. Using the example of Chat, `GetChat` will be sent to the server. The server will respond with an array of chat messages and `SocketListener` will listen for the response and add all the chats to the collection.

There are two extensions of Backbone in this function. The first is `Backbone.socket`. This is not set by default. We will have to create this property and set it to our Socket.IO connection. The other is the noun property of the collection. Again, this is not built into Backbone. We will manually have to add this.

Creating the model

We can now define our models, or in this case, model. We are not using a lot of different models, as plain JavaScript objects will work for rooms. Let's create the `User` model, as shown in the following code:

```
var User = Backbone.Model.extend({
   image: function(size){
      switch(this.get('type')){
         case 'local':
            return this.gravatar(size);
            break;
         case 'facebook':
```

```
        return this.facebook(size);
        break;
      case 'google':
        return this.gravatar(size);
        break;
    }
  },
  gravatar: function gravatar(size){
    return 'http://www.gravatar.com/avatar/' + md5(this.get('id')) +
'?d=retro&s=' + size;
  },
  facebook: function facebook(size){
    return 'http://graph.facebook.com/' + this.get('id') + '/
picture/?height=' + size;
  }
});
```

The `User` model needs to return a URL of an image from the `image` function.
We do a check to see what type of user they are. If it is Facebook, return Facebook's
photo, and if it is anything else, use Gravatar. This function is what the `UserView`
component used to create an `img` element.

We can now move on to creating the collections. This is where most of our Backbone
interactions will be.

 This code requires the MD5 library from `http://www.myersdaily.`
`org/joseph/javascript/md5-text.html`. You can also use the
Bower package, Cryptojs.

Creating collections

We are not going to add a lot extra functionality to our collections. We want to
extend Backbone Collection so that we get all the Backbone syncing and event
triggering. Let's create the first two collections:

```
var UserCollection = Backbone.Collection.extend({model: User});
var RoomsCollection = Backbone.Collection.extend();
```

The model option passed in when defining a collection will make sure that plain
objects passed in will be converted to this type.

`RoomsCollection` does not need this because the `room` objects are very simple. All we need from a room is its name.

There is one more collection we must define, `ChatCollection`. The following code is that collection:

```
var ChatCollection = Backbone.Collection.extend({
  parse: function(data){
    if (Array.isArray(data)){
      return _.map(data, function(d){
        d.user = new User(d.user);
        return d;
      });
    }else {
      data.user = new User(data.user);
      return data;
    } }
});
```

The `ChatCollection`, which is a Backbone Collection object, has something our other models did not have, a nested model. The `user` property returned from the server is a basic JavaScript object and we want it to be a `User` model. Adding an object to a collection will implicitly turn it into a Backbone model, but the collection cannot know how every property will map to the model definition. To do this, we use a `parse` method.

The `parse` method will first check whether the object coming in is an array. This happens when we initially enter a room. The server will send back an array of all the messages for that room. If so, we use the map underscore method to return an array of objects where the user property is a `User` model. Then, if the object is not an array, we just change the user property and return that.

This is all the Backbone models we are going to define. We have only created one model and three collections. We do not need very complex models on the frontend because we really only want the collections for the add/change events that they fire off. Most of the logic we needed was connecting Backbone to Socket.IO. What should happen is that `SocketListener` will listen for any events from the server, parse the response, add it to the collection, and the collection will emit an event that the component is listening for.

The Backbone router

Backbone has one more feature we will use. This is routing. A Backbone router will listen for hash changes in the URL and this will trigger events. The router can be configured to match certain patterns and even pull out parameters. Let's create the router, as shown in the following code:

```
var Router = Backbone.Router.extend({
  routes: {
    '': 'RoomSelection',
    'room/:room' : 'JoinRoom',
    '*default' : 'Default'
  }
});
```

Routers are built the same way as other Backbone objects; we extend the base router. The `Router` object really only needs a `routes` object that has patterns as the properties and the event name as the value. Routers allow the back button and deep linking to work in a single-page JavaScript application, just like the chat page we are building. For example, we could send out a link that was `/chat#room/test` and the application would start at the `JoinRoom` function instead of `RoomSelection`.

In this router, we only need two routes along with a catch-all. The first route will match when there is either no hash in the URL or a just the hash (`/chat#`). The next route will match `room/` and pass in whatever is after that as a parameter. Finally, the default route will match any and everything. Routes are processed in order, so this will catch all other routes.

Putting it all together

We have to create another file to initialize all our collections and render our views. Create `chat.js` along with the other JavaScript files present at `static/js/`. This will hold all the code we are going to cover next. The following code is the start of the file:

```
var PacktChat = window.PacktChat || {};
PacktChat.Chat = function(el){
  var $root = $('#' + el),
  socket = io.connect("http://localhost:3000/packtchat"),
  me = null,
  connected = false;
  //to be initialized
  var router,
```

```
    roomsCollection,
    userCollection,
    chatCollection;

  var GetMe = function GetMe(user){
    me = new User(user);
    Backbone.history.stop();
    startChat(me);
    Backbone.history.start();
    connected = true;
  };

  socket.on('connect', function(){
    if (!connected) socket.emit('GetMe');
  });
  socket.on('GetMe', GetMe);
```

The first thing we are going to do is create a namespace we can use called PacktChat. We get a reference to this by checking whether it is already defined on the window or creating a new object. We are only going to add one property, but if we had multiple things to add, we could use this statement before each one. The next step is to create our function, which will set everything up for our chat page.

Inside the function, we start setting up variables we will need. The first is the root element we will render from. It needs an element's ID that will be passed into PacktChat.Chat(). We connect to Socket.IO and create some variables for later.

The next function defined is GetMe. This will run from the 'GetMe' Socket.IO event. First, it will set me to a User model. Then, it will stop the Backbone history, which is used with tracking hash changes and the router. This will make sure a route is not executed before the data is loaded. Next, it will run startChat. Restarting Backbone's history is next followed by setting connected to true. This function is just making sure we have a reference to the current user (me) before we start the chat up.

Next is Socket.IO. This just registers the listeners needed.

We can now create the main function that will initialize everything, startChat. The following code is the first part of the function:

```
  var startChat = function startThis(){
    router = new Router();

    Backbone.socket = socket;
    Backbone.sync = SocketSync;
```

```
roomsCollection = new RoomsCollection();
roomsCollection.noun = 'Room';
userCollection = new UserCollection();
userCollection.noun = 'User';
chatCollection = new ChatCollection();
chatCollection.noun = 'Chat';

var roomsSync = new SocketListener('Room', roomsCollection,
socket);
var userSync = new SocketListener('User', userCollection, socket);
var chatSync = new SocketListener('Chat', chatCollection, socket);

roomsCollection.fetch();

var channel = postal.channel();
var roomJoin = channel.subscribe('Room.Join', roomFormEvent);
```

This section sets up all the collections and objects we will need to function. First, we create `Router`, which we just defined. Next, we prepare Backbone by adding our socket reference and sync function. Then, we create each collection we will need, along with setting the noun for each. Then, we create `SocketListener` for each collection and noun. Next, we run fetch off the room collection because we will most likely be rendering this view first. Fetch will use our sync function and the read method. This will create a Socket.IO event of `'GetRoom'`. Finally, we set up a postal channel to listen for the `'Room.Join'` event.

This brings us to the functions we need to define. The following are the four functions we need to add:

```
function roomFormEvent(message){
    roomsCollection.add({name: message.roomName, id: message.
roomName});
    router.navigate('room/' + message.roomName, {trigger: true});
    };

function RoomSelection(){
    roomsCollection.sync('create', {name: 'lobby', id: 'lobby'});
    React.unmountComponentAtNode($root[0]);
    React.renderComponent(RoomForm({rooms: roomsCollection}),
$root[0]);
    }

function JoinRoom(room){
    userCollection.reset();
    chatCollection.reset();
```

```
        roomsCollection.sync('create', {name: room, id: room});
        chatCollection.fetch({room: room});
        userCollection.fetch({room: room});
        React.unmountComponentAtNode($root[0]);
        React.renderComponent(ChatView({users: userCollection, chats:
    chatCollection, room: room, me: me}), $root[0]);
      };

      function DefaultRoute(){
        router.navigate('', {trigger: true});
      };
```

The first function, `roomFormEvent`, is wired up to the `'Room.Join'` postal event. This will take the room name passed and add it to `roomsCollection`. Then, it will use the router to fire off the function that is defined with joining a room, by using the navigate function and `{trigger: true}`. If the trigger was not sent with the method, the router would not execute the function for the route.

Next is `RoomSelection`. This function puts the user in the room named `lobby` (or creates it the room if it doesn't exist). Then, it will unmount any component rendered at the root element and render `RoomForm` there.

`JoinRoom` is very similar to this. First, we let the rooms collection know we have entered the room. The `create` command will fire off a Socket.IO event, telling the server to update the rooms sorted set and add the current user to that room. The next thing the function does is reset `chatCollection` and `userCollection`. Reset will remove all the current models in the collection. We need to do this, as each room will have different chat messages and users in them. After resetting each collection, we then fetch the messages and users for the room we just entered. Finally, we unmount the component at the root and render `ChatView` there.

The last function, `DefaultRoute`, will collect any other hash that does not match the others and send the route to room selection.

The following is that last bit of code for our `PacktChat.Chat` function:

```
    router.on('route:RoomSelection', RoomSelection);
      router.on('route:JoinRoom', JoinRoom);
      router.on('route:Default', DefaultRoute);
    };
  };

  var pc = new PacktChat.Chat('react-root');
```

We need to listen for each router event. The event will be prepended with `'route:'`.

Finally, we create a new object, `PacktChat.Chat`, passing in the name of the ID to render all the components from it. This will initialize all the other objects and listeners for us.

We now have built all our frontend JavaScript. We could have modularized this code more, but doing so would have been outside of the size and scope of this book. Another reason is that we only have one page that uses JavaScript, so it could have been considered overkill. If we were to modularize the code, we would break out each component, model/collection, and page integration object (`PacktChat.Chat`) into their own files. This would allow us to load only what we needed for each page and not have to copy and paste code.

At this point, though, our site is not ready. We have just a few other changes to be made to a couple files.

Updating CSS and the layout

We need to add two CSS rules to `style.css`, present in `static/css/`. Append the following to the file:

```
.chat-message {padding: 5px; margin: 5px 0;}
.chat-list {max-height: 500px; overflow: auto;}
```

These just make the chat page look better.

We will now need to add our `bower_components` directory to be served in Express. Open up `app.js` and add the following line after the current static line:

```
app.use(express.static(__dirname + '/static'));
app.use(express.static(__dirname + '/bower_components'));
```

When there are multiple references to static, Express will go through each directory in order to find the file.

Next, we need to add all our new JavaScript files to the layout and chat page. First, open `layout.ejs`, present in the `views/` folder, and make sure the following list of JavaScript files is in the head:

```
<script type="text/javascript" src="//cdnjs.cloudflare.com/ajax/libs/
socket.io/0.9.16/socket.io.min.js"></script>
<script type="text/javascript" src="/jquery/dist/jquery.js"></script>
<script type="text/javascript" src="/underscore/underscore.js"></
script>
<script type="text/javascript" src="/backbone/backbone.js"></script>
<script type="text/javascript" src="/react/react.js"></script>
```

```
<script type="text/javascript" src="/postal.js/lib/postal.js"></
script>
<script type="text/javascript" src="/momentjs/moment.js"></script>
<script type="text/javascript" src="/js/md5.js"></script>
```

This loads all our required libraries. We load them in the head because we will need them loaded before loading any application page-specific scripts.

Open up `chat.ejs` from the `views/` folder and make sure it looks like this in its entirety:

```
<div id='react-root'></div>
<script type="text/javascript" src="/js/models.js"></script>
<script type="text/javascript" src="/js/components.js"></script>
<script type="text/javascript" src="/js/chat.js"></script>
```

Here, we just load everything we need to run our chat page.

 Based on the scope of this book, some things have been simplified. Here, we have simplified loading the required libraries by putting them into the head and loading the application files by loading them on the page.

Adding a new worker

We have one small problem at this point. As time goes on, more and more rooms will be created and more messages will accumulate. Eventually, we will run Redis out of memory. We are not being good Redis citizens. We need to remove our Redis data and will do this with a new worker.

Create a file named `chat.js` under the `workers` directory. Start the function with the following code:

```
var client = require('../redis').client,
  log = require('../middleware/log');

var delta = 60 * 60 * 1000 * 3; //10800000
var interval = 60 * 60 * 1000 * 2; //7200000
```

We include our Redis client and logger. Then, we set up our delta and interval. We will remove any room, chat, or user that has been inactive or was created 3 hours ago (10,800,000 milliseconds ago). We will do this check every 2 hours (7,200,000 milliseconds). If we wanted, we could even make these values part of the config, so it could be configurable on each launch. Now, let's create the room check, as shown in the following code:

```
function RemoveRooms(){
  log.debug({message: 'Removing Rooms', ts: Date.now()});
  client.zrangebyscore('rooms', '-inf', ((new Date).getTime() -
delta), function(err, rooms){
    if (err !== null) log.error({message: 'Error in Remove Rooms',
err: err, ts: Date.now()});
    else {
      rooms.forEach(function (room) {
client.multi()
        .zrem('rooms', room)
        .del('rooms:' + room + ':chats')
        .exec();        });
}});
};
```

The first thing the function does is log a message. This is important as it runs in the background and we will never know whether it is working or not. Next, we run zrangebyscore, which will return only the elements that are between our values. We then loop over these values and remove the element from the rooms sorted set and the rooms:roomname:chats sorted set. At this point, the room does not exist as far as our application is concerned. Also, it will log any errors from the Redis command. We can run this like it is synchronous because we are not returning anything. The loop will eventually run our code. Next up is cleaning up the chat messages, as shown in the following code:

```
function CleanUpChatsFromRoom(){
  log.debug({message: 'Cleaning Up Chats', ts: Date.now()});
  client.zrange('rooms', 0, -1, function(err, rooms){
    rooms.forEach(function(room){
      client.zremrangebyscore('rooms:' + room + ':chats', '-inf',
((new Date).getTime() - delta));
    });
  });
};
```

We first get a list of all the rooms. We then check each room's chat sorted set for any messages over 3 hours and remove the chat. This function does not have the error check and logging in it for space reasons, but it can be added easily. The following is a user check:

```
function CleanUpUsers(){
   log.debug({message: 'Cleaning Up Users', ts: Date.now()});
   client.zrangebyscore('users', '-inf', ((new Date).getTime() -
delta), function(err, users){
     users.forEach(function(user){
       client.multi()
       .zrem('users', user)
       .del('user:' + user)
       .del('user:' + user + ':room')
       .exec();      });
   });
};
```

The `CleanUpUsers` function will delete any user that has been inactive for 3 hours. It will step through each user and remove them from the users sorted set and delete hash and user room keys. This will delete all the user's keys.

The following code shows how the `CleanUp` function will be executed every two hours by `setInterval`:

```
function CleanUp() {
   RemoveRooms();
   CleanUpChatsFromRoom();
   CleanUpUsers();
};

setInterval(CleanUp, interval);
CleanUp();
```

The `CleanUp` function kicks off all the other functions. We set it to run in `setInterval`, executing every 2 hours. The last thing we do is run it immediately, so the first run is not 2 hours from now.

Trying out our application

We should now be able to use our application. Load it up and browse to
`http://localhost:3000`. Log in to the site, and we should be redirected to
the chat page. We should see our room form component. We can add a room
here or we can load it up in another tab or browser and create a room there,
seeing it appear on the other window in real time.

We can then join one of the rooms in both windows and chat with ourselves.
Each chat message should appear in real time.

Summary

We have used React and Backbone to create a user interface. All our React
components are reusable and easily extended. For example, we can easily
implement a profile page that will display more information about a user
when you click on their name. A few lines in `UserView` and a route in the
`Router` and we are literally almost done.

Backbone models were hacked up a little to get them to work with Socket.IO.
There are libraries to do this, but I wanted to walk through what had to be
done. We are not using the full capacity of Backbone models, so this could
be something that can be improved with more time.

We have pushed a lot of code. At this point in our journey, we will have built
an entire working Node.js application from the ground up. We have taken a
few detours to investigate different features of libraries. Some other things have
been passed over for brevity (full logging and testing come quickly to mind).

In the next chapter, we will look at some best practices that will make our
application a little bit more production-ready.

8
JavaScript Best Practices for Application Development

Some readers may be getting nervous at this point in the book. I don't blame them. This is because there are still some very large, glaring issues with our code base. The question, "Will our application work anywhere but in localhost?" should encapsulate many of the issues. The answer is no. This is a problem, and this chapter is the solution. We are going to cover how to build a reproducible and scriptable build system that runs in one step. All the adjectives in the last sentence are important. We have to be able to run one command which will do exactly what we need to build our application. If we start introducing manual build steps, we risk introducing bugs into building and deploying. This will waste time and stress us out. Here is what we will cover in this chapter:

- Setting up tests
- Extracting the differences between environments
- Setting up Grunt
- Preprocessing our code
- Linting our code
- Concatenating and minifying our code
- Static files and CDNs

Node package versions

We have some new packages to install. All the packages are related to Grunt, which is a JavaScript automated task runner that is based on Node.js. We will define tasks and Grunt will carry them out. We will use the following versions:

- `grunt-cli`: 0.1.13
- `grunt-contrib-clean`: 0.5.0
- `grunt-contrib-concat`: 0.4.0
- `grunt-contrib-jshint`: 0.8.0
- `grunt-contrib-uglify`: 0.4.0
- `grunt-preprocess`: 4.0.0
- `grunt-contrib-nodeunit`: 0.4.0
- `istanbul`: 0.3.0
- `nodeunit`: 0.9.0

Add these dependencies to `package.json`. This time we will create a new property named `devDependencies`. It is an object just like dependencies that is meant for development or testing. In `package.json`, `devDependencies` should look as follows:

```
"devDependencies": {
    "grunt-cli": "0.1.13",
    "grunt-contrib-clean": "0.5.0",
    "grunt-contrib-concat": "0.4.0",
    "grunt-contrib-jshint": "0.8.0",
    "grunt-contrib-nodeunit": "0.4.0",
    "grunt-contrib-uglify": "0.4.0",
    "grunt-preprocess": "4.0.0",
    "istanbul": "0.3.0",
    "nodeunit": "0.9.0"
},
```

We can then run `npm install` to install all our packages.

Setting up tests

So far, we have not done any testing. This is bad and not a best practice. We will rectify this here. We will only build a few tests, but it will demonstrate how to create tests. Create a directory named `tests` and create the `routes.js` file.

Open the file and paste the following code:

```
var routes = require('../routes'),
  config = require('../config'),
  nodeunit = require('nodeunit'),
  Request = require('./request'),
  Response = require('./response');

exports.indexRouteTest = function(test){
  var res = new Response();
  test.equal(res.view, undefined);
  routes.index({}, res);
  test.equal(res.view, 'index');
  test.equal(res.viewData.title, 'Index');
  test.done();
};
```

Here, we are testing the index route. It should call render on the response object passing in index as the view and an object that has `title` set to `Index`. To test this, we are not going to set up an entire Node.js and Express stack. We are just going to mock up what we need. We need a response object, so we create one with a fake render function that will store what was passed into it. We will need to create the response object now before we run the test. Create a file named `response.js` under the `tests` directory and add the following code:

```
module.exports = function Response(){
  return {
    url: '',
    locals: {},
    redirect: function(redirectUrl){this.url = redirectUrl;},
    render: function(view, viewData){
      this.view = view;
      this.viewData = viewData;
    },
    redirect: function(url){this.url = url;}
  }
};
```

This is just a function that returns an object that has mocked up all the properties and functions our tests are expecting. In order to mock up an object, we look at the code, see what is going to be executed, and then create an object that has those functions. In addition to this, we need a way to test whether the function was executed correctly.

In our example of `render`, we create properties of `view` and `viewData` that we can then check to see whether the correct string and object were passed. We will use this object in any test that needs a request. We will now create a file named `request.js` in the same directory and add the following code:

```
module.exports = function Request(){
  return {
    logoutCalled: false,
    flashCalled: false,
    body: {},
    session: {isAuthenticated: false,passport: {}},
    logout: function(){this.logoutCalled = true},
    flash: function(f, m){
      this.flashName = f;
      this.flashMessage = m;
      this.flashCalled = true;
      return f;
    },
    csrfToken: function(){return 'csrf';}
  };
}
```

This is mocked up in a similar fashion to respond. We need something to be executed and a way of telling when that something was executed.

The actual test is an exported function that has a test object passed in. We run our asserts on the test object and when completed, `test.done()`. Here, we call the index route with a blank object as the request and our response object. We then check what it was called with. We can see whether this passes by running it from the command line:

`$node_modules/.bin/nodeunit ./tests/routes.js`

If `nodeunit` is installed locally, we can call it from the local `bin` folder. This should output the next screenshot:

Next, create a file named `tests/middleware.js`. Add the following code to it:

```
var util = require('../middleware/utilities'),
    config = require('../config'),
    nodeunit = require('nodeunit'),
    Request = require('./request'),
    Response = require('./response');

exports.requireAuthTest = nodeunit.testCase({
    setUp: function(cb){
        this.req = new Request();
        this.res = new Response();
        this.nextExecuted = false;
        this.next = function(){this.nextExecuted = true}.bind(this);
        cb();
    },
    'Not Authenticated': function(test){
        this.req.session.isAuthenticated = false;
        util.requireAuthentication(this.req, this.res, this.next);
        test.equal(this.res.url, config.routes.login);
        test.equal(this.nextExecuted, false);
        test.done();
    },
    'Authenticated': function(test){
        this.req.session.isAuthenticated = true;
        test.equal(this.nextExecuted, false);
        util.requireAuthentication(this.req, this.res, this.next);
        test.equal(this.res.url, '');
        test.equal(this.nextExecuted, true);
        test.done();
    }
});
```

This one is a little more complex. We need to define both the request and response for the next tests. We then use `nodeunit.testCase` to build a group of tests. This group of tests will test the `requireAuthentication` middleware. Before each test is run, the `setUp` function executes, which will create the objects we need for each test. This is done before each new test.

The first test simulates someone that is not logged in. It makes sure `this.res.redirect` is executed with the `config` login URL. Then, it checks to make sure `next()` has not been executed. The other test does the opposite. It checks the redirect URL and whether `next()` has been executed. This test can be executed with the following command:

```
$node_modules/.bin/nodeunit ./tests/middleware.js
```

We should have tests for every function we create. This will include all our middleware, routes, Redis, passport auth functions, and so on. We need not test Express' static middleware. If we are only executing a libraries function, then we do not need to test, but if we add to them, a great example being Passport, we will need to test them. Most of the time, we will avoid creating an entire Node.js server to test one function. This is where JavaScript's dynamic nature is useful. We can just mock up any object and property that we know the function will need. This leads to a great question, "How do we know we have tested everything?"

 In the code that accompanies this book, I have added more tests. It would be very tedious to list out all the different tests here.

Using Istanbul for code coverage

Code coverage is a tool that allows developers to know how much of their code is tested. It will watch and track each line that is executed. It will then report a percentage of total lines that were executed during the tests.

Istanbul should already be installed. We tell Istanbul to run our tests through `nodeunit` and it will do the rest. If our tests are all in the `tests` folder, we will run the following command:

```
./node_modules/.bin/istanbul cover node_modules/nodeunit/bin/nodeunit --
tests/
```

This will start the tests exactly like running `nodeunit` by itself. The only difference is that we get a little summary of the coverage at the end. This is shown in the next screenshot:

```
============================= Coverage summary =============================
Statements   : 67.5% ( 54/80 )
Branches     : 28.57% ( 4/14 )
Functions    : 43.48% ( 10/23 )
Lines        : 67.5% ( 54/80 )
============================================================================
```

The preceding screenshot displays a useful breakdown of how much of the code is tested. There is one caveat here, though; it is only for the files that have been tested. Some code coverage tools will look at an entire directory and include everything, but Istanbul is only using a few files. Another way to fix this is to create a test for everything!

In addition to a summary, Istanbul creates a coverage directory that includes an HTML page with the breakdown of what lines have been tested. In the root of the project, navigate to `coverage/lcov-report/index.html`. Open this in any browser and we should see a page similar to the next screenshot:

Code coverage report for **All files**

Statements: **67.5%** (54 / 80)   Branches: **28.57%** (4 / 14)   Functions: **43.48%** (10 / 23)   Lines: **67.5%** (54 / 80)   Ignored: none

File ▲		Statements		Branches		Functions		Lines	
grunt_stuff/		100.00%	(2 / 2)	100.00%	(0 / 0)	100.00%	(0 / 0)	100.00%	(2 / 2)
grunt_stuff/middleware/		100.00%	(20 / 20)	100.00%	(4 / 4)	100.00%	(5 / 5)	100.00%	(20 / 20)
grunt_stuff/passport/		43.33%	(13 / 30)	0.00%	(0 / 4)	0.00%	(0 / 10)	43.33%	(13 / 30)
grunt_stuff/routes/		67.86%	(19 / 28)	0.00%	(0 / 6)	62.50%	(5 / 8)	67.86%	(19 / 28)

Generated by istanbul at Sun Aug 10 2014 16:28:28 GMT-0400 (EDT)

We can click on each folder, which will then list out the files that have been tested. Each file has detailed information about which line has been executed and how many times. This is shown in the next screenshot:

```
20  1  function register(req, res){
21  1    res.render('register', {title: 'Register', message: req.flash('error')}});
22     };
23
24  1  function registerProcess(req, res){
25       if (req.body.username && req.body.password)
26       {
27         user.addUser(req.body.username, req.body.password, config.crypto.workFactor, function(err, profile){
28           if (err) {
29             req.flash('error', err);
30             res.redirect(config.routes.register);
31           }else{
32             req.login(profile, function(err){
33               res.redirect(config.routes.chat);
34             });
35           }
36         });
37       }else{
38         req.flash('error', 'Please fill out all the fields');
39         res.redirect(config.routes.register);
40       }
41     };
42
```

Green means executed, red is not executed, and yellow is a function that has not been tested. Once we are using code coverage, identifying our next test becomes easy. We find a file, require it in a test, look at all the lines highlighted in red in the file, and slowly create tests until all the red highlights are gone.

Nodeunit is great for testing Node.js. We also want to test frontend code, as well. Qunit (`http://qunitjs.com/`) is a great choice.

Setting up different environments

We will continue with our opening problem. Our application is only accessible from one computer—our own. To fix this, we need to find all the differences that would exist between environments and abstract them out. We need this process to be automated. We cannot go through and find all references to localhost and change them out every time we want to deploy. We will follow the advice given by Twelve Factor App (`http://12factor.net/`).

Twelve Factor App

Twelve Factor App was written by the people behind Heroku (`https://www.heroku.com/`). Heroku is a **Platform as a Service** (**Paas**), which means they can easily host and scale out application with very little modification to code. This ability is exactly what we want for this application. Twelve Factor App contains many best practices learned by the people at Heroku the hard way, through experience.

The main best practice we want from here is configuration. Configurations will be very different between environments. For example, in development, Redis, RabbitMQ, and Socket.io all connect through localhost. In production, these services will be on at least two servers, if not three. We want to collect every config setting that will change and store them in environment variables. This is recommended in Twelve Factor App.

Storing config settings in the environment allows us to easily have many different deploys. The most important part of this is that the code base will be exactly the same between each deploy. We will not have to manually change files between them.

Fixing the config file

The first place we can easily identify settings is the `config` file. Open up `config.js` and modify the file to look like this:

```
var config = {
  port: process.env.PORT,
  secret: process.env.SECRET,
  redisPort: process.env.REDIS_PORT,
  redisHost: process.env.REDIS_HOST,
  routes: {
    login: '/account/login',
    logout: '/account/logout',
    register: '/account/register',
      chat: '/chat',
```

```
        facebookAuth: '/auth/facebook',
        facebookAuthCallback: '/auth/facebook/callback',
        googleAuth: '/auth/google',
        googleAuthCallback: '/auth/google/callback'
    },
    host: process.env.HOST,
    facebook: {
      appID: process.env.FACEBOOK_APPID,
      appSecret: process.env.FACEBOOK_APPSECRET
    },
    google: {
      clientID: process.env.GOOGLE_APPID,
      clientSecret: process.env.GOOGLE_APPSECRET
    },
    crypto: {
      workFactor: 5000,
      keylen: 32,
      randomSize: 256
    },
    rabbitMQ: {
      URL: process.env.RABBITMQ_URL,
      exchange: process.env.RABBITMQ_EXCHANGE
    }
  };

  module.exports = config;
```

A lot of properties changed, but only in one way. We have added `process.env.`
`VARIABLE_NAME` for each setting we are going to set in the environment. Before we
start the server up again, we will need to set all the environment variables.

Creating our environment files

We will create two files for each environment we want to support. The first will be
public variables. The other will have more sensitive information. Our Facebook app
ID is a great example of this. We split these up so we do not have to check sensitive
information into our version control system.

 The next part will only work on Linux and Mac OS X.
The same basic things will need to happen in Windows,
but they will not be detailed here.

Let's create our first environment file in the root of our project. We will name it
dev.env. Here is the file:

```
export NODE_ENV=development
export SECRET=secret
export PORT=3000
export HOST='http://localhost:3000'
export SOCKETIO_URL='http://localhost:3000/packtchat'
export GIT_HEAD=`git rev-parse HEAD`
export STATIC_URL='http://localhost:3000'
export AWS_BUCKET='packtchat'
```

We are exporting the variables so they will be available to the next shell we spawn, if
needed. It is important to know there can be no spaces between the variable name and
the equals sign, and the value or the environment variable will not be set correctly.

There is one variable that is set differently; GIT_HEAD. GIT_HEAD is set to the output
of the git rev-parse HEAD command.

The reason these settings were chosen to go into this file is that each one will not
cause app keys or passwords to be changed if they were to get out. A good test to
see where an environment variable should be set is if we can open source our code
in our repository without having to redact it. There is nothing in this file that
requires redaction. Let's create the other environment file, dev_secret.env,
as shown in the following code:

```
export SECRET=secret
export REDIS_HOST=localhost
export REDIS_PORT=6379
export RABBITMQ_URL='amqp://guest:guest@localhost:5672'
export RABBITMQ_EXCHANGE='packtchat.log'
export FACEBOOK_APPID='APP_ID'
export FACEBOOK_APPSECRET='APP_SECRET'
export GOOGLE_APPID='APP_ID'
export GOOGLE_APPSECRET='APP_SECRET'
export AWS_ACCESS_KEY_ID='AWS_KEY' #to be set
export AWS_SECRET_ACCESS_KEY='AWS_SECRET_KEY' #to be set
```

We set these the same way. All these keys would force us to reset app keys and
change passwords, so they are in this file. This file should never be checked into
git or any other version control system. This does pose a problem with how other
programmers get this file, and is best answered case by case. Some organizations
will have a shared drive where it resides. Then, add a document that will point a
new programmer where to look.

Open a terminal and go to our project's directory. Type in the following command:

```
$source dev.env
$source dev_secret.env
```

Source just reads through the file like it was typed into the terminal and adds the variables to our environment. Then, we can start our server configured. At this point, anytime we run a server locally we will need to add these variables to our environment before launching our application. If not, it will not be fully configured.

Adding more environments

We can easily add more environments because the config file loads from the environment. We just change the environment and the server is configured differently. This is easy because each environment should be separate. We won't be running development and production on the same server (except when testing here). Let's create the prod environment files. Name the dev.env and dev_secret.env copies prod.env and prod_secret.env, respectively. Right now, keep them the same except for the first line of prod.env. Change this line to the following:

```
export NODE_ENV=production
```

Once we have our production URL, Redis, RabbitMQ, Facebook App, Google App, and Amazon Web Service keys, we can update the environment files.

Introducing Grunt

Our environment is set up; let's do something with it. We need something that will automatically run tasks. This is where Grunt comes in. We can give it a list of tasks that Grunt will execute. The first thing we need to do is create a Gruntfile.js file.

Building a basic Grunt file

Gruntfile.js configures Grunt. It tells Grunt what tasks to carry out, how to run each task, and in what order. We can now create a basic Gruntfile.js file in the root of the project. Add the following code snippet to the file:

```
module.exports = function(grunt) {
  grunt.initConfig({
    pkg: grunt.file.readJSON('package.json')
  });
```

```
grunt.loadNpmTasks('grunt-contrib-uglify');
grunt.loadNpmTasks('grunt-contrib-concat');
grunt.loadNpmTasks('grunt-contrib-jshint');
grunt.loadNpmTasks('grunt-preprocess');
grunt.loadNpmTasks('grunt-contrib-clean');
grunt.loadNpmTasks('grunt-contrib-nodeunit');

// Default task(s).
grunt.registerTask('default', []);
grunt.registerTask('prep', []);};
```

Grunt runs on Node.js, so it uses the same module system. We will configure the `grunt` object that is passed into this file with `grunt.initConfig`. This object will have all our tasks defined as properties on it. For now, we are just loading `package.json`, which has information we can use in other tasks, such as the name of the project, version, and author. Next, we load all the other Grunt packages we installed. This allows us to use each in a task. Finally, we create task lists. Each one is empty, but this is where we can define what tasks will run in what order. The default task will run when Grunt is called with no arguments. The other task can be run when called with the name as the argument, like Grunt prep, for example.

Automating our tests

We have just created some tests and Grunt can automate them. Add this code to `grunt.initConfig` right after the `pkg` property:

```
pkg: grunt.file.readJSON('package.json'),
nodeunit: {
    all: ['tests/*.js']
}
```

Do not forget this is a new property in an object, so the previous property will need a comma after it. We can probably guess what this does. It tests all the JavaScript files in the directory `tests`. Next, we need to tell Grunt when to run this task:

```
grunt.registerTask('default', ['nodeunit']);
grunt.registerTask('prep', ['nodeunit']);
```

We want to run this anytime Grunt runs. A failed test will stop Grunt from running any other tasks. We can test this if we add this line to any of the test functions:

```
test.equal(true, false);
```

This will fail and Grunt will immediately halt processing. This is exactly what we want.

Preprocessing our files

A glaring issue we need to change is the hardcoded `Socket.io` URL in `chat.js`. It is pointed to localhost, which will not work for production. We do not want to go down the road of manually changing this back and forth between development and production. We will use `grunt-preprocess`, which will parse certain files and add, remove, or change things inside each. This is exactly what we need to change the Socket.io URL to match the environment. We will also use it to load different versions of our JavaScript files.

The first thing we are going to need to do is move all our JavaScript files. We need to do this because we are going to build the files and another task will move them back to the static folder. Create a `js_src` directory with a `src` directory under that in the root of the project. Next, copy `chat.js`, `components.js`, `md5.js`, and `models.js` to `js_src/src`. Then, rename `chat.js` to `chat.pre.js`. Open up `chat.pre.js` and modify it to look like this:

```
socket = io.connect('/* @echo SOCKETIO_URL */'),
```

Preprocess will run through the files we give it and look for certain keywords. `@echo` is one. By default, preprocess will use environment variables as its context, which is great because we have already defined `SOCKETIO_URL` in the environment. Preprocess will replace this statement with what is defined in the variable.

The next file we are going to process is the layout. Rename `views/layout.ejs` to `views/layout.pre`. Change these lines in the head element:

```
<!-- @if NODE_ENV='production' -->
    <script type="text/javascript" src="<!--@echo STATIC_URL -->/js/
Frameworks.<!-- @echo GIT_HEAD -->.min.js"></script>
    <!-- @endif -->

    <!-- @if NODE_ENV!='production' -->
    <script type="text/javascript" src="<!--@echo STATIC_URL -->/js/
Frameworks.js"></script>
    <!-- @endif -->
```

Preprocess will also execute the `if` loop. Here, we check whether we are in production or not and change what JavaScript file is included. In production, we will use a minified file (which we have yet to create) and use a nonminified version anywhere else. This is helpful because in development, we want useful line numbers if something throws an error. It will also let us set breakpoints in the code. Also, add this right before the closing body tag:

```
<div class="container">
<small>Commit: <!-- @echo GIT_HEAD --></small>
</div>
</body>
```

At the bottom of every page, we should see our git commit that the server is using. It will be prominent on our pages because there is not much on them to begin with. We can hide it or set it in a JavaScript variable to capture during logging errors.

Next, rename `views/chat.ejs` to `views/chat.pre`. Change the file to the following:

```
<div id='react-root'></div>
<!-- @if NODE_ENV='production' -->
<script type="text/javascript" src="<!--@echo STATIC_URL -->/js/
ChatPage.<!-- @echo GIT_HEAD -->.min.js"></script>
<!-- @endif -->

<!-- @if NODE_ENV!='production' -->
<script type="text/javascript" src="<!--@echo STATIC_URL -->/js/
ChatPage.js"></script>
<!-- @endif -->
```

This does the exact same thing as the layout was doing.

We can now create the Grunt task to process these files. Open up `Gruntfile.js` and add this code as a property of `initConfig` right after `nodeunit`; do not forget to add a comma after the `nodeunit` property:

```
preprocess: {
      dist: {
        files: {
          'views/chat.ejs' : 'views/chat.pre',
          'views/layout.ejs' : 'views/layout.pre',
          'js_src/src/chat.js' : 'js_src/src/chat.pre.js'
        }
      }
    }
```

Preprocess is the task that including Grunt-preprocess gives us. We configure the `dist` target to use the files listed. The value of each property is the source and the property name is where preprocess will create the processed file at. We can see it will put each renamed file back where it should be. We can now tell Grunt to run this task.

Add preprocess to each array for each task:

```
grunt.registerTask('default', ['nodeunit', 'preprocess']);
grunt.registerTask('prep', ['nodeunit', 'preprocess']);
```

We can test this by running Grunt from the terminal. Remember to source our environment files if it is a new terminal. We should see a new `layout.ejs`, `chat.ejs`, and `chat.js`.

Using Grunt to clean out a folder

We have a `clean static/js` folder right now. We will need this each time we build our JavaScript. Grunt is going to add the git commit in the filename of the minified file and we do not want this directory to keep growing in size.

This is where `clean` comes in. We can give it a directory and it will delete everything in that directory. Add this to `initConfig`, again adding a comma after the last property preprocess:

```
clean:{
    dist:{
       src: ['static/js/*.js']
    }
  }
```

These options are very clear. All files with the `.js` extension will be deleted out of `static/js`. We can now add it as the next task for default and dev:

```
grunt.registerTask('default', ['nodeunit', 'preprocess', 'clean']);
grunt.registerTask('prep', ['nodeunit', 'preprocess']);
```

We do not run this for `prep`, as we will load the files from somewhere else (which we will get to). This also shows that we can have different task lists.

JSHinting our source files

The next task we will run is JSHint. JSHint will go through our JavaScript and let us know if there are any possible bugs or issues. This is also known as linting. JavaScript is a very flexible language and can run with some issues. Linting finds these and flags them before we run the code and get errors in the browser. It is very useful and we should always lint our code. Grunt will let us do this automatically.

Add this to `Gruntfile.js` after the clean property:

```
jshint: {
    dist:{
       src: ['js_src/src/*.js', '!js_src/src/md5.js']
    }
  }
```

This is very similar to `clean`. We just pass a list of files that should be run through JSHint. The last statement is an exclude. It will exclude `md5.js` from being linted. We are doing this because we did not write this code and it fails linting.

If something fails this step, Grunt will stop processing the other tasks. This forces us to fix the issues. I did not lint the code I was writing so far, as I knew we were going to cover this. There should be some issues that come up when first running JSHint. Here is a screenshot of an error:

```
Linting js_src/src/chat.pre.js ...ERROR
[L19:C4] W033: Missing semicolon.
    }
```

Register this task with the others using this code:

```
grunt.registerTask('default', ['nodeunit', 'preprocess', 'clean',
'jshint']);
grunt.registerTask('prep', ['nodeunit', 'preprocess']);
```

We are only going to run this for development.

There are two things we can do with linting that are recommended. The first is to 'use strict'. This forces the linter and browser to make JavaScript more unforgiving. Certain errors that would run before will throw an error now. It is another protection against hard-to-track-down runtime errors. All we have to do is add the line, use strict, before any other statements in a file or function. This will put that file or function in the strict mode. The other is to lint all the Node.js files. Right now, we are only linting the frontend files, but everything else is JavaScript and would benefit from being linted.

Concatenating our code

Our JavaScript code is processed and linted, so now we are going to group it together into two files. The first will be all the code required for our chat page and the other is all the frameworks. Previously, we were making six library and four application code requests. We are going to cut that down to two requests. Let's add the concat task:

```
concat:{
    app: {
        src: ['js_src/src/md5.js', 'js_src/src/components.js', 'js_
src/src/models.js', 'js_src/src/chat.js'],
        dest: 'static/js/ChatPage.js'
    },
    frameworks: {
        src: ['bower_components/jquery/dist/jquery.js', 'bower_
components/underscore/underscore.js',
```

```
          'bower_components/backbone/backbone.js', 'bower_components/
react/react.js',
          'bower_components/postal.js/lib/postal.js', 'bower_
components/momentjs/moment.js'],
        dest: 'static/js/Frameworks.js'
      }
    }
```

This task is a little different from the others. It has two targets, apps, and frameworks. These will do different things when called. App will collect all the files in our `js_src/src` folder and concatenate them into one file at `static/js/ChatPage.js`. This file can then be served by Node.js.

`Frameworks` does the same thing, except they go through all our `bower_component` folders that collect the library files. There will now be one file that has all the libraries our page will need.

Now, we can add concat to the task lists:

```
grunt.registerTask('default', ['nodeunit', 'preprocess', 'clean',
'jshint', 'concat:app', 'concat:frameworks']);
  grunt.registerTask('prep', ['nodeunit', 'preprocess']);
```

We could have just added concat and that would have run both targets, but I wanted to show how we can run each target separately.

Minifying our code

Minification will be the last step for Grunt. This will go through each file and remove all the helpful human features (such as whitespace, new lines, descriptive variable names, and more) so that the file is much smaller. Before we build the task, we need to add another property to `initConfig` after `pkg`:

```
pkg: grunt.file.readJSON('package.json'),
git_head: process.env.GIT_HEAD,
```

Grunt can use variables in its tasks and use `initConfig` as the context. We add `git_head` in this context so we can use it in our minifying task, which we will create right now:

```
uglify: {
  dist: {
    files: {
```

```
        'static/js/ChatPage.<%= git_head %>.min.js' : '<%= concat.app.
    dest %>',
        'static/js/Frameworks.<%= git_head %>.min.js' : '<%= concat.
    frameworks.dest %>'
        }
    }
}
```

This task has a few new things in it. The first uses variables in each filename. Grunt will replace what is inside `<%= %>` with the value of the variable. For `git_head`, it will be a long hexadecimal number, which will be the head revision of our current commit. This will make each minified file unique for every commit. Next, we use the value of the destination of our `concat` command. This is useful if we ever decide to change the filename, as this task will not error out. Again, we need to add them to the task list:

```
grunt.registerTask('default', ['nodeunit', 'preprocess', 'clean',
    'jshint', 'concat:app', 'concat:frameworks', 'uglify']);
grunt.registerTask('prep', ['nodeunit', 'preprocess']);
```

Here is what `uglify` should do to our files:

```
Running "uglify:dist" (uglify) task
File static/js/ChatPage.4ab2340aa3394a13c6bb25699fb9ee31dad585c8.min.js created:
 15.06 kB → 9.91 kB
File static/js/Frameworks.4ab2340aa3394a13c6bb25699fb9ee31dad585c8.min.js create
d: 1.29 MB → 337.82 kB
```

We have gone from 10 requests and over 1.3 MB in size to 2 requests and 347 KB in size, only 20 percent of the requests and 26 percent of the size.

Grunt summary

We have collected a few tasks that would be tedious to do every time we wanted to start up our server and automated them. Our JavaScript will be linted, concatenated, and minified every time we test our server. In addition to this, the preprocessor will make sure that Socket.io connects to the correct URL and loads the full JavaScript versions of our code for development and the minified for production, all of this done with one command.

One last feature of Grunt that is useful is `watch`. We just need to add `grunt-contrib-watch` to `package.json` and define a task similar to the others we have created. After that, we can run Grunt `watch`, and anytime a watched file is changed it will automatically run tasks on it. If we were to do this, we would watch all the files in `js_src/src` and then use lint and `concat`. As we added code, we would know immediately if we made a mistake and it would be put into our static directory to be served. Here is an example task that you can add to `Gruntfile.js`:

```
watch: {
    files: ['js_src/src/*.js'],
    tasks: ['default']
}
//do not forget to load grunt-contrib-watch
grunt.loadNpmTasks('grunt-contrib-watch');
```

`files` is an array of the files that should be watched. `tasks` is what task needs to be run. We can test this by running `grunt watch` and then changing any JavaScript file in `js_src/src`.

Static files and CDNs

We are currently using Express' static app to serve our JavaScript and CSS. A best practice for scalable sites is to push any static content onto a **Content Delivery Network (CDN)**. If you have ever used Facebook (they do have a pretty large user base), you have used a CDN. If you inspect your Facebook profile, you will see a domain come up again and again, `fbstatic-a.akamaihd.net`. This is the CDN that Facebook uses for static assets. A CDN will have multiple servers across the world with the same content. Based on where the request comes from, the CDN will return the closest source. We are going to do something similar with this application using Amazon Simple Storage Service (S3).

Some of you out there might say S3 is not a CDN, and you are correct. Amazon has CloudFront to do this. S3 will be better than serving static assets with Node.js, and until an application grows beyond a certain size and scope, S3 will fill the need of a CDN.

Creating an S3 bucket

We create storage areas in S3 using buckets. We will run through that process here. The same warning applies here as in other tutorials; the layout and website copy are correct at the time of writing this book. I expect that Amazon will, at some point, change the process for any of these next steps. The basic flow should still apply, though. The first thing we have to do is sign up for an **Amazon Web Services** (**AWS**) account at `http://aws.amazon.com/`. If this is the first time you are signing up, you will get a year of low usage for free (although you do need to enter a credit card). Then, when you have an account, log in to your AWS console, which will show you all the services you can use. Under **Storage & Content Delivery**, click on **S3**:

From there, click on **Create Bucket** and give your bucket a name. This name has to be globally unique, so you will probably want to add an application identifier to it, for example, `packtchat-s3-cdn-bucket`. Then, click on **Create**. We have an S3 bucket!

Now, we will set up a user. Either go back to the console starting page or use the menu to select **Identity and Access Management** (**IAM**). From the IAM starting page, click on **Users** in the menu on the left and then **Create New Users**. We only need one, so enter a username. Click on **Create**. We will need to either click on **Download Credentials** or copy the **Access Key ID** and **Secret Access Key**. After you click on **Close Window**, you will not be able to get this information again. You can reset it and create new credentials, though, so all is not lost. Here is a screenshot of a user that I have:

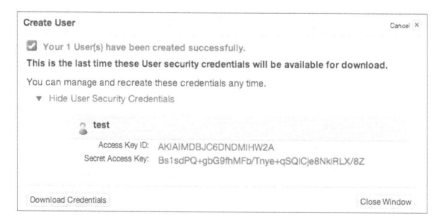

Now that we have AWS credentials, we can add them to our secret environment files. Add the credentials to the AWS_ACCESS_KEY_ID and AWS_SECRET_ACCESS_KEY variables.

The next step is to set permissions on our new bucket. Click in the bucket's row and not the actual link. If done correctly, a list of properties should appear on the right. If not, it will jump to the bucket's contents. In the property list on the right, expand **Permissions** and click **Edit Bucket Policy**. AWS policies can be difficult to set and the documentation is confusing. Here is the policy that should be used:

```
{
  "Statement": [
    {
      "Sid": "PublicReadForGetBucketObjects",
      "Effect": "Allow",
      "Principal": {
        "AWS": "*"
      },
      "Action": "s3:GetObject",
      "Resource": "arn:aws:s3:::bucket_name/*"
    },
    {
      "Sid": "PacktchatUserFullPermissions",
      "Effect": "Allow",
      "Principal": {
        "AWS": "arn:aws:iam::user_number:user/user_name"
      },
      "Action": "s3:*",
      "Resource": [
        "arn:aws:s3:::bucket_name",
        "arn:aws:s3:::bucket_name/*"
      ]
    }
  ]
}
```

There are two policies here. The first allows anyone to get any object in the bucket we created. This is important because without it, all requests will be denied. The next one gives access to our newly created user to complete any action inside of this bucket. We will focus on more AWS in the next chapter. Also, note that everywhere user_name, user_number, or bucket_name is specified will be replaced with the values chosen. The user number will be in IAM.

Python and installing virtual environments

Our next step is to build a Python script that will collect all the files in a directory and push them to our S3 bucket. Before we build the script, we will need to create a virtual environment for Python. We want to only install packages locally for the current project, so we can have multiple projects running different versions of the same package. Python does this with `virtualenv`. This install will be for Mac OS X, which runs Python 2.7.5. Open a terminal and run the following two commands:

```
$sudo easy_install pip
$pip install virtualenv
```

Pip is a package manager for Python and we install that first, so we can use it to install `virtualenv`. At this point, we can create a virtual environment. Run the following commands:

```
$virtualenv venv
$source venv/bin/activate
```

The first command creates a virtual environment in the `venv` directory and the next activates it. If it worked correctly, we should see (venv) in front of our prompt. This lets us know we are in the virtual environment. The activation script basically changes our PATH to point to Python inside our newly created directory. Then, when we install new packages, they will reside under that directory and not globally. We will now create a file that lists out all the requirements for this script, aptly named `requirements.txt`. Create this file and add the following line to it:

```
boto==2.29.1
```

Then, run the following command in the terminal:

```
pip install -r requirements.txt
```

Pip should install the specific version 2.29.1 of Boto, which is a Python library that will interact with AWS. Now, we can write our Python script. Create a file named `static.py` and add this code to it:

```
import boto
import os

from boto.s3.key import Key

root_dir = './static/'
```

```
def upload(file_name):
    k = Key(bucket)
    k.key = file_name
    k.set_contents_from_filename(root_dir + file_name)
    print 'Uploading %s' % root_dir + file_name


def walk(directory):
    for (source, dirs, files) in os.walk(directory):
        #remove first directory
        d = source.replace(directory, '')
        for file in files:
            if (file != '.DS_Store'):
                file_list.append(d + '/' + file)
        map(walk, dirs)


def clean_js():
    for key in bucket.list(prefix='js/'):
        key.delete()

conn = boto.connect_s3()

#the AWS keys are in the env
bucket = conn.get_bucket(os.environ['AWS_BUCKET'])

clean_js()
file_list = []
walk(root_dir)
map(upload, file_list)
```

Here is a quick rundown of what is happening. First, import the libraries that we need and set the directory we are going to upload. The upload function takes a filename and creates an object (key in the script) in the S3 bucket. walk will recursively go through a directory and load the files. It needs to remove the leading directory name because we want our files to be created at the root of the bucket and not at static in the bucket. Next, it makes sure that the file is not named .DS_Store (a Mac OS X system file) and adds them to a list. The clean_js function will delete all the files in the js directory before uploading new ones. This is the same thing Grunt does, because we have unique filenames. At last, we get to the actual execution. First, we connect to S3. This function can take credentials or it will look for environment variables, which we have set in our secret environment files.

Next, we get the bucket name from the environment and then process all the files. We can test whether this works by running this in our terminal:

```
(venv)$source prod.env
```

```
(venv)$source prod_secret.env
```

```
(venv)$python static.py
```

We need to source our environment files because the Python script is looking for variables defined in them. If everything is set correctly, we should see the script upload our CSS and JavaScript files to S3. We can now leave the virtual environment by running the following command in the terminal:

```
(venv)$deactivate
```

We can now set our production STATIC_URL to point to S3. Open up prod.env and change this line:

```
export STATIC_URL='https://your_bucket_name.s3.amazonaws.com'
```

Depending on the environment files loaded, our views files will load different JavaScript files. For example, layout will load the uniquely named and minified frameworks JavaScript file from S3 in production and a localhost file in development.

Scripting our new tools

We have automated some tasks, but we have created an issue where we must run two to three commands to accomplish each task. We want to always shoot for one command. We will create a script to launch our development server and collect the static files. First, create a file named set_env.sh. This file will load our environment files so that we can then run our different commands. Paste this into it:

```
#!/bin/bash
if [ $# -ne 1 ]; then
  echo "Please pass in the environment as the first argument"
  exit 1
fi

source ./$1.env
source ./$1_secret.env

if [ $? != 0 ]; then
  echo "Create the needed environment files"
  exit $?
fi
```

This uses `bash` and if you have never scripted with `bash` before, it can look a little strange. The first `if` condition checks the number of passed-in arguments (`?#`) to see if it is not equal to `1`. If that is true, exit and let the user know the environment should be passed in. The next step is to build the name of the environment files from the first argument (`$1`) and then source them. The next `if` condition checks to see if the exit status (`$?`) of the previous command is not equal to `0` and then exits if it is not. If the files exist, then the exit status will be `0`.

Next, create a file named `server_prep.sh` and run the following command to make it executable:

$chmod a+x server_prep.sh

Then, paste this into it:

```
#!/bin/bash

source ./set_env.sh $1
./node_modules/.bin/grunt prep
```

The `./node_modules/.bin/grunt prep` script makes use of `set_env.sh`. We just source it to get all our environment variables available. This script then uses the locally installed Grunt and runs the prep task ensuring that all the preprocess files are correct and ready:

$./server_prep.sh 'dev'

We should be able to check `layout.ejs` and `chat.ejs` to make sure they are created.

Now, we can build the script that will upload our static files to S3. Create a file named `collectstatic.sh` and paste this code into it:

```
#!/bin/bash
source ./set_env.sh $1

./node_modules/.bin/grunt

virtualenv venv
source venv/bin/activate
pip install -r requirements.txt

python static.py
deactivate
```

It is very similar to the previous script; first, we prep the environment by sourcing our environment variables. The next step is to make sure that all the JavaScript files have been concatenated and minified. Then, we make sure we have a virtual environment with the needed packages. Finally, we run the Python script to upload the files.

Each of these scripts will work differently based on the environment variables set. If we were to create a staging environment, we would just change the variables that would be different and run each script with staging as the argument.

Summary

Our application is slowly becoming more maintainable. We have created some much-needed tests and automated them. Before this chapter, we could only start the application from localhost. Now, it is ready to be deployed to different environments. We did this by extracting out all the differences between environments (URLs, connection strings, and app IDs are some). Then, we used Grunt to create automated tasks that build the application for each environment. The tasks also force us to use best practices when doing this. Finally, we scripted these tasks so that each one would only consist of one command instead of three to four for each.

In the next chapter, we will actually deploy our application somewhere other than localhost.

Deployment and Scalability

We have finally reached the point where we can actually deploy our application using Amazon's **Elastic Compute Cloud** (**EC2**). EC2 is a popular cloud provider. Right now, our application only lives on our computer. We will use Ansible to install all the dependencies and deploy our code on EC2 instances. Then, we will take a look at how and why our application is ready to scale. Here is what we will cover in this chapter:

- What EC2 is and how to create instances
- Ansible
- Ansible roles
- How to scale

We have a lot to cover, so we are just going to jump right in.

Creating servers on EC2

EC2 is the compute portion of Amazon's public cloud. We will ask Amazon to create a server for us, and we will manage what is on it and what it does. Our plan is to not utilize any specific EC2 image to be used, other than the newest version of Ubuntu. This allows us to easily create more instances in order to serve more demand.

We will use our AWS account, which we created in the last chapter. Log in to our AWS console and under **Compute & Networking**, click on **EC2**.

Then, under **Instances**, click on **Instances**. An instance is one machine running a specific image.

We will now create a new instance. Click on **Launch Instance**. This should open up a dialog to configure the instance. We will use QuickStart and the latest Ubuntu image, which at the time of this writing is Ubuntu Server 14.04 LTS. Use 64-bit and select this image. Next, we will choose **Type**. Here, we will just want to use **t2.micro**. This is the smallest and the cheapest option, but it is enough for now.

Click on **Next: Configure Instance Details**. We do not need to enter anything here, so click on **Next: Add Storage**. This is where more drives can be added, but we will not do so now. Although it is a good idea to bump up the current drive's size from 8 GB to 16 GB, one thing to remember is that the storage for this instance will be erased and will revert to the base image when stopped. This is a reason why we will need Ansible. Click on **Next: Tag Instance**. This will be a key part of our deployment. We will want to add these tags to our instance, the format being key:value with the following entries:

- Redis:Role
- RabbitMQ:Role
- Chat:Deploy
- Worker:Deploy
- prod:Env
- HAProxy:Role

We are tagging the instance so that later, Ansible can target certain instances to configure. Then, click on **Next: Configure Security Group**. We can create a new group; we just need to make sure that SSH, HTTP, and port 3000 are open to everyone. The final rule is to allow this group to connect with itself. We do this by adding all the TCPs and then for the IP, type sg and a list of all the security groups will come up. Select the security group we are using currently. This will allow any instance in this group to connect to any other instance using the internal EC2 IP address (usually, 10.X.X.X) or the public DNS name.

 If we want to be more secure, we can lock down SSH to just our current public IP address. This can cause issues if the IP address ever changes. Having this open to the public ensures that our scripts will run, but it is a security issue.

Next, click on **Review and Launch** and finally click on **Launch**. The next screen will ask us to either create or use a specific key pair. If this is the first instance, we will want to create a pair. Keep track of this key! This is how we can SSH into the instance, and we will be using it with Ansible. I put my private key in the .ssh directory. After this, the instance is finally ready and will launch. The launch will take anywhere from a few seconds to a few minutes.

Once the instance is up, we can view some information about it. Click on the box on the far left and it will load information about the instance in the lower pane. The first tab, **Description**, will have the public DNS name. It should be in the format of ec2-IP-ADDRESS.compute-1.amazonaws.com. Copy this address, open a terminal, and SSH into the machine using the following command:

```
$ssh ubuntu@ec2-IP-ADDRESS.compute-1.amazonaws.com -i ~/.ssh/aws_key.pem
```

The Ubuntu image uses Ubuntu as the default user, so we must use this to log in. We must also tell SSH to use our newly created AWS key. This should connect us and we should get a shell. We have created our first server in the cloud and are ready to start building our server.

AWS EC2 summary

There are a lot of features in EC2. We have only done the bare minimum of creating a server. If we wanted much more control, we could create our own images (AMIs or Amazon Machine Images), although the base Ubuntu AMI will work fine for this project.

One issue that could create problems is that the Ubuntu AMI uses an instance store. The data on the drive will only persist while the instance is running. If the instance is stopped or terminated, the data is lost. Most of the servers we will build should be ephemeral. This means that they do not store any state and can be brought up or down without any concern. Certain roles cannot operate this way. A database server is a great example. We will need to create a separate **Elastic Block Store** (**EBS**) and then attach it to the image. The EBS volume will persist separately from the instance. All system administration tasks will still need to be done. For example, the first time when the volume is mounted, it will need to be formatted and full backups should still be done. Just because it is in the cloud does not mean that it is impervious to issues or requires no administration.

For our application, we will not need any persistent data. All the application data will be stored in Redis, which is temporary. RabbitMQ only stores logging information so it does not need to persist either. If we needed this information to persist, we would just attach an EBS volume and makes sure our configuration files pointed the Redis and RabbitMQ config to the correct path.

It is important to note that this is not a High Availability deployment. If Redis ever goes down, the entire application will go down. It is outside the scope of this book to set this up. Redis Sentinel and, when it attains stablility, Redis clustering will provide High Availability.

What is Ansible?

Ansible is going to be the tool we use to manage our servers and deploy our code. It is written in Python and will handle config files, installing software, pulling code from Git, and almost anything else you can think of. Another great feature is that Ansible is agentless. It uses SSH, so we don't have to prepare and install something before we start. Let's install Ansible so that we can start building our deploy scripts.

Installing Ansible

Since Ansible uses Python, we can use our virtual environment that we created earlier. We will want to add Ansible to a new file named `dev-requirements.txt`. Here is what the file should contain:

```
-r requirements.txt
ansible==1.6.3
```

Then, we can install it with `pip`:

```
$source venv/bin/activate

(venv)$pip install -r dev-requirements.txt
```

The reason we do this is because we don't need to install Ansible on the production server, but we still want it to be explicitly declared. Here, we are using the option to include another requirements file in this file. We can then choose the group of packages to install based on the chosen requirements file.

The way we are going to use Ansible is through a playbook. A playbook is a list of tasks that get applied to a list of servers. The first thing we need then is a list or inventory of servers. We are going to use an Ansible-created EC2 inventory script (https://raw.githubusercontent.com/ansible/ansible/devel/plugins/inventory/ec2.py or Google Ansible EC2 inventory script). Create a new directory named `ansible` in your project root and save this file as `ec2.py`. This script goes through your EC2 instances and builds groups based on availability zones, instance names, keys used, instance type, and most importantly, tags. The first thing we will do is create an `ansible` directory in the root of our project and drop the downloaded `ec2.py` file into it. This script is written in Python, and it uses boto to communicate with AWS. This is perfect because we should already have boto installed in our virtual environment. The next step is to create another file named `ec2.ini` in the `ansible` directory with `ec2.py`. This is a config file for `ec2.py`. Enter the following code in the file:

```
[ec2]
regions = us-east-1
```

```
regions_exclude =
destination_variable = public_dns_name
vpc_destination_variable = ip_address
route53 = False
cache_path = ~/.ansible/tmp
cache_max_age = 0
```

Most of the settings are correctly named. The only two settings that we will change are `regions` and `cache_max_age`. The `regions` setting should be the region or regions in which we created our instances. The value of the `Cache_max_age` setting will be zero so that any changes get picked up.

Before we test this script, we will need to get credentials that have access to EC2 actions. The script will take a look into the environment for AWS credentials because it is using boto. We can, therefore, either give access to our previously created user or create a new user and give access to this user. If we create a new user, then we will want to create a different environment file so that we can load the credentials separately. This file can be called `ec2_secret.env`. Remember, this is confidential information and we do not want to put it into version control.

Giving access to a user is quite easy. Go to **IAM**, select **Users**, select the user you want, click on the **Permissions** tab, and then select **Attach User Policy**. Inside this dialog, there is a policy template named **Amazon EC2 Full Access**. Choose this template and apply it to the user. This user can now query, create, or destroy AMIs. We can now test our inventory script. Open a terminal and enter these commands, assuming we are outside the virtual environment to begin with:

```
$source venv/bin/activate
(venv)$source dev_secret.env #or wherever our AWS credentials are in
(venv)$cd ansible
(venv)$chmod u+x ec2.py
(venv)$./ec2.py
```

We should see a bunch of lists that reference all our current instances. The same instance will be in many different lists. We also should see lists for each tag, for example, `tag_Redis_Role`. When we see all our tags as groups, we are ready to run our first Ansible command. Open a command prompt and enter the following command:

```
(venv)$ansible all -m ping -i ec2.py --private-key=~/.ssh/aws_key.pem -u ubuntu
```

Let's break this down quickly. `All` is a host pattern, which matches all surprisingly. Next, `-m ping` tells Ansible to use the `ping` module on each host. The `ping` module is not the same as the `ping` command. This is an Ansible module that will let us know if it can communicate with each host. The next two options are self-explanatory. If this works, you should see something similar to the next screenshot:

```
ec2-50-19-156-37.compute-1.amazonaws.com | success >> {
    "changed": false,
    "ping": "pong"
}
```

In this command, we are specifying which private key to use for SSH authentication. This will be the key we received from Amazon. We can continue to add the `--private-key=` parameter for every command, or we can run this to add it to our SSH keys:

`$ssh-add ~/.ssh/aws_key.pem`

Remember to replace `aws_key.pem` with the filename for the key that we downloaded from Amazon. The rest of the commands for this chapter will make the assumption that we have done this.

Using Ansible roles

We can now start to build our servers. Ansible has two great abstractions named roles and playbooks. We can define a role that only worries about a single responsibility. We can then target specific servers to apply this role to. Another way to look at this is that a role is a component or a building block of our architecture, and playbooks are a group of components and tasks that get executed together. The playbook lists which tasks get applied to the servers in the role. Let's create the first role, Redis.

Create a new directory in the root of our project named `ansible`. Inside this directory, create another directory named `roles`. Then, in `roles`, create a directory named `redis`. The final directory will be `tasks`, inside `redis`. This structure and filenames are dictated by Ansible, so we want to stick to these. Finally, create a file named `main.yml` in `tasks`.

Here is how our directory structure should look:

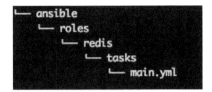

YML stands for **Yet Another Markup Language (YAML)**. Ansible uses it extensively to define everything about our playbook. Paste the following code in `main.yml`:

```
---

 - name: Install Redis
   apt: name=redis-server=2:2.8.4-2 state=present

 - name: Bind to all Interfaces
   lineinfile: dest=/etc/redis/redis.conf regexp=^bind  line='bind
0.0.0.0'
   register: redisconf

 - name: Redis Started
   service: name=redis-server state=started enabled=yes

 - name: Redis Restarted
   service: name=redis-server state=restarted
   when: redisconf.changed
```

These are the lists of tasks we want to run through in order to install Redis. As we can see, Ansible uses a declarative syntax. It is really easy to follow along. Each task has a name and command or module to execute. Each task can have multiple options that modify it. The first task uses `apt` to install a specific version of `redis-server` from the default repository. We are pinning our versions here as well. We do not want an updated package to cause issues.

Use Ubuntu's package search to find the name and version available at (http://packages.ubuntu.com/).

The next task makes sure that the `bind 0.0.0.0` line is in the `redis config` file. It also registers itself as `redisconf` so that other tasks can check to see whether this file has changed or not.

The next task checks to make sure that `redis-server` is started and is set to start on boot.

The last task is conditional. If `redisconf.changed` then restart the service, if not let it run.

Now that we have our tasks defined, we can define which servers they apply to. Create a file named `redis.yml` in the `ansible` directory. In this file, paste the following code:

```
- hosts: tag_Redis_Role
  remote_user: ubuntu
  sudo: yes
  roles:
    - redis
```

Here, we have a `hosts` pattern that will target a specific tag. All we have to do is make sure that the servers we want to be running Redis are tagged appropriately. We then specify that the user Ubuntu should be used and to use `sudo` for each command. Finally, we have a list of roles. Ansible will know that it needs to look in the `roles` directory, find `redis`, and load the tasks from `main.yml`. Open a terminal and run this command:

```
(venv)$ansible-playbook -i ec2.py redis.yml --limit tag_prod_Env
```

We should see something similar to the next screenshot for each task:

As a quick reminder, this command does not have the `--private-key` parameter. This will fail if we have not run `ssh-add` or appended `--private-key`.

What is great about Ansible is that it will check for the current state before running tasks. The first time when Ansible goes through the playbook, it has to install/check everything. The next run through Ansible will effectively do nothing.

Let's build the RabbitMQ role now.

Installing RabbitMQ

This will be very similar to Redis. The first thing we need to do is create a directory structure under roles for RabbitMQ, although this time, we will create two directories under `rabbitmq`: `files` and `tasks`. Including the files we are going to create the directory structure for, `rabbitmq` under `roles` should look like the next screenshot:

```
├── rabbitmq
│   ├── files
│   │   └── rabbitmq.config
│   └── tasks
│       └── main.yml
```

Now, we can create the YAML file that will use this role. Create `rabbitmq.yml` in our `ansible` directory. This should be at the same level as `redis.yml`. The following code goes inside this file:

```
- hosts: tag_RabbitMQ_Role
  remote_user: ubuntu
  sudo: yes
  roles:
    - rabbitmq
```

The key part of this file is to use a tagged role. Now, we can create the `rabbitmq` role. Inside `rabbitmq/tasks`, create `main.yml` with the following code:

```
---
- name: Install RabbitMQ
  apt: name=rabbitmq-server=3.2.4-1 state=present

- name: Rabbitmq.config
  copy: src=rabbitmq.config dest=/etc/rabbitmq/rabbitmq.config
  register: rabbitmqconfig

- name: RabbitMQ Started
  service: name=rabbitmq-server state=started

- name: Enable RabbitMQ management
  shell: rabbitmq-plugins enable rabbitmq_management

- name: Restart RabbitMQ Service
  service: name=rabbitmq-server state=restarted
```

```
- name: Force RabbitMQ to Reload Config
  shell: rabbitmqctl {{ item }}
  with_items:
    - stop_app
    - reset
    - start_app
  when: rabbitmqconfig.changed
```

This file introduces a few new things. The first thing is the copy action. It will copy a local file to the remote host if the file doesn't exist or if it is different. Here, we are copying a `rabbitmq.config` file. As we are using Ansible's `roles` feature, we do not have to define the full path to the file to be copied. Ansible will look for it in the `files` directory under this role.

The next new item is the shell action. This will run any arbitrary shell command. Here, we are enabling the RabbitMQ management plugin.

The final new idea is to use a list of items and looping. Each item is `{{ item }}` in the the loop. We are just using simple items, but the items can be more complex with properties as well. Here, we are forcing RabbitMQ to reload the config as configuration changes do not take effect with a service restart.

The other steps have been introduced with the `redis config` file. The last thing we have to do is create the `rabbitmq.conf` file in the `rabbitmq/files` directory. Here is how it should look:

```
[{rabbit, [
  {default_user,<<"nonguest">>},
  {default_pass,<<"uniquepassword">>}
]},
{rabbitmq_management, [{listener, [{port, 15672}]}]}
].
```

RabbitMQ's config file syntax is a little strange, but here we are changing the default user, password, and management port. This should be the bare minimum for our production server. We can now run the playbook and install RabbitMQ using the following command:

```
(venv)$ansible-playbook -i ec2.py rabbitmq.yml --private-key=~/.ssh/aws_
key.pem --limit tag_prod_Env
```

Just like our Redis playbook, Ansible should go through the installation and configure RabbitMQ.

If we want to use the web management interface, we will have to modify the security group attached to our instance. In the AWS console, go to **EC2** and click on **Security Groups**. We can then edit the inbound rules from the **Actions** dropdown. We will use the **Custom TCP** rule that is mapped to port 15672, and we can select **My IP** to only allow our computer to connect. We can load http://OUR-EC2-IP-ADDRESS:15672 and log in using our new nonguest user.

We now have our backend services built. If we had a database, we could build out the Ansible playbook in a similar way. Install the binaries, set up the config, and make sure that it is set to start on boot.

Installing our application

We now have the foundation for our application; so, we can push the code out and start Node.js. We are going to use multiple roles as there are a few steps in deploying the application. The first role is nodejs. Create a directory under ansible/roles named nodejs with another directory named tasks. Create main.yml under tasks. Here is the code for main.yml:

```
---
  - name: Install Node.js
    apt: name=nodejs-legacy state=present update_cache=yes

  - name: Install NPM
    apt: name=npm state=present update_cache=yes
```

We have one new statement in these commands, update_cache. This tells apt-get to update and use the latest version of Node.js and npm. Sometimes, apt cannot install the application due to security updates. Next is git, which is what I have been using for version control for this project and I recommend that you use it, especially because our deployment depends on it. Create a git role with a tasks directory and main.yml. Here are the git tasks:

```
---
  - name: Install Git
    apt: name=git state=present

  - name: Check app path
    file: path={{ project_path }} mode=0755 state=directory

  - name: Directory for SSH
    file: path=/root/.ssh/ state=directory
```

```
    - name: Copy SSH key over
      copy: src=~/.ssh/ssh_key_for_git dest=/root/.ssh/key mode=600

    - name: Git Clean
      shell: removes={{ project_path }}/.git cd {{ project_path }} &&
  git clean -xdf

    - name: Git checkout
      git: repo={{ project_repo }}
           dest={{ project_path }}
           version={{ branch }}
           accept_hostkey=yes
           key_file=/root/.ssh/key
```

Git Clean uses an option named removes. If the directory or file in removes does not exist, it removes this task from execution. During the first run through the .git directory will not exist, so this task will be skipped.

The next thing to note is that we are using variables here for project_path, project_repo, and branch. We will define the variables shortly. The file module allows us to check whether a file or directory already exists and to create it if not. The git module will check out a specific repository and branch into a directory that we pass in. We must also copy the SSH key that has access to the Git repository.

Deploying the code

The next role that we will create is appdeploy. Create the role directory along with tasks and templates. Create the main.yml file in tasks and add this code:

```
    ---
    - name: Create App user
      user: name={{ project_user }}

    - name: Copy Secret Environment file
      template: src=../../../../{{ deploy_env }}_secret.env dest={{
  project_path }}

    - name: Copy Normal Environment file
      template: src=../../../../{{ deploy_env }}.env dest={{ project_
  path }}

    - name: Run Server Prep
      command: chdir={{ project_path }} ./server_prep.sh {{ deploy_env
  }}
```

```
    - name: Create Project etc
      file: path=/etc/{{ project_name }} state=directory

    - name: Create start_server.sh
      template: src=start_server.j2 dest=/etc/{{ project_name }}/start_
server.sh mode=755

    - name: Create stop_server.sh
      template: src=stop_server.j2 dest=/etc/{{project_name}}/stop_
server.sh mode=755

    - name: Install forever globally
      command: creates=/usr/local/bin/forever chdir={{project_path}} npm
install -g forever

    - name: Create init script
      template: src=init_script.j2 dest=/etc/init.d/{{project_name}}
mode=755

    - name: Create rc.d links
      shell: update-rc.d {{ project_name }} defaults 80

    - name: Restart Service
      shell: service {{ project_name }} restart
```

These are a lot of little tasks that use many different variables. We will quickly run through these tasks, jumping over to any relevant files.

The first is the user module. It does exactly what you think it does, makes sure that a user exists.

Then, we copy our secret environment file. We go up enough directories to load the .env files in the root of our project. Having two files that are the same in a code base is a recipe for disaster. It is almost guaranteed that the files will have divergent data. There should always be a definitive copy. The astute reader that you are, you might have probably noticed that the environment file is called as a template. We do this so that we can modify our secret file. We will only need to modify the lines that set REDIS_HOST and RABBITMQ_URL in prod_secret.env:

```
{% for role in groups['tag_Redis_Role'] %}
  {% for server in groups['tag_prod_Env'] %}
    {% if role == server %}
export REDIS_HOST={{ hostvars[server]['ec2_private_ip_address'] }}
    {% endif %}
  {% endfor %}
```

```
{% endfor %}
{% for role in groups['tag_RabbitMQ_Role'] %}
  {% for server in groups['tag_prod_Env'] %}
    {% if role == server %}
export RABBITMQ_URL='amqp://nonguest:uniquepassword@{{
hostvars[server]['ec2_private_ip_address'] }}:5672'
    {% endif %}
  {% endfor %}
{% endfor %}
```

Here, we are looping through two different groups, `Redis_Role` and `prod_Env`, to find the server that matches both. The same is done for RabbitMQ. What this does is it allows us to dynamically spin up instances with the correct tags and Ansible will figure out the IP addresses of the servers for us. If not, we will have to modify the secret file every time we want to deploy.

Note that although we did this with the `prod_secret` file, usually we will not need to do this as we would have a static IP address and a DNS name. This is also true for local development. We know that everything is localhost, so we don't need to add the template loops. If there are no template tags, the file will be copied as is in Ansible. This is perfect for any environments that will be created right before deployment, as we will not know the IP addresses beforehand. Also, note that if there are template tags in the file, it cannot be used with our shell scripts locally (`server_prep.sh` or `collectstatic.sh`).

The same is done with the regular environment file. Here is what we want to process in `prod.env`:

```
{% for role in groups['tag_HAProxy_Role'] %}
  {% for server in groups['tag_prod_Env'] %}
    {% if role == server %}
export HOST='http://{{  hostvars[server]['ec2_public_dns_name'] }}/'
export SOCKETIO_URL='http://{{  hostvars[server]['ec2_public_dns_
name'] }}/packtchat'
    {% endif %}
  {% endfor %}
{% endfor %}
```

Again, we are doing this for `prod`; however, in actual production, we will have a public DNS name that we can statically set (at least we should!).

The next step is running `server_prep.sh` in our deploy environment, because we just loaded our environment files. Remember `server_prep` runs Grunt to preprocess our JavaScript, layout, and chat view.

The next three tasks are related. We want a start up script and shutdown script that will launch our application. We create a new directory in `etc` with our project name. Then, we create a `start_server.sh` file from this template, `start_server.j2`, as follows:

```
#!/bin/bash

cd {{ project_path }}
source {{ deploy_env }}.env
source {{ deploy_env }}_secret.env

forever --pidFile /home/{{ project_user }}/{{ project_name }}.pid -a
-l /home/{{ project_user }}/{{ project_name }}.log start {{ project_
path }}/{{ project_exec }}
```

This script just uses `prep` for the environment before launching `forever`, which is a Node package that will start an application and monitor it. If the thread dies, it will relaunch it. This is exactly what we need. We start forever telling it to drop a `.pid` file and logfile of the console. If we SSH into our server and run this script, our application will be available over port 3000.

Here is the code for `stop_server.j2`:

```
#!/bin/bash
forever stop {{ project_path }}/{{ project_exec }}
```

We do not need to use `prep` in the environment as we are just stopping our Node process.

If we are going to use `forever`, we need to install it. We are using `npm` to install forever globally. The `creates` option lets us check whether a certain file exists or not; if it does, skip the step and if not, run the command.

The last three steps are related as well. The first step creates an `init` script from a template. Here is the template, `init_script.j2`:

```
#!/bin/bash

start() {
    echo "Starting {{ project_name }}"
    su - {{ project_user }} /etc/{{ project_name }}/start_server.sh
    RETVAL=$?
}
```

```
stop() {
    if [ -f /home/{{ project_user }}/{{ project_name }}.pid ];then
        echo "Shutting Down {{ project_name }}"
        su - {{ project_user }} /etc/{{ project_name }}/stop_server.sh
        rm -f /home/{{ project_user }}/{{ project_name }}.pid
        RETVAL=$?
    else
        echo "{{ project_name }} is not running."
        REVAL=0
    fi
}

restart() {
    stop
    start
}

case "$1" in
    start)
        start
        ;;
    stop)
        stop
        ;;
    restart)
        restart
        ;;
    *)
        echo "Usage: {start|stop|restart}"
        exit 1
        ;;
esac
exit $RETVAL
```

This is a bash script, and hence, the different syntax. The two main parts of this script are `start` and `stop`, where we run the scripts we created. Each time we run one of the scripts, we use `su`, which will change the user that executes the next command. This is important from a security standpoint as the user running the application has the least amount of privileges (read-only). If, for any reason, this process gets compromised, there will be very little that the user can do. The `stop` function checks for the `.pid` file and stops the server or echoes out that the server is not running. This script will be put in the `/etc/init.d/` directory. We can now run `service project_name` `start`, `stop`, or `restart`.

`update-rc.d` will set our script to automatically run on boot for different run levels.

Finally, we restart the service to make sure that the server is serving the latest version of the code.

We have gone over all the roles, so now let's create the script that brings them all together. Create `appdeploy.yml` inside your `ansible` directory. Here is how this file should be:

```
- hosts: tag_Chat_Deploy
  remote_user: ubuntu
  sudo: yes
  vars_files:
    - vars.yml
  roles:
    - nodejs
    - git
    - appdeploy
- hosts: tag_Chat_Deploy[0]
  remote_user: ubuntu
  sudo: yes
  vars_files:
    - vars.yml
  tasks:
    - name: Install Pip
      apt: name=python-pip state=present

    - name: Install Virtualenv
      shell: pip install virtualenv

    - name: Collect Static
      command: chdir={{ project_path }} ./collectstatic.sh {{ deploy_env }}
```

Again, we will step through this detouring where needed. We are targeting any instance with the Chat Deploy tag. We now can see where all our variables were defined, in `vars.yml`. We will look at that file now:

```
project_name: nodechat
project_path: /var/node/chat
project_repo: git@bitbucket.org:user/project.git
project_user: nodechat
project_exec: app.js
```

Here, we just add all the variables with their values. All of the roles used here will have access to these variables.

Then, we define all the roles in the order in which they need to run, `nodejs`, `git`, and `appdeploy`.

Next, we define a new group of hosts with more tasks. We are doing this because we have to upload our minified JavaScript to S3 each time there is a new commit. If we don't do this, the views will try to load a nonexistent JavaScript file. `tag_Chat_Deploy` is a group of instances and because of this, we can specify an index. We choose the zero or the first instance in the group. This is important, because if we did not do this and had 10 instances in the group, we would upload the static files 10 times. In this way, we will only do it once. We need `pip` and `virtualenv` installed so that we can run `collectstatic.sh`.

Wait, you might say, "where are the `deploy_env` or `branch` variables?" It was not in our `vars.yml` file. These variables are passed in the command line, which brings us to the command we can use to test this step:

```
(venv)$ansible-playbook -i ec2.py appdeploy.yml --limit tag_prod_Env
--extra-vars "deploy_env=prod branch=master"
```

We can pass extra variables in the command line, which all tasks and roles will have access to.

After we have executed this role, we should be able to view the site at `http://EC2-IP-ADDRESS:3000`. Socket.io will not work because it will try to connect on port 80 instead of 3000. We will cover how to listen on port 80 shortly; before this, we need to cover creating the workers.

An important thing to note is that there is no `npm install` or `bower install`. The npm FAQ states the following:

> *Use npm to manage dependencies in your dev environment, but not in your deployment scripts.*

This means that we should include `node_modules` and `bower_components` in our Git repository. This chapter's code has all the modules installed and ready for deployment.

Installing the workers

Our application needs two workers, one that pulls the logs from RabbitMQ and another that cleans up Redis every few hours. This task will actually be the easiest as it does not require any new roles. We will reuse roles that are already defined. This is the reason why we broke up the application deployment into three different roles. Small role definitions facilitate composition. Create `worker.yml` in the `ansible` directory. Here is what should be present in this file:

```
- hosts: tag_Worker_Deploy
  remote_user: ubuntu
  sudo: yes
  gather_facts: false
  vars_files:
    - vars.yml
  roles:
    - nodejs
    - git
    - { role: appdeploy, project_name: nodechat_worker_chat, project_
exec: workers/chat.js }
    - { role: appdeploy, project_name: nodechat_worker_log, project_
exec: workers/log.js }
```

This looks a lot like `appdeploy.yml`. This is to be expected because we are using the same code base and the workers run on Node. The difference lies in the last two role tasks. Here, we are using the `appdeploy` role, but we are changing certain context variables for each role. A new `project_name` service will create separate `init` scripts for each, and `project_exec` will point to the worker script that needs to be executed. After running through these, our instance should have three `forever` applications running.

Load balancing multiple application servers

If we have 10 application servers running, how do we create one specific URL that someone can load? This is done through load balancing. We will install a load balancer (HAProxy) that will be the public-facing server. The load balancer knows about each application server and will send the requests to all different backend servers. If, at any point, our servers cannot handle the requests coming in, we can spin up another EC2 instance and tell the load balancer about it, which will then start sending it requests.

We will need a new role, so create the `haproxy` directory under `ansible/roles` and add `files`, `tasks`, and `templates` under this directory. Create `main.yml` under `tasks` and add the following to it:

```
---
  - name: Install HAProxy
    apt: name=haproxy=1.4.24-2 state=present

  - name: Enable HAProxy
    copy: src=haproxy_default dest=/etc/default/haproxy

  - name: Create config
    template: src=haproxy.cfg.j2 dest=/etc/haproxy/haproxy.cfg

  - name: HAProxy Restart
    service: name=haproxy state=reloaded
```

This is a simple list of tasks. Install HAProxy and then configure it. The second task needs the `haproxy_default` file, so create this under `haproxy/files`. This file only has one line:

```
ENABLED=1
```

This will allow HAProxy to be controlled by its `init` script.

The next task requires a template; so, let's take a look at the template we need to create. After creating `templates/haproxy.cfg.j2`, add this code to the beginning of the file:

```
global
    chroot /var/lib/haproxy
    user haproxy
    group haproxy
    daemon

defaults
    log global
    contimeout 5000
    clitimeout 50000
    srvtimeout 50000

listen stats :1936
    mode http
```

```
stats enable
stats hide-version
stats realm Haproxy\ Statistics
stats uri /
stats auth user:password

frontend public
  mode http
  bind *:80
  option httplog
  option dontlognull
  option forwardfor
  acl is_websocket path_beg /socket.io
  acl is_websocket hdr(Upgrade) -i WebSocket
  acl is_websocket hdr_beg(Host) -i ws
  use_backend ws if is_websocket
  default_backend node
```

Most of this is just boilerplate HAProxy config settings. The interesting parts are the **Access Control Lists (ACLs)**. The ACLs check whether the request is for socket.io if the upgrade header is for WebSocket or the host header begins with ws. This should catch any WebSocket traffic. We then specify the ws backend to be used if it is websocket and backend node if not. Now, let's create the backend that does the load balancing:

```
backend node
  mode http
  cookie SERVERID insert
  balance leastconn
  {% for role in groups['tag_Chat_Deploy'] %}
    {% for server in groups['tag_' + deploy_env + '_Env'] %}
      {% if role == server %}
      server {{ server }}
        {{hostvars[server]['ec2_private_ip_address'] }}:3000
        cookie {{ server }}
        {% endif %}
        {% endfor %}
        {% endfor %}
```

Backends have a list of servers that HAProxy will balance the load across. This backend will use the `leastconn` balancing, which will pick the server with the least connections for each new connection. We also use our double for loops to find all the servers that are in our deployed environment. The line cookie `SERVERID` insert will create a cookie with the server's public DNS name based on the server line. We do this so that we can see which server is responding to a request. Doing this will also turn on sticky sessions. This means that once a browser has connected to a server, HAProxy will send all the requests to the same server. Here is the WebSocket backend:

```
backend ws
  mode http
  option http-server-close
  option forceclose
  no option httpclose
  balance leastconn
  cookie SERVERID insert
  {% for role in groups['tag_Chat_Deploy'] %}
  {% for server in groups['tag_' + deploy_env + '_Env'] %}
    {% if role == server %}
    server {{ server }} {{  hostvars[server]['ec2_private_ip_address']
}}:3000 cookie {{ server }}
    {% endif %}
    {% endfor %}
    {% endfor %}
```

The backend is essentially the same. We want a list of all our Socket.io servers.

The next step is to create a `haproxy.yml` file in the root of `ansible`. Here is how it should look:

```
- hosts: tag_HAProxy_Role
  remote_user: ubuntu
  sudo: yes
  roles:
    - haproxy
```

Now that we have everything ready we can run the HAProxy role. Open a terminal and run this command:

```
(venv)$ansible-playbook -i ec2.py haproxy.yml --limit tag_prod_Env
--extra-vars "deploy_env=prod branch=master"
```

Our production HAProxy server will have a static IP and a DNS name, so we should be able to load it in our browser and the application should work. To test load balancing, we will want to create another instance, add the tags (Chat Deploy and prod Env), and run our `appdeploy` and `haproxy` roles. After HAProxy restarts, we should be able to load up the application in different browsers and check the cookie to see different servers responding.

> Don't forget to add the correct security group so that the servers can communicate. Also, if we are just testing this out and do not have a static IP, we can just go to our instance list and get the IP from there.

The next screenshot shows the cookie that will be set:

SERVERID	54.88.29.185

Automating roles

We have six roles with five different task files. We can create another hierarchy of files that can run multiple roles at a time. Create two files, one named `site.yml` and the other named `deploy.yml`. Here is what will go in `site.yml`:

```
---
    - include: redis.yml
    - include: rabbitmq.yml
    - include: appdeploy.yml
    - include: worker.yml
    - include: haproxy.yml
```

Here is `deploy.yml`:

```
---
    - include: appdeploy.yml
    - include: haproxy.yml
```

We can then run them just like another task file using the following command:

```
(venv)$ansible-playbook -i ec2.py site.yml --limit tag_prod_Env --extra-vars "deploy_env=prod branch=master"
```

We can automate this even more. Create a file named `deploy.sh` in the root of the project. First, run this command to make it executable:

```
$chmod a+x deploy.sh
```

Then, add this code to it:

```bash
#!/bin/bash

if [[ $# -ne 3 ]]; then
  echo "Please pass in the playbook, environment, and git branch"
  exit 1
fi

source $2_secret.env

source venv/bin/activate

cd ansible

ansible-playbook -i ec2.py $1 --limit tag_$2_Env --extra-vars "deploy_
env=$2 branch=$3"

if [ $? -ne 0 ]; then
  echo "Did you remember to add the SSH key with ssh-add? Do you have
an $2_secret.env file with the AWS credentials? Are the instances
tagged with tag_$2_Env?"
fi
```

This is a bash script that will automate the setting up of the environment and running Ansible. If our `secret.env` file has some Python templating, the script will complain about not finding `{%`, but it will still process the reason why we want to source it, the AWS credentials. We can then run it as follows:

$./deploy.sh site.yml prod master

This will run `site.yml` in the production environment from the Git branch master.

A summary of Ansible

Ansible is very powerful and extensible. With our current setup, we can easily create an entirely new environment from nothing in just a few minutes. We will now review what we learned about Ansible.

First is roles. Roles allow us to group hosts and tasks together. Inside a role, there is a directory structure that we can follow, which makes loading relative assets easy. We can also use variables to make roles reusable. We did this with the `appdeploy` role. It was used for the main application and workers. We could even use this in another project that requires Node.js and `forever` running.

Any time we want to add another role or database, for example, we just have to create a new directory under roles and create tasks, files, templates, and anything else. This brings us to the next point: Ansible's inventory groups. Our inventory was built from EC2 that groups the servers together by tags. This allows us to split our servers by role and environment. If we needed another production web server, we just create a new instance with the needed tags and run our Ansible task. If we were not using EC2, we could still use inventory groups. We will just need to create an inventory file that looks as follows:

```
[tag_Chat_Deploy]
10.0.0.1
10.0.0.2
[tag_Redis_Role]
10.0.0.3
[tag_RabbitMQ_Role]
10.0.0.4
[tag_HAProxy_Role]
10.0.0.1
[tag_Worker_Deploy]
10.0.02
```

We just need to match the tags that Ansible is looking for with a list of IP addresses. In all the Ansible commands we have been running, we have used a `--limit` parameter. If our inventory only has one environment in it, we could drop this from the Ansible command. For example, if we created `prod_inventory` and `dev_inventory`, we could use this command:

```
$ansible-playbook -i prod_inventory site.yml --extra-vars "deploy_
env=prod branch=master"
```

With Ansible, if we can script and run something locally, then we can do this remotely on our server. There are many modules that we haven't even touched and even a repository for roles named Galaxy (`https://galaxy.ansible.com/`). Ansible is free, but it does have a product that we can purchase. This product just eases management even more.

Creating new environments

We can easily create a new environment for our application. Let's say, we want a test environment. All that we will have to do is create the environment files (regular and secret), create the instance(s) with the correct tags, and launch the deploy script. Because we use tags, we can easily create an environment that exists on only one instance. We will not even have to add the environment files to version control as the script will copy them over if they exist.

Scalability

We have automated the rolling out of our code to servers in the cloud, but how is this scalable? The first thing we take a look at is a diagram of how our application looks:

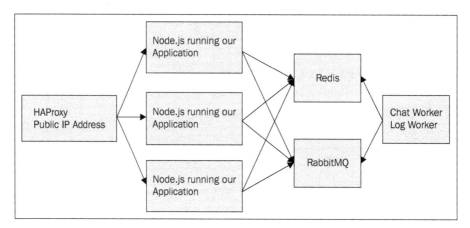

The front public-facing address of our site will be the server that is running HAProxy. In this setup, we will only want one server running HAProxy, and if it is production, this site should have a static IP and a public DNS record. HAProxy is very efficient at load balancing, and one of them can handle a lot of traffic. Eventually, we can run two behind a balanced DNS record, for example, but this is out the scope of this book.

HAProxy will then send the requests to one of our application servers behind it. These servers do not need a public-facing DNS record. They only need to communicate with the HAProxy server (and technically our computer so that SSH/Ansible will work). Each one of these servers will only be running one instance of Node and our application. We could even configure Ansible to kick off multiple instances of Node. Node.js is single-threaded, so most computers should be able to easily handle Node.js running once for each core. We will only need to update our `start` script and the HAProxy config to do this.

Each Node.js instance will create a connection to Redis. This is important as it keeps `state` out of the application layer. Redis is the only server that has complete knowledge of who is logged in (through connect sessions) and what rooms and messages exist (our application). Our application layer just takes a request, asks Redis what's going on, and returns a response. This high-level view is true if Node.js or Socket.io serves the response. If the session only lived in the memory on one machine, then when another machine responded to the request, the machine would not know that the user was logged in.

RabbitMQ is used for logging. Exactly like Redis, each application server creates its own connection. I will admit that this is not a great example of RabbitMQ's abilities. We can consider an example though.

Our example uses RabbitMQ for e-mails. Currently, our application does not send any out. E-mails can be resource-intensive. This does not mean that it will take up a lot of CPU cycles, but rather it relies on another server to respond. If we sent an e-mail during an HTTP response, a timeout could cause our application to appear slow and unresponsive. Let's say that we want to send out an e-mail when someone first signs up and when someone sends a direct chat (a feature we don't currently have). The first thing to do is create a worker that will watch an e-mail queue, which we create in RabbitMQ. Then, we will create a code that will easily add a message to this queue. This would be similar to our logging code. Each layer would only worry about what it was designed to do. We also could quickly change our e-mail processor. We just stop the e-mail worker and run our deploy script for the worker.

This brings us to the last layer of our application, workers. The setup for these is very similar to that of the application layer, Node.js, `start` and `stop` scripts. The difference is that the workers respond to RabbitMQ queues or a time interval.

Different types of scalability

There are two different types of scaling, horizontal and vertical. We will discuss which applies to our application layers.

Horizontal

Horizontal scaling involves adding more servers to respond. This method is harder to implement, but it can scale indefinitely. Our layer with Node.js web servers scales horizontally. If we notice that our application is timing out or is slow, we can spin up more instances to handle the load.

Horizontal scaling requires that no application state be stored on the server. This makes sense because we can never be sure if the same server will respond to requests.

The worker layer also can scale horizontally. If the workers cannot keep up, then we can create more workers.

Vertical

Vertical is the simplest way to scale. The downside to this is that it has a finite limit. If we use AWS as our provider, we can only currently create instances up to a certain number of CPUs and GBs of RAM (32 and 244 currently). It involves giving more resources to a server. In our build HAProxy, Redis and RabbitMQ can all scale vertically. If we run out of memory for Redis, then we can use a larger instance to run Redis. With the current maximum resources that AWS has, we should not run into a ceiling until we have a very, very large site.

 All the vertical scaling servers can scale horizontally as well. The topic is just outside the scope and length of this book. HAProxy can handle a lot of traffic out of the box. If necessary though, we could run multiple HAProxys balanced behind a round-robin DNS entry. Redis could be sharded. Sharding involves splitting requests based on a factor of the request. RabbitMQ can be clustered to serve more requests.

Summary

We covered how to create and launch instances in AWS. If we did not want to use AWS, there are many other cloud providers such as DigitalOcean and OpenShift. Then, we created Ansible scripts to install and deploy our application. Finally, we covered how this application setup can be scaled horizontally and vertically.

In the next chapter, we will discuss how we can troubleshoot and debug our application.

10
Debugging and Troubleshooting

We are finally at the last chapter. We started with an empty directory and built a full application. We will not be adding anything else to the application. We will investigate how to debug and find memory leaks in our code. Here is what we will cover in this chapter:

- Inspecting requests
- How to set debug breakpoints in our codebase
- CPU profiling
- Heap snapshots to help track down memory leaks

Node packages

This will be a completely separate, new application. We will need to create a new root directory. We are going to purposefully create issues so that we can investigate them. We are going to introduce two Node packages, `node-inspector` and `webkit-devtools-agent`. Add these two packages to our new `package.json` file under `devDependencies`. We will build small example Express applications to test with. Here are the versions at the time of writing this:

- `node-inspector`: 0.7.4
- `webkit-devtools-agent`: 0.2.5
- `express`: 4.5.1

Then, just run `npm install`. We may want to install `node-inspector` and `webkit-devtools-agent` globally by using the `global` flag with `npm install`. This will allow us to debug any Node.js application on our machine.

Using Chrome Developer Tools

We will need Google Chrome (http://www.google.com/chrome) for this chapter. It is a free download, and if you currently do not have it, install it before proceeding.

Chrome has great developer tools that allow us to see exactly what is going on with the HTML, CSS, and JavaScript on any page. We will introduce tools quickly here before really digging into them later in the chapter. The first thing to do is to get the developer tools to show. The easiest way is to right-click anywhere on a web page and select **Inspect Element**. A pane should come up from the bottom of the screen by default. There should be eight different tabs across the top of the pane, as shown in the following screenshot:

| Q | Elements | Network | Sources | Timeline | Profiles | Resources | Audits | Console |

 Google is always updating Chrome and the name, order, and functionality could change at any point in the future. Although, for the most part, the core task of each tab has remained static for a while now.

Elements

The **Elements** tab allows us to see every HTML element that is on the page. It will highlight the elements in the page as we hover over them, and if we click on them, it will load more information to the right. The additional information shows what styles are applied and/or ignored and what the actual computed values are. We will not use this for our debugging, but it is indispensable for any CSS/frontend troubleshooting.

Network

The **Network** tab displays every request made. If this tab is blank, we will need to reload the page. It will only capture this information when it is open. We should be able to follow the entire loading process with this tab. The first request will be the HTML. Then, we should see many requests for CSS, JavaScript, fonts, and so on depending on the page. There is a lot of information that can be picked up from here. First, the HTTP method, the HTTP status code, what the type was, what made the request, whether or not the file was cached, and the timing of the request. Then, when we click on each request, we can get even more information. We can then see the request and response headers, the raw response, and any cookies set. We will look at a few of these features later. This tool is really useful when we need to see requests. A great example of this is during an Ajax call. The **Network** tab will log all the information about a request that we will need to help troubleshoot these calls.

Sources

The **Sources** tab will be where we will spend a lot of time. Because of this, we will not spend much time in the introduction. All of the source for the JavaScript loaded in a page will be here. We can then set break points and start debugging, step in, step out, and step over. The node-inspector package will allow us to do this for JavaScript on the server, instead of just in the browser.

Timeline

Timeline has three different ways of capturing events and data. This is shown in the next screenshot:

This tool captures data as it happens on the page, so we can inspect it later. Events will capture every event that happens on the page irrespective of whether it is a JavaScript event, network, or render and layout. It will track how long and in what order these will happen. This is information that was impossible to gather before. Frames is great for animation. It will break down what is happening in each rendering frame. This is helpful if we have to track down why an application is not rendering at 60 fps. Finally, memory will track the heap and a summary of what is stored in the heap. The summary includes documents, HTML elements, and listeners. We will not be using this much.

Profiles

Profiles is the detailed memory information that **Timeline** does not give us. We can take heap snapshots and inspect every object that is currently in the heap. This tool even lets us take multiple snapshots and compare them. We will be doing this later in the chapter. In addition to heap snapshots, we can record heap allocations and watch changes in the heap as they happen. Both of these tools are indispensable when tracking down memory leaks.

Finally, this tab has CPU profiling to find out which functions are the most CPU intensive. We will cover this feature later in this chapter.

Resources

The **Resources** tab lists out all of the items that the browser is tracking locally. This includes cookies, local storage, Web SQL, and anything in the application cache. I had used this in *Chapter 1, Backend Development with Express,* and *Chapter 9, Deployment and Scalability,* to show the cookies that were set. We will be very happy this exists when we are building anything that uses these stores. Again, we will not cover this here.

Audits

The **Audits** tab is essentially a performance best practice validator. It will run through the currently loaded page and let us know what we can do to make our page load more efficient and performant. The options and recommendations are self-explanatory, so we will not spend time here.

Console

The final tab is **Console**. This is the often-referenced console in `console.log`. Anything sent through `console.log` will show up here. Logging to console should always be preferred to using an alert. If what we want to debug is an object, the console will allow us to expand all the properties and dig into the object, whereas an alert will display `[object Object]`.

We also can run JavaScript directly in the console. It is an easy-to-use REPL. We can test the code to see how it will execute. One thing to remember is that it will run in the global scope. This means that we will not have access to any functions and variables that are hidden inside closures or immediately invoked functions. Many JavaScript libraries make sure that they only expose the bare minimum of variables to the global scope. We will look at how to view these variables in scope later in the chapter.

We have gone through each of the developer tools that Chrome ships with. Each tool was only slightly touched on. These tools have a lot of options and use cases that we cannot cover here. If we need to know what is happening in JavaScript in a browser, Chrome has a tool for it.

Inspecting requests

HTTP is request based. The browser makes a request and our web server responds with a response. This interaction is hidden from users in all browsers, for a good reason. When developing applications, we will have the need to view this interaction. For this we will use Chrome's **Network** tab.

This will be our first new application, so create a directory named `requests`. This directory will be the root of our project. The first thing we will do is use a basic Express server. This code is right from Express' API documentation. It is the most basic functioning `'hello world'` we can build. Create an `app.js` file and add the following code to it:

```
var express = require('express');
var app = express();

app.get('/', function(req, res){
  res.send('hello world');
});


app.listen(3000);
```

Next, open Chrome Developer Tools and the **Network** tab. Then, open `http://localhost:3000`. We should see something like the next screenshot:

Name Path	Method	Status Text	Type	Initiator	Size Content	Time Latency	Timeline
localhost	GET	200 OK	text/html	Other	197 B 11 B	5 ms 4 ms	

This is a great summary of info that we care about as web developers. We can quickly see the method, status, and the timing of the request. If our page had sent some Ajax requests, each one would be here with this information. 5 years ago, this data was difficult to get.

Next, click on the actual request to see both the request and response headers. Knowing what headers were sent and what headers were received so easily is invaluable.

Now, let's poke around. We will add a header and change the status code. Modify the response as follows:

```
app.get('/', function(req, res){
  res.set('Important-Header', 'test-value');
  res.send(500, 'hello world');
});
```

This is completely contrived, but illustrative of the ease in which we can see the browser to server exchange. Our **Network** tab should now look as follows:

We can see our new status being set if we click on the network request.

```
▼ Response Headers      view source
   Connection: keep-alive
   Content-Length: 11
   Content-Type: text/html; charset=utf-8
   Date: Mon, 07 Jul 2014 03:00:34 GMT
   ETag: W/"b-222957957"
   Important-Header: test-value
   X-Powered-By: Express
```

The final thing we will do is to mock up an example Ajax request. First, remove the 500 status code from our response as follows:

```
res.send('hello world');
```

Then, we will have to create a POST route for our Ajax request. Add this method to app.js right under the GET route as follows:

```
app.post('/', function(req, res){
  res.send('<h1>POSTED</h1>');
});
```

Reload Node.js and our page. Next, paste the following code into the JavaScript console:

```
var xhr = new XMLHttpRequest();
var data = new FormData();
data.append('test', 'test-value');
xhr.open('POST', '/', true);
xhr.send(data);
```

This is a very basic asynchronous XML HTTP request (the first A and X in Ajax) sent with a simple form attached. If we switch over to the **Network** tab, we should see that it logged our request.

| localhost | POST | 200 OK | text/html | Other | 168 B 6 B | 3 ms 2 ms |

This looks like the request we just made. Let's click on the request we just made and view the headers. The headers should show that the content-type is multipart/form-data and also have a request payload of the data we set. Another thing we can view is the rendered and raw response. Preview will show how the browser would have rendered this and Response is the raw response sent. These can be very helpful if we need to see the output. An example of this would be when we create a server error in development and the returned response has a stack trace.

Something to note is that as far as JavaScript is concerned, this Ajax request was not fully processed. We only started the request, but never set any listeners for state changes for the response. Everything we just looked at is what Chrome tracked. Even if there is some JavaScript code three layers down that we did not write that makes an Ajax request on our page, we can follow it.

Be careful when using XMLHttpRequest and FormData. Each browser has their own idiosyncrasies with these objects. In the case of FormData, the browser might not even support it. More code is required to use XMLHttpRequest if we care about the response that comes back. In our examples, we are using the current version of Chrome, so both of these should work.

Incidentally, this is where jQuery can bring a lot of value when supporting multiple browsers.

This was a quick overview, but we touched on the key features that every web developer will need at some point during troubleshooting. This tool will save hours of debugging. There will never be a question about whether a request was made and with what headers and payload.

Debugging

Breakpoints are a developer's best friend. They are much more useful than using `console.log()` everywhere. We will explore how to set a breakpoint on both the front and backend.

Frontend debugging

First up is frontend debugging. Before we can do this, we must create some JavaScript to debug. Create a new directory named `static` with a file named `debug.js` in the directory. Here is the code that will be in `debug.js`.

```
(function(){
  var body = document.body;
  (function(){
    var div = document.createElement('div');
    body.appendChild(div);
  })();

})();
```

Two simple self-executing functions (to create different scopes) that will add a div to the page. Nothing exciting here. Next, we must add this script to our response. Open up `app.js` and add or change the following lines:

```
var express = require('express');
var app = express();

app.use(express.static(__dirname + '/static'));
app.get('/', function(req, res){
  res.set('Important-Header', 'test-value');
  res.send('hello world<script src="/debug.js"></script>');
});

app.post('/', function(req, res){
  res.send('<h1>POSTED</h1>');
});

app.listen(3000);
```

We are building this very quickly and dirtily. This is not valid HTML, but Chrome will process it. Reload Node.js and Chrome. Open up developer tools, click on the **Sources** tab, and expand **localhost:3000**. We should see our new JavaScript file there, as shown in the next screenshot:

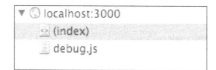

Click on `debug.js` and it will load in the panel. Then, set a breakpoint on line **4** by clicking on the line number. A blue arrow should appear showing that a breakpoint is set.

```
debug.js ×
1  (function(){
2    var body = document.body;
3    (function(){
4      var div = document.createElement('div');
5      body.appendChild(div);
6    })();
7
8  })();
9
```

Reload the page and processing should stop at line **3**. From here, we can resume execution, step over, step into, and step out, as shown in the next screenshot:

 If these concepts are unclear, review Google's debugging documentation at `https://developer.chrome.com/devtools/docs/javascript-debugging`.

Step over the first line and we should then be able to see each scope under Scope Variables. There will be **Local**, **Closure**, and **Global**. Any variable that can be referenced will be here under the appropriate scope. We can expand each object and see its properties and methods, as shown in the following screenshot:

```
▼ Scope Variables
▼ Local
   ▶ div: div
   ▶ this: Window
▼ Closure
   ▶ body: body
▶ Global
```

If we are looking for a specific property, we can Watch Expressions to quickly view it. Let's resume the page execution and then click on **Elements**. We should see that a blank div has been added to the end of the body.

Reload the page again so that it stops at our breakpoint again and step over to line 5. We will now click on the **Console** tab. In the console, type the following line of code:

```
div.id = 'console-test';
```

Then, return to **Sources** and let the execution resume. Lastly, go back to **Elements** and notice that our `div` now has an ID of `console-test`. This demonstrates that when debugging, the console executes in the context of the breakpoint and not the global context. If we use this code in the console after the page is loaded, we will get a reference error as `div` does not exist in the global scope. The value of this should be clear without explicitly running through every possibility.

 Chrome even makes debugging minified code easy as it has Pretty Print that will make the code human readable again. We can even make minified code look like the source code with a source map. We can automate the creation of a source map with Grunt using `grunt-concat-sourcemap`.

Backend debugging

Debugging the frontend is easy to perform, as Chrome loads JavaScript from the server to parse and compile it. The browser is already doing this. How do we debug JavaScript that runs on Node.js? We do this with `node-inspector`. This is installed locally or we can install it globally with the following command:

```
npm install -g node-inspector
```

Once this is installed, we can then run this command to debug our application. We should stop the current Node.js server to let this one start serving.

```
node-debug app.js
```

Chrome might open up a tab to debug. If not, we can manually connect to the debugger at `http://localhost:8080/debug?port=5858` by default. The page that loads is a subset of the full developer tools available in Chrome. It has **Sources** and **Console**. If we think about it, this makes sense. There is no DOM or Network, so these tools are not useful.

We will set the breakpoint on line 7. When we load up our application in another tab, it will break. Debugging Node.js is exactly the same as debugging frontend JavaScript. The same tools and layout are here. We can step through our code, inspect any variable that has a reference in the current scope, and even load up any `node_module` code and set breakpoints.

Once the code is paused at the breakpoint, switch over to the **Console** tab. Then, run the following line of code in the console:

```
res.set('console-test', 'test');
```

After the code executes, resume the execution of the code with the debugging tools. Jump back over to our tab that is loading the site and look at the **Network** tab. We should see a new response header `console-test: test`. In the exact same fashion as the frontend, we can execute the code in the context of the paused scope.

Debugging summary

Node-inspector allows us to use Chrome developer tools to debug the code running in Node.js. This is awesome and very powerful. If you currently use Chrome to debug JavaScript, then I am sure you are already sold on this. If you are not using any JavaScript debuggers, Chrome and `node-inspector` will make your job much easier.

CPU profiling our application

Our next troubleshooting method is going to be CPU profiling. This will let us know what functions are the most CPU intensive. For this, we will use `webkit-devtools-agent`. The setup for this tool is a little more difficult than the last.

The first thing we need to do is add a reference to the module. Open up `app.js` and add this line to the top, as highlighted in the following code:

```
var agent = require('webkit-devtools-agent');
var express = require('express');
var app = express();
```

Technically, this is all we need to add to our code. If this was a production codebase, we could check whether we were in development or not and load this module. We can start the node at this time.

The next step is to send a USR2 signal to the process-running node. Signals are a way to notify a process. A common signal is TERM that tells the process to start shutting down and to terminate. USR2 is a user-defined signal. This means that developers can decide what to do when the signal is received. `Webkit-devtools-agent` uses this signal to start debugging. We can do this with a few different commands. If the `pgrep` command is available, we can use it. Open another terminal and run the following command:

```
pgrep node
```

This should return the PID (Process ID) of node. If `pgrep` does not exist on our system, we can use the next command:

```
ps -A | grep -m1 'node app.js' | awk '{print $1}'
```

This will do the same thing as `pgrep`. It will list out the whole process, then use `grep` for our command that started the server, and finally only print out the PID.

We can take either of these and then pipe that into the `kill` command, which will send the process a signal. If we are running Linux, this will kill -SIGUSR2 and Mac OS X will kill -USR2. Here is what the two different commands look like on Mac OS X:

```
pgrep node | xargs kill -USR2
ps -A | grep -m1 'node app.js' | awk '{print $1}' | xargs kill -USR2
```

The `xargs` command will take the input from the piped-in command and use it as an argument for the next command. If Node is running with the `webkit-devtools-agent` module loaded, we should see an output like the next screenshot in our Node terminal:

If we send the USR2 signal again, it will turn off the agent. The next step is to load up `http://c4milo.github.io/node-webkit-agent/26.0.1410.65/inspector.html?host=localhost:9999&page=0` in our browser. If everything worked correctly, we should see Chrome Developer Tools. The only tab we can really use here is the **Profiles** tab. We will use **Collect JavaScript CPU Profile** in this section. Make sure that the radio button for this is selected and click on **Start** at the bottom of the page. Then, load our site a few times in another tab. Lastly, click on **Stop**. We should get an item under **CPU PROFILES** in the left column. We can click on this to get a breakdown of the percentage of the time that was spent during processing. In this example, most of the time was spent doing nothing because our application is not very CPU intensive. We will change that.

In `app.js`, create a new function called `CPUWaster` and execute it on the root `GET` route. Here is what it should look like:

```
function CPUWaster(){
  var j;
  for(var i=0; i < 10000000; i++){
```

```
      j = Math.sqrt(Math.pow(i, i));
    };
  }

  app.get('/', function(req, res){
    CPUWaster();
    res.set('Important-Header', 'test-value');
    res.send('hello world<script src="/debug.js"></script>');
  });
```

This function just loops 10 million times and gets the square root of the squared counter. A true CPU-wasting function. Note that this will happen asynchronously to the response that is returned. This is fine for our example as the CPU will still process through the loop.

Stop Node and restart it. Our **Profiles** tab will show a **Detached from the target** message. We will need to resend the signal to the process, because it is a new process, and reload our **Profiles** tab.

After everything has reloaded, start our CPU profile again and load the root page 10 to 20 times. Our profile should have a new second place function, `CPUWaster`. The actual percentage will vary, but we should see roughly 25 to 35 percent taken up by `CPUWaster`. The function name, file, and line number should also be shown. It should look similar to the next screenshot:

Self ▾	Total	Aver...	Calls	Function	
64.85%	64.85%	64.85%	0	(program)	
34.98%	34.98%	34.98%	0	▶ CPUWaster	/Users/jjohanan/django/finalChapters/debug/requests/app.js.7

Like most of the other examples in this chapter, this is very contrived, but illustrative. CPU spikes can create issues in Node.js as we can tie up the event loop. This stops Node.js from being able to serve any more clients and making any current requests seem very slow. We have the tools to investigate any slowness or CPU spikes. If we must do a task that is very CPU intensive, we can always use a message queuing system to offload this process elsewhere.

Taking heap snapshots

In JavaScript, a heap snapshot will have all the objects that are not going to be garbage collected. This is perfect for tracking down memory leaks. We had briefly touched on memory leaks in *Chapter 6, Using Bower to Manage Our Frontend Dependencies*. Here, we will create some memory leaks on both the backend and frontend to see what they look like.

First, we will create a memory leak in Node.js. Create a new file named `leak.js` and put the following code into it:

```
var agent = require('webkit-devtools-agent');
var express = require('express');
var app = express();
var http = require('http');
var server = http.createServer(app);

server.setMaxListeners(1000000);
app.use(express.static(__dirname + '/static'));

app.get('/', function(req, res){
  //no-op listener
  for(var k=0; k < 1000; k++){
    server.on('request', function(e){var t = express;});
  }
  res.set('Important-Header', 'test-value');
  res.send('hello world<script src="/debug.js"></script>');
});

server.listen(3000);
```

This is very similar to `app.js`. The main difference is that each GET request will add a thousand event listeners to the request event of the server. What's even worse than just adding the listeners is that each one is an anonymous function that creates a closure. Once we have added an anonymous function as a listener, it is very difficult to remove it as we do not have a reference to the function anymore. Closures are very useful, but they are also dangerous. If we are not careful, we can make objects that will not be garbage collected.

Start Node.js running this code, send it a USR2 signal, and load our profiling tools in Chrome. This time, we will select **Take Heap Snapshot** instead of CPU profiling. After selecting the radio button, click on **Start**. Click on the snapshot to view all the different types of objects in it. My snapshot is 7.2 MB. This might vary as Chrome can have extensions loaded, which will increase the size. The actual size is not the important part as we just want a baseline of how much memory is being used. The table to the right will give us more information about how that 7.2 MB is taken up. We should see something similar to the next screenshot:

Constructor	Di...	Objects Count		Shallow Size		Retained Size	
▶ Object	2	529	1%	16 248	0%	5 835 520	77%

The first column is what type of object the row is summarizing. In our example, it is a generic object. Next is distance. This is the distance from the garbage collector root. Then, it is the count, which is explanatory. Next is **Shallow Size**. This is the amount of memory that the objects are taking up. Finally, there is **Retained Size**. This is the amount of memory that will be freed up if these objects were garbage collected. This can be larger as objects will have references to other objects. This reference will keep the other object from being garbage collected. In our example, I selected the top row and these 529 objects account for 77 percent of all the memory taken.

Searching for memory leaks involves taking a baseline snapshot, the snapshot we just took, and then taking an action. We will load the root page in a browser for our action. Then, we take another snapshot and check to see what has changed. If there are no memory leaks, we should not see more objects being retained. If there are more objects, this means our action is keeping a reference to something it should not. Reiterating what I stated in *Chapter 6*, *Using Bower to Manage Our Frontend Dependencies*, event listeners are a major source of memory leaks and this is our leak here. Let's catch it.

Load up our site in a browser three times. Then, go back to the developer tools and take another heap snapshot by clicking on the record button at the bottom left.

This snapshot will be larger. This is usually not good. Sometimes, it is alright for memory to grow. An example of this is if we lazy load a database connection. Our first snapshot will not include the memory allocated for this connection. The request can then load the database connection allocating more memory. A key point to take from this is that each request should not take more and more memory. Once a resource is loaded, it should not continue to eat up memory.

It is impossible to track down the leak looking at the entire snapshot. We want to see what changed using the comparison view. At the very bottom of the page, there should be a dropdown on **Summary**. Click on it and change it to **Comparison**. If we had more snapshots, we could choose which one to compare to, but as there are only two, it will compare with the other.

The comparison view changes the columns. There is now a column named **Delta**. This will show us the difference in counts between the two snapshots. Click on the column header and this will make the table sort by **Delta** from high to low. This is usually a good place to start when looking for memory leaks. We want to know where the largest change in objects occurred. In our example, this will bring up closure with a delta of 3028.

We can then expand the row and the first object. It shows that it was an anonymous function that is holding on to the express and server variables.

▼ (closure)	3 031	3	+3 028	218 232	216	+218 016
▼ function() @98237	·			72		
▶ express :: function cr						
▶ server :: Server @6262?						
▶ shared :: (shared funct						
▶ 64 :: function() @1039?						
▶ __proto__ :: function E						

The following table shows a list of objects which will have the retaining tree. This is a list of objects that is holding a reference to the object we are currently investigating. In our example, we see it is an Array in request in _events of the Server object, as shown in the following screenshot:

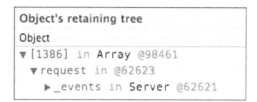

This is our leak. We know that we are adding a thousand listeners on every request and we made three requests. This lines up very nicely with our delta of 3,000 extra closures. We will probably never have such an easy memory leak to track down in real life. Memory leak hunting is all about searching the heap for objects that should have been garbage collected. It definitely helps to know what objects should be there. Another useful practice is to avoid anonymous functions as much as possible. We can track the objects better if each one had a name. Most leaks will not add a thousand extra objects after each action. Most likely, it will be a few or even one. This means that we need to take an action a few thousand times to create enough data to search.

Frontend memory leaks

Frontend memory leaks were not a problem. If we go back in time, web pages would be reloaded many times throughout a visit. This would reset any memory leaks. Today, there are many single-page applications (much like the one we built) where a user will not reload a page during their entire visit. Memory leaks will grow and can cause problems.

We will now create some leaks on the frontend. We will continue to use the same server and just create a static JavaScript file. Create a file at `static/feleak.js` and put the following code into it:

```javascript
var badArray = [];
var body = document.body;

function createLeak(){
  var div = document.createElement('div');
  body.appendChild(div);
  div.addEventListener('click', function(){body.innerText='HEY!';});
  badArray.push(div);
  body.removeChild(div);
}

function bigLeak(){
  for(var i=0; i<10000; i++){
    createLeak();
  }
}
```

This is a very heinous leak. Not only will it keep a reference to each div that is created, but it will also keep a closure for each. Now, we have to load this script on the page. Modify the GET route in `leak.js` to this:

```javascript
app.get('/', function(req, res){
  res.set('Important-Header', 'test-value');
  res.send('hello world<script src="/feleak.js"></script>');
});
```

We can now load this page up in our browser and start using the built-in frontend tools in Chrome. After the page is loaded, open the developer tools and go to the **Profiles** tab. Select **Take Heap Snapshot** and click on **Take Snapshot**. This first snapshot should be very small, somewhere around 2 MB. Depending on which extensions are loaded, this could be larger. We can now create the leak. Click over to the **Console** and run this three or four times.

```javascript
bigLeak()
```

Then, take another snapshot. This should add multiple megabytes of memory. We can see what changed by changing the view from **Summary** to **Comparison**. This should all sound familiar. We should see **array, closure, HTMLDivElement,** and **Detached DOM** tree near the top if we sort by objects created between the snapshots. It should look similar to the following screenshot:

Constructor	# New ▼	# Delet...	# Delta	Alloc. Size	Freed Size	Size Delta
▶ (array)	62 282	544	+61 738	2 451 860	66 988	+2 384 872
▶ (system)	34 466	1 800	+32 666	326 584	30 460	+296 124
▶ (closure)	32 226	926	+31 300	1 160 136	33 336	+1 126 800
▶ Object	30 187	76	+30 111	485 832	2 240	+483 592
▶ HTMLDi...	30 001	0	+30 001	600 016	0	+600 016
▶ Detache...	30 000	0	+30 000	0	0	0

The array is keeping a reference to each `div`. Even though we remove it from the DOM, it is still kept around. This is where the detached DOM trees are coming from. A detached DOM is almost never good. It usually means that we removed an element, but something is still referencing it. The closures are held because the click listener references a variable in the outer scope. Each listener is an anonymous function, so each one will have its own closure.

Most of the time, we will not come across such large memory leaks. All it takes is one reference that we did not account for. For example, when using jQuery, it is very easy to select many elements and forget about them. If we remove or replace the element, it will still be held onto. Memory leaks also come from poor closure management. JavaScript is very forgiving and will allow us to reference variables in many different scopes. If the function sticks around, it will keep all the other scopes alive along with it.

We can clean up our leak here by getting rid of `badArray`. Load up the console again and execute the following line:

```
badArray = null;
```

Then, take another snapshot and all the elements and closures should be gone.

Memory leak summary

Finding memory leaks is not easy. There is no shortcut. Even a page with just a few lines of JavaScript will have thousands upon thousands of objects in the heap. When searching, it helps if we can execute an action thousands of times. This will make very small leaks more apparent. Once a leak is identified, we must walk through the logic and ask if each reference is required. Can we pass the value instead of referencing a closure? Can we encapsulate an action with the variables it needs? There is no way to answer these questions without thinking hard about our application.

Summary

At the time of writing this, Chrome has, in my opinion, the best developer tools. We can capture, track, and inspect almost anything about a web page. Firefox, Opera, Safari, and Internet Explorer all have developer tools that would have blown away any developer a few years ago. The fact that there are multiple great browsers makes right now a great time to be a web developer.

In this chapter, we looked at how to view the network exchange between browser and server. Then, we looked at debugging. We can debug JavaScript on both the server and browser. Finally, we looked at profiling the CPU and memory. Both of these resources are becoming more and more important to track as JavaScript applications become larger and longer lived.

This concludes our journey. We have touched on a lot of different topics. There is no way that we could have comprehensively covered each topic. We did cover what any developer should know about each of these topics. This knowledge can now be easily built on as these are not new concepts anymore. We have built an application from start to deployment. We can build on this experience and knowledge to build more applications.

Index

A

Access Control Lists (ACLs) 263
acknowledgements, Socket.IO app 54-56
AddRoom event 194
addUser function 169
Advanced Message Queuing Protocol
    (AMQP) 116
Amazon Web Services (AWS)
  URL 236
Ansible
  about 246
  environments, creating 267
  installing 246-248
  roles, using 248-250
  summarizing 266, 267
Ansible-created EC2 inventory script
  URL 246
Ansible roles
  application, installing 253, 254
  automating 265, 266
  multiple application servers,
    load balancing 261-265
  RabbitMQ, installing 251-253
  using 248-250
  workers, installing 261
app
  config file, setting up 42
  config file, setting up for 42
  updating, for config usage 43-45
application
  extending, methods used 45, 46
  Google authentication, adding to 98-101
  trying 216

application, Ansible
  code, deploying 254-260
  installing 253, 254
application-specific events
  adding 79
application state
  storing, in Redis 173
apt-get tool 146
Audits tab, Chrome developer tools 274
authentication
  about 36-41
  building 84
  Google, used for 94-98
authorization
  used, in Socket.IO 75
authorization handler
  using 75
AWS EC2
  summarizing 245

B

Backbone
  about 184
  collections, using 186, 187
  models, using 185, 186
Backbone models
  about 203
  collections, creating 206
  creating 205, 206
  summarizing 208-212
  syncing, with Socket.IO 203, 204
Backbone router 208
backend debugging 280, 281

basic file, Grunt
  building 227, 228
Bower
  installing 176
  using 176
Bower package
  versions 189, 190
browser side
  adding 52-54

C

cards
  charging, in real time 131-133
CDN 235
chatAdd function 202
Chrome developer tools, using
  about 272
  Audits tab 274
  Console tab 274
  Elements tab 272
  Network tab 272
  Profiles tab 273
  Resources tab 274
  Sources tab 273
  Timeline tab 273
CleanUp function 215
CleanUpUsers function 215
client
  building 49, 50
code coverage
  Istanbul, using for 222
code, Grunt
  concatenating 232
  minifying 233, 234
collection property 198
collections, Backbone models
  creating 206, 207
componentDidUpdate function 202
componentWillMount attribute 181
componentWillMount function 182
config
  Socket.IO, adding to 72-74
  used, via app update 43-45
config file
  fixing 224, 225
  setting up, for app 42

config file, setting up
  app, updating for config usage 43-45
  route mapping 43
Console tab, Chrome developer tools 274
Content Delivery Network. *See* **CDN**
cookies
  about 76
  used, in Express 23-25
Cosmo
  URL 21
CPU profiling 281-283
CPUWaste function 282
Create Read Update Delete (CRUD) 195
creates option 257
Cross-Site Request Forgery (CSRF) 34-36
Crypto 103
CSS
  updating 212, 213

D

database
  adding 110
data structures, Redis
  application, building 150-157
  using 149
data types, Redis
  hash data type 149
  lists 149
  sets 149
  sorted set 149
  string 149
  using 149
debugging
  about 277
  backend debugging 280, 281
  frontend debugging 278-280
  summarizing 281
DefaultRoute function 211
denial-of-service (DOS) 33
destroy function 204
disconnect event
  using 58
Document Object Model (DOM) 177

E

EBS 245
EC2
  about 243
  servers, creating on 243-245
Elastic Block Store. *See* EBS
Elastic Compute Cloud. *See* EC2
Elements tab, Chrome developer tools 272
Embedded JavaScript (EJS) 18
environment files
  creating 225, 226
environments
  adding 227
  config file, fixing 224, 225
  setting up 224
  Twelve Factor App 224
environments, Ansible
  creating 267
error.log queue 133
EXPIRE command 162
Express
  and Socket.IO, using 72
  cookies, using 23-25
  middleware, creating 15-17
  middleware, using 14
  Redis, session store 28-30
  sessions, adding 25-27
  sessions, using 23
  used, in Node 12-14

F

Facebook
  authenticating, Passport used 88-94
Facebook application
  registering 85-88
files, Grunt
  preprocessing 229, 230
flash messages 40
FLUSHDB command 160
forms
  Cross-Site Request Forgery (CSRF) 34-36
  processing 31-33
frontend debugging 278, 279

frontend memory leaks
  about 286
  creating 287, 288
fully qualified domain name (FQDN) 89

G

Galaxy
  URL 267
getChat function 193
getDOMNode function 181
GetMe function 209
GetRoom function 194
Google
  used, for authentication 94-98
Google authentication
  adding, to application 98-101
Google Chrome
  URL 272
Grunt
  about 227
  basic file, building 227, 228
  code, concatenating 232, 233
  code, minifying 233, 234
  files, preprocessing 229, 230
  Node package versions 218
  source files, JSHinting 231, 232
  summarizing 234
  tests, automating 228
  used, for emptying folder 231
  watch feature 235

H

HAProxy 270
hash, Redis data types 149
hash, Redis schema
  using 159
heap snapshots
  frontend memory leaks 286-288
  obtaining 283-286
  used, for tracking memory leaks 289
Heroku
  URL 224
Homebrew
  URL 116
horizontal scaling 269

I

Identity and Access Management (IAM) 236
interaction
  creating 51
Istanbul
  using, for code coverage 222, 223

J

join event 64
JoinRoom function 211
JSHint 231

K

keys, Redis
  about 159
  rooms 167
  users 167

L

layout
  about 20-22
  implementing 20-22
  updating 212, 213
libraries function
  executing 222
Linux
  RabbitMQ, installing on 118
  Redis, installing on 146, 147
lists, Redis data types 149

M

Mac OS X
  RabbitMQ, installing on 116, 117
  Redis, installing on 145, 146
management interface
  using 123, 124
memory leaks
  creating, on frontend 286-288
  tracking down, with heap snapshots 289

message queue

message queue
  about 120-123, 140
  adding, to PacktChat 133-139
  management interface, using 123, 124
  messages, queuing 125, 126
  messages, sending 124
  Redis, using as 163-167
  topic exchange, using 133-139
  worker, adding 126
  worker, building 138, 139
messages
  cards, charging in real time 131-133
  broadcasting 56, 57
  queuing 125, 126
  sending 124
  sending back 127-129
  StartServer, creating 129, 130
  worker, building 130, 131
methods
  used, for extending application 45, 46
middleware
  creating 15-18
  used, in Express 14
multiple application servers
  load balancing 261-265
MVC (Model, View, Controller) 45

N

namespace client
  building 61-65
namespaces
  about 69
  and rooms, using 71
  creating 59-61
  finding 70
  namespace client, building 61-65
  using 69
Network tab, Chrome developer tools 272
Node
  Express, using 12-14
Node.js
  about 9-11
  URL 9
Node Package Manager. *See* npm

Node packages
about 10
versions 271
Node package versions 47, 83, 115, 175
Node package versions, Grunt 218
Node package versions, Redis 143
npm
about 9-11
using 260

O

OAuth
about 112
process 112
providers, adding 101

P

package
installing 48
package.json file 11
PacktChat
message queues, adding to 133-139
Redis, adding to 167
pageCount session variable 28
parse method 207
partial function 40
Passport
used, for authenticating Facebook 88-94
Password-Based Key Derivation Function 2
(PBKDF2) 103, 112
passwordCheck function 103
passwordCreate function 103
password-storing theory 111
Personal Package Archive (PPA)
feature 147
using 147
ping event 64
Ping-Pong 51
Platform as a Service (Paas) 224
postal.js 180
Profiles tab, Chrome developer tools 273
Python
used, for serving site 50
Python script
building 238-240

Q

Qunit
URL 223

R

RabbitMQ
about 116
installing 251-253
installing, on Linux 118
installing, on Mac OS X 116, 117
installing, on Windows 119, 120
message queuing 139, 140
URL 115
RabbitMQ management plugin 118
React
about 176-184
components, creating 195-198
features 177
summary 203
URL 177
React components
creating 196-202
Read Evaluate Print Loop (REPL) 167
Redis
about 143
adding, to PacktChat 167
application state, storing in 173
features 172
installing 144
Node package versions 143
used, for storing Socket.IO 79, 80
using, as message queue 163-167
Redis, adding to PacktChat
about 167
functions, creating 168-172
structures, defining 167
Redis application
building 150-157
Redis functions
creating 168-172
Redis installation
about 144
on Linux 146, 147

on Mac OS X 145, 146
on Windows 148
on Windows, URL 148
Redis keys
expiration method 161
removing 160-163
Redis persistence
about 160
Redis keys, removing 160
Redis schema
building 158
hash, using 159
keys 159
keys, adding 158
Redis, session store 28-30
Redis structures
defining 167
registration
adding 108-110
**relational database management
system (RDBMS)** 143
removeAllRooms function 192
removeClick function 181
removeFromRoom function 192
removeUserFromRoom function 171
render function 179, 201, 203
representational state transfer (REST) 195
requests
inspecting 274-277
making 74
Resources tab, Chrome developer tools 274
roomFormEvent function 211
rooms
adding 66-68
and namespaces, using 71
finding 71
using 69, 70
RoomSelection function 211
route mapping 43

S

S3 bucket
creating 236, 237

scalability
about 268
types 269
secret option 27
secure local authentication
adding 102-107
database, adding 110
registration, adding 108-110
servers
creating, on EC2 243-245
sessions
about 76
adding 25-27
used, in Express 23
SET command 162
SETEX command 163
set function 186
sets, Redis collection types 161
sets, Redis data types 149
settings, app
URL 19
socketAuth function 191
Socket.IO
adding, to config 72-74
and Express, using 72
authorization handler, using 75
authorization, used in 75
Backbone models, syncing with 203, 204
cookies 76
drawbacks 81
finishing 190-195
obtaining 77, 78
sessions 76
storing, Redis used 79, 80
working 80
Socket.IO app
building 48
Socket.IO app, building
acknowledgements 54-56
browser side, adding 52-54
client, building 49, 50
interaction, creating 51
package, installing 48
Ping-Pong 51
Python, used for serving site 50

Socket.IO, working
 WebSockets 80
sorted set, Redis collection types 161
sorted set, Redis data types 149
source files, Grunt
 JSHinting 231, 232
Sources tab, Chrome developer tools 273
StartServer
 creating 129, 130
static files 235
string, Redis data types 149

T

templates
 adding, to mix 18-20
 layout, implementing 20-22
tests
 Istanbul, using for code coverage 222, 223
 setting up 218-221
tests, Grunt
 automating 228
this.MULTI() function 153
Timeline tab, Chrome developer tools 273
tools
 scripting 240-242
topic exchange
 using 133-137
Twelve Factor App
 about 224
 URL 224
types, scalability
 horizontal 269
 vertical 270

U

Ubuntu 146

V

vertical scaling 270
VirtualBox
 URL 148
virtual environment, for Python
 creating 238, 239

W

watch feature, Grunt 235
WebSockets 80
Windows
 RabbitMQ, installing on 119, 120
 Redis, installing on 148
wireEvents function 64
worker
 adding 126-215
 building 130-139
workers, Ansible
 installing 261

Y

Yet Another Markup Language (YAML) 249

Thank you for buying
Building Scalable Apps with Redis and Node.js

About Packt Publishing

Packt, pronounced 'packed', published its first book "*Mastering phpMyAdmin for Effective MySQL Management*" in April 2004 and subsequently continued to specialize in publishing highly focused books on specific technologies and solutions.

Our books and publications share the experiences of your fellow IT professionals in adapting and customizing today's systems, applications, and frameworks. Our solution based books give you the knowledge and power to customize the software and technologies you're using to get the job done. Packt books are more specific and less general than the IT books you have seen in the past. Our unique business model allows us to bring you more focused information, giving you more of what you need to know, and less of what you don't.

Packt is a modern, yet unique publishing company, which focuses on producing quality, cutting-edge books for communities of developers, administrators, and newbies alike. For more information, please visit our website: www.packtpub.com.

About Packt Open Source

In 2010, Packt launched two new brands, Packt Open Source and Packt Enterprise, in order to continue its focus on specialization. This book is part of the Packt Open Source brand, home to books published on software built around Open Source licenses, and offering information to anybody from advanced developers to budding web designers. The Open Source brand also runs Packt's Open Source Royalty Scheme, by which Packt gives a royalty to each Open Source project about whose software a book is sold.

Writing for Packt

We welcome all inquiries from people who are interested in authoring. Book proposals should be sent to author@packtpub.com. If your book idea is still at an early stage and you would like to discuss it first before writing a formal book proposal, contact us; one of our commissioning editors will get in touch with you.

We're not just looking for published authors; if you have strong technical skills but no writing experience, our experienced editors can help you develop a writing career, or simply get some additional reward for your expertise.

Node Cookbook
Second Edition

ISBN: 978-1-78328-043-8   Paperback: 378 pages

Over 50 recipes to master the art of asynchronous server-side JavaScript using Node.js, with coverage of Express 4 and Socket.IO frameworks and the new Streams API

1. Work with JSON, XML, and web sockets to make the most of asynchronous programming.

2. Extensive code samples covering Express 4 and Socket.IO.

3. Learn how to process data with Streams and create specialized streams.

4. Packed with practical recipes taking you from the basics to extending Node with your own modules.

Node Web Development
Second Edition

ISBN: 978-1-78216-330-5   Paperback: 248 pages

A practical introduction to Node.js, an exciting server-side JavaScript web development stack

1. Learn about server-side JavaScript with Node.js and Node modules.

2. Website development both with and without the Connect/Express web application framework.

3. Developing both HTTP server and client applications.

Please check **www.PacktPub.com** for information on our titles

Mastering Node.js

ISBN: 978-1-78216-632-0   Paperback: 346 pages

Expert techniques for building fast servers and scalable, real-time network applications with minimal effort

1. Master the latest techniques for building real-time big data applications, integrating Facebook, Twitter, and other network services.

2. Tame asynchronous programming, the event loop, and parallel data processing.

3. Use the Express and Path frameworks to speed up development and deliver scalable, higher quality software more quickly.

Using Node.js for UI Testing

ISBN: 978-1-78216-052-6   Paperback: 146 pages

Learn how to easily automate testing of your web apps using Node.js, Zombie.js, and Mocha

1. Use automated tests to keep your web app rock solid and bug-free while you code.

2. Use a headless browser to quickly test your web application every time you make a small change to it.

3. Use Mocha to describe and test the capabilities of your web app.

Please check **www.PacktPub.com** for information on our titles

www.ingramcontent.com/pod-product-compliance
Lightning Source LLC
LaVergne TN
LVHW081334050326
832903LV00024B/1153